Nature and Agriculture in the European Union

CURRENT ISSUES IN ECOLOGICAL ECONOMICS

General Editors: Sylvie Faucheux, *Professor of Economic Science* and Martin O'Connor, *Associate Professor of Economic Science, C3ED, Université de Versailles–Saint Quentin en Yvelines, France*, John Proops, *Professor of Ecological Economics, School of Politics, International Relations and the Environment, Keele University, UK* and Jan van der Straaten, *Retired Senior Lecturer, Department of Leisure Studies, Tilburg University, The Netherlands*

The field of ecological economics has emerged as a result of the need for all social sciences to be brought together in new ways, to respond to global environmental problems. This major new series aims to present and define the state-of-the-art in this young and yet fast-developing discipline.

This series cuts through the vast literature on the subject to present the key tenets and principal problems, techniques and solutions in ecological economics. It is the essential starting point for any practical or theoretical analysis of economy–environment interactions and will provide the basis for future developments within the discipline.

Titles in the series include:

Greening the Accounts
Edited by Sandrine Simon and John Proops

Nature and Agriculture in the European Union
New Perspectives on Policies that Shape the European Countryside
Edited by Floor Brouwer and Jan van der Straaten

Nature and Agriculture in the European Union:

New Perspectives on Policies that Shape the European Countryside

Edited by
Floor Brouwer

Head of the Research Unit Management of Natural Resources, Agricultural Economics Research Institute (LEI), The Hague, The Netherlands

Jan van der Straaten

Assistant Professor, Department of Leisure Studies, Tilburg University, The Netherlands

CURRENT ISSUES IN ECOLOGICAL ECONOMICS

Edward Elgar
Cheltenham, UK • Northampton, MA, USA

Published by
Edward Elgar Publishing Limited
Glensanda House
Montpellier Parade
Cheltenham
Glos GL50 1UA
UK

Edward Elgar Publishing, Inc.
136 West Street
Suite 202
Northampton
Massachusetts 01060
USA

A catalogue record for this book
is available from the British Library

Library of Congress Cataloguing in Publication Data
Nature and agriculture in the European union : new perspectives on policies that shape the European countryside / edited by Floor Brouwer, Jan van der Straaten.
    p. cm. -- (Current issues in ecological economics)
    Includes bibliographical references and index.
    1. Agriculture--Economic aspects--European Union countries. 2. Agriculture--Environmental aspects--European Union countries. 3. Agriculture and state--European Union countries. I. Brouwer, Floor. II. Straaten, Jan van der. III. Series.
    HD1917 .N38 2002
    338.1'094--dc21
                                                           2001050110

ISBN 1 84064 235 1

Typeset by Manton Typesetters, Louth, Lincolnshire, UK.
Printed and bound in Great Britain by Biddles Ltd, *www.biddles.co.uk*

Contents

PART III   MITIGATION AND REGULATION

PART IV   OUTLOOK

List of figures

List of tables

List of contributors

Nikos Beopoulos is Associate Professor, Department of Rural Economics and Development, Agricultural University of Athens, Iera Odos 75, GR- 11855 Athens, Greece (e-mail: beopoulos@auadec.aua.gr).

María Blanco is Assistant Professor, Department of Agricultural Economics, Polytechnic University of Madrid, Cuidad Universitaria s/n, ES - 28040 Madrid, Spain (e-mail: mblanco@eco.etsia.upm.es).

François Bonnieux is a Research Leader at Institut National de la Recherche Agronomique (INRA), Centre de Rennes, INRA Economie, Rue Adolphe Bobierre CS 61 103, F 35 011 Rennes Cédex, France (e-mail: francois. bonnieux@roazhon.inra.fr).

Floor Brouwer is Head of the Research Unit Management of Natural Resources, Agricultural Economics Research Institute (LEI), P.O. Box 29703, 2502 LS The Hague, The Netherlands (e-mail: f.m.brouwer@lei.wag-ur.nl).

Claudia Carter is Research Associate, Cambridge Research for the Environment (CRE), Department of Land Economy, University of Cambridge, 19 Silver Street, Cambridge CB3 9EP, United Kingdom (e-mail: cec29@cam. ac.uk).

Bob Crabtree is a Consultant specializing in economic impact analysis and in the design and evaluation of policies for environmental management, CJC Consulting, 45 Southmoor Road, Oxford OX2 6RF, United Kingdom (e-mail: r.crabtree@totalise.co.uk).

Carel P.C.M. van der Hamsvoort is Senior Research Scholar Natural Resource Economics and Public Finance, Agricultural Economics Research Institute (LEI), P.O. Box 29703, 2502 LS The Hague, The Netherlands (e-mail: c.p.c.m.vanderhamsvoort@lei.wag-ur.nl).

Ingo Heinz is Senior Researcher in environmental economics and specialized on water issues at the Institut für Umweltforschung (INFU), Universität

Dortmund, Otto-Hahn-Strasse 6, D-44221 Dortmund, Germany (e-mail: iheinz@infu.uni-dortmund.de).

Markus F. Hofreither is Professor of Economics, Department of Economics, Politics and Law, University of Agricultural Sciences Vienna, Gregor-Mendelstrasse 33, A – 1180 Vienna, Austria (e-mail: hofreith@edv1.boku.ac.at).

Leonidas Louloudis is Assistant Professor, Department of Rural Economics and Development, Agricultural University of Athens, Iera Odos 75, GR-11855 Athens, Greece (e-mail: louloudis@auadec.aua.gr).

Jan Luijt is Senior Research Scholar in land economics and forestry, Agricultural Economics Research Institute (LEI), Department of Public Issues, P.O. Box 29703, 2502 LS The Hague, The Netherlands (e-mail: j.luijt@lei.wag-ur.nl).

Maurizio Merlo is Professor of Forest Economics and Policy and Director of the Centre for Environmental Accounting and Management in Agriculture and Forestry, Faculty of Agriculture, University of Padova, Agripolis, Corte Benedettina, Via Roma 34 a, 35020 Legnaro, Italy
(e-mail: merlo@agripolis.unipd.it).

Clive Potter is Reader in Environmental Policy at Imperial College, London and a Member of the Environmental Policy and Management Group, RSM Building, Prince Consort Road, London SW7 2AB, United Kingdom (e-mail: c.potter@ic.ac.uk).

Pierre Rainelli is a Research Director, Institut National de la Recherche Agronomique (INRA), Centre de Rennes, INRA Economie, Rue Adolphe Bobierre CS 61 103, F 35 011 Rennes Cédex, France (e-mail: Pierre.Rainelli @roazhon.inra.fr)

Clive L. Spash is Director of Cambridge Research for the Environment (CRE), Department of Land Economy, University of Cambridge, 19 Silver Street, Cambridge CB3 9EP, United Kingdom (e-mail: cec27@cam.ac.uk).

William M. Stigliani is Professor of Chemistry and Director of the Center for Energy and Environmental Education (CEEE), University of Northern Iowa, Cedar Falls, Iowa 50614–0293, United States of America (e-mail: william.stigliani@uni.edu).

Jan van der Straaten is Assistant Professor, Department of Leisure Studies, Tilburg University, P.O. Box 90153, 5000 LE Tilburg, The Netherlands (e-mail: j.vdrstraaten@kub.nl).

José Sumpsi is Professor in Agricultural Economics, Department of Agricultural Economics, Polytechnic University of Madrid, Cuidad Universitaria s/n, ES – 28040 Madrid, Spain (e-mail: jsumpsi@eco.etsia.upm.es).

Consuelo Varela-Ortega is Professor in Agricultural Economics, Department of Agricultural Economics, Polytechnic University of Madrid, Cuidad Universitaria s/n, ES – 28040 Madrid, Spain (e-mail: cvarela@eco.etsia.upm.es).

Preface

Nature and agriculture both shape the European countryside. One of the main challenges for the years to come will be to strengthen their interactions in the future development of rural areas. Economics and ecology play a vital role in sustaining the interactions between agriculture and nature, and this understanding should guide the identification of suitable policy instruments.

The current book has been put together following the observation from the editors that a solid understanding of economic–ecological interactions is vital for the perspectives on agriculture and nature policies in the EU. The book provides a state-of-the-art overview of the present understanding of linkages between agriculture and nature in the context of EU policy. Dilemmas facing European agriculture are identified and their economic and ecological consequences are explored. This understanding will be crucial in identifying potential options for the future role of agriculture and nature policy in the EU. It is our view that current difficulties should be coped with by a sound mixture of nature policy and agricultural policy.

We are grateful to the authors who were prepared to contribute to this book. They promptly responded to our proposals for change. This allowed us to strengthen the balance across individual contributions.

We hope this book will broaden the understanding of the vital role of economics and ecology in the interaction between agriculture and nature.

Floor Brouwer and Jan van der Straaten
Summer 2001

1. Agriculture and nature in conflict?

Floor Brouwer and Jan van der Straaten

CURRENT RELATIONSHIPS BETWEEN NATURE AND AGRICULTURE

Agriculture delivers a range of societal needs. It supplies food for the market, also contributing value added and employment to the national economy. Furthermore, farmers play an important role in sustaining the rural country-side. Agriculture is a dominant user of land in most European countries. More than three-quarters of the territory of the European Union (EU) is agricultural or wooded land. Forests cover about a third of the total land area in the EU. In marked contrast to the situation in other parts of the world, a large proportion of the land area of Europe has been farmed for several millennia. Agriculture was practised in both Southern and Northern Europe as early as the late Neolithic period. Originally confined to the flattest and most accessible land, arable and pastoral farming spread out to cover all but the most difficult terrain in many regions. By the middle of the late Roman empire (around AD 400), a majority of France, over half of Germany, most of the low countries, the Iberian peninsula, Italy and Greece, and the southern UK were all in farming use. Only the extreme north and the most mountainous areas, including Sweden, Finland, the northern tip of the UK and the Alpine regions of France, Italy, Austria, Switzerland and southern Germany, remained almost completely covered by forest or other natural vegetation, as recently as 100 years ago. In short, agriculture is a very important phenomenon and its societal significance cannot be overlooked.

As a result of its longstanding management of the land, farming in Europe has co-evolved with its ecology, landscapes and other environmental resources. Today, many of Europe's species and their characteristic habitats are dependent upon continued management to sustain their diversity. European landscapes are primarily cultural, heavily influenced by centuries of farm and woodland management. However, this largely positive relationship between management and environmental quality has depended upon low-input farming practices, in terms of use of capital and nutrients, while labour inputs were relatively high by comparison to the current situation.

1

The loss of biodiversity and cultural landscapes are issues of major significance in the EU, and a high priority for policy. A high proportion of flora and fauna depend upon semi-natural habitats and mosaics of farmed and forested land cover. More than a third of bird species are in decline, mainly due to habitat degeneration and land use changes caused by agricultural intensification. In Europe, many of the most valuable areas for wildlife and landscapes are those which have been settled and farmed for many centuries, in which species have co-evolved with traditional agricultural management and where landscapes are dependent on regular management for their variety and interest. Losses of biodiversity and landscape quality have also been widespread because of the removal of landscape features, loss of permanent grassland and destruction of other semi-natural habitats, as well as agricultural intensification on production farmland. The policy response is divided between the EU, national and more local levels.

At present there are two main threats to sustaining the interaction between agriculture and nature: abandonment and intensification (European Commission and Eurostat, 1999). Agricultural production intensified and concentrated over time, especially in regions with competitive advantages. Concentration of production resulted from intensification and specialization of production, involving the development of capital-intensive and geographically specialized farming. Such mechanisms are mainly observed in regions where agriculture is most productive. Competitive advantages might arise because of better biophysical conditions, more rationalized farm structures, and integration of primary production with food processing industries and well developed farm extension services. Agrochemicals (among others, including fertilizers, pesticides and feed additives) were increasingly applied to increase production, and also to reduce the risks of crop losses and the occurrence of pests and diseases. Marginalization and abandonment are also a problem in some regions and tend to occur in remote areas with unfavourable economic or social conditions, or on less fertile land where traditional extensive agriculture is threatened by its inability to compete effectively with intensive production in other regions. In Spain, for example, the abandonment of agricultural land potentially affects 12 million ha of land (Varela-Ortega and Sumpsi, 1998). Declining trends in agricultural production might be affected by a combination of environmental, demographic, geographic, socio-economic and political conditions. Such conditions could reduce the viability of farming, which might eventually cause the cessation of farming, usually leading to a change in land use or even land abandonment. Land abandonment can induce a loss of valuable habitats and species diversity. In addition, soil erosion and declining biodiversity are concerns in some marginal areas (Baldock *et al.*, 1996).

In conclusion, agricultural practices have a strong relationship with the availability of natural resources, also considering the quality of nature. Many

European landscapes, such as the Waddensea, the Alps and many wetlands and river deltas, are clearly recognized as nature. Public policies control the activities permitted in most of these nature areas. In addition, many of these national parks and nature reserves are managed by nature conservation groups or specialized national authorities. Agriculture tends to have limited impact on these nature reserves, as certain land management practices are regulated. This is not to say that there are no conflicts between national parks and farmers.

AGRICULTURE SUSTAINING THE RURAL COUNTRYSIDE

More complex is the situation outside the clearly recognized and defined nature reserves. Approximately 100 years ago, agriculture and nature were strongly interconnected, and in fact, it was very difficult to indicate which part of the land was nature and which part of the land was used agriculturally. By that time, land used agriculturally had a high nature value. This was maintained by the extensive use of agricultural land. The word 'extensive' can easily be misinterpreted. The type of farming practices applied was extensive due to the limited pressures it caused on nature values. This was not the intention of the farmers. On the contrary, they tried to maximize food production within the constraints they faced and the options that were available. However, natural barriers against the intensification of agriculture remained high and could not be controlled due to the limited expertise available then. This type of agriculture was very labour intensive. At that time, farming was labour intensive, but very capital extensive (with limited use of machinery and agrochemicals like pesticides and fertilizers). The output provided was food and a high quality of nature.

In the course of time, the composition of inputs in the agricultural projects changed dramatically. Agriculture became increasingly dependent on capital (machinery, fertilizers and pesticides), allowing increasing production at the expense of labour. By doing so, the nature values of the farmland decreased considerably. Of course, there was also a loss of nature values and biodiversity in strict nature areas. However, the loss of biodiversity of farmland is widespread and dramatic (Tucker and Heath, 1994; Vos and Stortelder, 1992; Presser, 2000; Gasc, 1997; Hagemeijer and Blair, 1997).

Agriculture in the EU is characterized by a wide range of farming types. By 1997, the EU had almost 7 million agricultural holdings, and farm size in the EU on average was around 18 ha. The number of agricultural holdings shows a declining trend, with increasing specialization of production and more intensive farming practices applied. The number of agricultural holdings has dropped between 1975 and 1995 by almost 20 per cent. Farm size has increased from 15 to 18 ha during the period between 1975 and 1995, which was an increase of about 20 per cent.

Farm structure differs markedly between Member States. Farm size on average ranges between 4 ha (Greece) and 69 ha (United Kingdom). It is smallest in Greece, Italy and Portugal. In these countries, around 70 per cent of the agricultural holdings are smaller than 5 ha. In contrast, about a third of the holdings are larger than 50 ha in the UK.

Farming systems in Europe are important for landscape maintenance and voluntary incentives are offered funding specific land management practices, needed for landscape, biodiversity and general environmental objectives.

THE POLICY CONTEXT OF AGRICULTURE AND NATURE

This intensification process of agriculture was mainly policy and technology driven. Because of this, a conflict in the policy field itself became apparent. The loss of nature values also became a source of concern for national states and the European Union. Non-Governmental Organizations (NGOs) in the field of nature protection, in particular the World Wide Fund for Nature and Greenpeace, gained societal support. Conventions were undersigned and Ministries for Environment and Nature Management were established. In addition, national parks and nature reserves became increasingly a concern for public policies. This, however, did not imply an increase of nature values in Europe in quantitative and qualitative terms. On the contrary, nature on farmland in particular is still decreasing year after year. The main reason is that the intensification is an ongoing process. On the other hand, this intensification process takes place only in those regions where agricultural circumstances are favourable. Farmers concentrate on these regions. In remote, hilly and mountain areas a process of extensification can be recognized. Farmers abandon land or cease their enterprises.

The process of extensification has a negative influence on the biodiversity of this land, in particular in Southern regions. When extensification starts, the maintenance of stone walls, terraces and wells is also terminated. An increase in erosion and landslides is the result. Furthermore, this abandoned land has in most cases shrub vegetation without the vulnerable species of the extensively used farmer land. From this analysis we can conclude that farmland is under the threat of a loss in biodiversity due to a process of extensification and intensification. In both processes the impetus of support from the Common Agricultural Policy (CAP) can be recognized.

Agricultural policy making includes agricultural ministries and the Agriculture Directorate-General of the European Commission. The network of the decision-making process of environmental policy making includes the environment ministries and the Environment Directorate-General. Agricultural and environmental decision-making processes are largely separate (Table 1.1).

Table 1.1   Milestones in the development of EU agri-environment policy

Agricultural policy	Environmental policy
	1973 First Environmental Action Programme has recognized the need to tackle emerging problems of agricultural pollution
1975 Less Favoured Areas Directive 75/268, to compensate farmers for working in mountain areas and hill farming and farming in certain less-favoured areas	
	1979 Birds Directive (79/409/EEC)
	1980 Drinking Water Directive (80/778/EEC) which specifies maximum allowable concentrations for nitrates and pesticides
1985 Commission's Green Paper which proposed that agricultural policy should 'take account of environmental policy, both as regards the control of harmful practices and the promotion of practices friendly to the environment'	
	1991 Nitrates Directive (91/676/EEC)
	1992 Habitats Directive (92/43/EEC)
1992 Agri-environmental regulation (2078/92) introduced as part of the MacSharry reform of 1992	1992 The 5th Environmental Action Programme 'Towards Sustainability' identifies the need for environmental integration into sectoral policies. Agriculture is one of the five target sectors

Source: Lowe and Baldock (2000)

Sustainable development has been made an explicit objective of the EU in the Amsterdam Treaty. The requirement to integrate environment into EU sectoral policies (including CAP) arises from Article 6 of the Consolidated Treaty, and applies to all policy sectors. The European Council at Cardiff in June 1998 endorsed the principle that major policy proposals made by the Commission should be accompanied by an appraisal of their environmental impact. At the same meeting the Council considered a Commission Communication entitled 'A Partnership for Integration: A Strategy for Integrating Environment into EU Policies' (European Commission, 1998). This proposed a strategy to implement the requirements of Article 6, and which directs attention to sectoral practices as being the origin of most environmental problems and therefore the source of the solutions. It reiterates that sustainable development is a concept that brings together concerns for social and economic development alongside protection of the environment, and that policies which result in environmental degradation and depletion of natural resources, are unlikely to be a sound basis for sustainable economic development.

THE ORGANIZATION OF THE BOOK

It is against the backcloth of linkages between agriculture and nature that the present volume has been compiled. In particular, it addresses our current understanding of linkages between agriculture and nature in the context of EU policy. Dilemmas facing agriculture are examined and their implications for the economic–ecological interaction are explored. This understanding will be crucial in identifying potential options for the future role of agriculture and nature policy in the EU context. The book has four parts: (i) methodological, (ii) cases on the interaction between agriculture and nature, (iii) mitigation and regulation, and (iv) outlook.

The first part reviews interactions between agriculture and nature from the perspective of an economic, ecological and policy point of view.

Chapter 2 examines the interface between agriculture and nature from an economic point of view. François Bonnieux and Pierre Rainelli state that it was the aim of the CAP to stimulate an undercapitalized agricultural economy. This has been achieved through an increase in productivity, and has been accompanied by a higher use of agrochemicals (fertilizer and pesticides) and an orientation towards mechanization. This trend was harmful to the environment, because water quality deteriorated due to the leaching of pesticides and fertilizers to groundwater and surface water. Furthermore, biodiversity and landscape quality has suffered from this type of agriculture. We may therefore conclude that harmful external effects on the physical and natural

environment accompanied agriculture. The Polluter Pays Principle was formulated in the 1970s to relate such externalities to the production methods
applied. However, we should not ignore the difficulties faced in defining the
property rights of nature and the environment in society. Difficulties in particular apply to agriculture.

The authors investigate farmers' response to market incentives, in particular when price relations of inputs and outputs are changed. They conclude
that, given the current societal interests to promote the beneficial relationships between nature and agriculture, instruments need to be chosen that are
least distorting. For that reason, a systematic use of economic incentives at
farm level has to be given a high priority. Efficiency gains could be achieved
in the allocation of available resources by decoupling support from production. This could be achieved mainly by a reduction of price support measures
in favour of direct payments (area-based payments or headage payments).
However, agricultural policy reform, which lessens intensification, is a necessary but insufficient step to remedy all environmental impacts originating
from agriculture. Decoupling support from production cannot solve any problem occurring from production shifts. For that reason, economic incentives
must be used to internalize costs and benefits. The challenge is to find the
optimal mix of the policy variables, including zoning, eligibility criteria,
prescriptions and monitoring, control and penalties for non-compliance in
order to minimise social costs, but without forgetting the social benefits.

In Chapter 3, William Stigliani discusses the Iowa agricultural system from
the aspects of economy, environment and energy. This North-American case
is dealt with in this book on EU policy, giving evidence that nutrient control
measures are also critical factors in agricultural production in other parts of
the world. Agriculture in Iowa has a strong emphasis on maximization of
crop yields and livestock production for increasing profits. This is achieved at
the expense of the environment at state, continental and global level. Also,
large amounts of energy are consumed by agriculture. The analysis in this
chapter focuses on the mass flows of two important components of the
agricultural system, the input of synthetic nitrogen fertilizer (N-fertilizer),
and the output of hog manure. The analysis shows the impacts of excess
amounts of nitrogen fertilizers applied and the poor application of livestock
manure. The author introduces a more ecological system of agriculture management. He argues that the current way that N-fertilizer and hog manure are
used in Iowa can only be justified when short-term economic interests are the
overriding consideration without paying sufficient attention to the effects on
water quality in, for example, the Gulf of Mexico, resulting from this type of
agriculture. When the current agricultural practice is compared with the
alternative, more ecological system, it becomes clear that substantial benefits
result from the application of this alternative model. Local impacts such as

water pollution, soil erosion and hog manure stench are reduced, as is Iowa's contribution to the 'dead zone' in the Gulf of Mexico.

It can be concluded that environmental pressures related to intensive live-stock production in the EU and in the USA are rather similar. Responses to harmful effects of agricultural practices on the environment have been reactive in the sense that measures were introduced in response to emerging or documented problems. This is applicable to most policies designed to internalize external effects from agriculture practice, irrespective of differences in cultures and preferences in the EU and the USA.

This chapter provides evidence that meeting ecological objectives in agricultural policy also creates additional benefits for the farm economy and energy conservation. Reduced use of synthetic fertilizer, particularly nitrogen, is good for the environment, saves farmers' money, and lowers the energy demand required for its production. Likewise, use of manure either as a fertilizer or an energy source can reduce water pollution, provide income, lower the stench, and improve the on-farm energy balance.

Chapter 4, by Clive Potter, examines the influence of the CAP on farmers and the countryside. It is argued that this policy has directed the countryside into a productivist direction, moulded by the commodity regimes and wedded to intensive, environmentally destructive systems of agricultural production. According to the policy mind set which gave rise to this state of affairs, agricultural output and productivity are the ultimate benchmarks of success, the primary purpose of rural policy being to raise the living standards of farmers through modernization.

Rebalancing policy and reforming institutions in order to give greater priority to environmental protection and less agri-centric forms of rural development, has been a slow process. There has been a complicated co-evolution of public attitudes and policy approaches, in which mounting criticism of agriculture's environmental impact has been met with a series of policy adaptations and adjustments. The result is that today we have a wide range of policy instruments being used to tackle environmental problems in agriculture which can only be understood if they are analysed within the broader agricultural policy context.

The author describes how current agri-environmental policy approaches came into existence. He analyses how policymakers have traditionally viewed the relationship between agriculture and the environment and the way in which the environment has been treated within the productivist policy model. By recognizing farmers as producers of public environmental goods, policymakers were able to justify from an early stage an essential voluntaristic strategy of subsidizing them for the environmental services they provided. In the agri-environmental policy field measures have tended to be bolted on to a CAP, which is basically productivist in its design and operation. Nevertheless, the outline of a more sustainable and better integrated rural policy which will eventually come to replace the current CAP is now apparent.

The coming years will see further evolution towards a more integrated application of policy instruments within a broad EU framework setting down standard operating procedures and basic principles. With large amounts of public resources, spent on farm support being recoupled to agri-environmental incentive schemes, pressure will increase for improved monitoring and enforcement. Better ways of delivering schemes to farmers and a broader client base of land managers will need to be found as well as mechanisms for bringing in groups of managers in order to conserve entire landscapes and watersheds.

Chapter 5 by Clive Spash and Claudia Carter examines to what extent economic methods can be used to give a monetary value to non-market values of nature and the environment. The authors offer a critical assessment of methods of environmental valuation which have been proclaimed as relevant to answering rural management issues when nature and the environment is at stake. In doing so, they outline a range of values associated with agricultural production and rural land use change. They also set out the methods of cost–benefit analysis (CBA) appropriate for assessing land use activities while referring to empirical work and explain the main problems associated with these methods. Additionally, they recommend the most appropriate methods for empirical work to evaluate the monetary benefits and costs of land use changes.

In particular the authors pay attention to the way in which the economic value of nature and the environment can be regarded. They provide an overview of the environmental values related to rural land use and divide these into market, non-market and non-economic values. Non-market values include a range of the environmental side-effects which might be associated with managing the countryside, such as wildlife habitat conservation. They summarize the principal methods for generating estimates of the non-market values and major problems in their application. The techniques discussed are the Travel Cost Method (TCM), the Production Function Approach (PFA), Hedonic Pricing (HP), and stated preference techniques, mainly the Contingent Value Method (CVM). They emphasize the limitations of these methods, which therefore demand prudent use in any policy context.

Finally, they give an overview to what extent these techniques can be used in different fields of policy concern where non-market values may be relevant such as aesthetics, cultural and historic values, health and safety, ecosystems functions and biodiversity, peace and quiet, recreation and tourism, and water and air quality. In this list CVM has the highest potentials in the view of the authors. They argue that perhaps the greatest contribution this technique currently offers is in terms of forcing economists to reconsider the content and meaning of both observed and intended human behaviour with regard to a plurality of environmental values. Of course, this is *ipso facto* also the case for policymakers in the EU dealing with the direction of EU policy in the fields of nature and agriculture.

The second part reviews four cases that offer empirical evidence on the interactions between agriculture and nature. Chapters 6–9 provide four case studies in various European countries.

Chapter 6, by Consuelo Varela-Ortega and her co-authors examines the availability of water in the Mediterranean region. The interactions between agriculture and nature are reviewed with a case study of the Tablas de Daimiel, which is an important RAMSAR qualified wetland area in the Castilla-La Mancha region in Spain. Farmers in the neighbourhood of this national park use water for irrigation purposes. By doing so, they increase the productivity of their farmland. However, they also diminish the water quantity available for the wetland and reduce in this way its ecological quality.

The authors seek for instruments integrating environmental objectives and economic objectives for a well-balanced cost-effective policy choice. Among the policy alternatives of the EU, agri-environmental programmes (AEP) have attained the environmental goal of reducing water abstractions and thus have contributed to recovering wetland ecosystems and have, in turn, produced economic and social stability.

From the case study it can be concluded that all policy options are more cost-effective than the measures, which currently apply, with the 1992 CAP reform direct payments, complemented with agri-environmental support measures. This policy was implemented in the Castilla-La Mancha region. Unquestionably, the incorporation into the CAP programmes of water saving agri-environmental payments has met the policy's environmental goal of water conservation. However, from a public perspective, this policy is expensive for the EU budget. If less water is available in the farms, irrigation will be reduced, crop profitability will diminish and farm income will decline. Therefore, farmers will voluntarily join this programme only if direct compensation payments are offered to them. Conversely, if cross-compliance options, as foreseen in Agenda 2000, were applied in the area, they would attain the desired reduction in water extractions at half of the expenses of the public funds.

Looking at the private sector, all policy options will inflict some income losses to the farmers if compared to the currently applied policy. In fact, in this policy, as farmers are eligible to a dual direct payment source of income (CAP reform of 1992 and agri-environmental support measures), they actually obtain higher income gains than with the baseline policy. Being an expensive policy, it remains socially questionable whether farmers will have to be additionally compensated for meeting environmental standards that are beneficial for nature's protection and for long term social well-being.

In general, the question that arises from this case study in the framework of Mediterranean water policies is a matter of policy choice. It is well known that all international agencies that deal with natural resources conservation call for a more efficient management of water resources, while the Mediterranean basin is one of the most fragile natural water environments. Deciding who will have to pay for the cost of reducing water use in agriculture is a major question of policy choice, where economic efficiency, nature preservation for future generations and social equity will have to be considered.

Chapter 7 presents a case study on agricultural policy and nature conservation in the UK. In his contribution, Bob Crabtree argues that habitat protection took a major step forward in the 1980s with two major pieces of regulation. The first, the 1981 Wildlife and Countryside Act, strengthened instruments for the protection of Sites of Special Scientific Interest (SSSIs) from potential damaging operations, especially on farmland. The act was not designed to provide for the more general protection of valued countryside from changes in land use. Since agriculture was outside the planning system, farmers were free to do much as they wished with their land. The second piece of legislation established a system of fixed payments that was to become the benchmark for future agri-environmental intervention in the UK.

There can be no doubt that the major agri-environmental schemes in the UK have produced nature conservation benefits. They have proved politically acceptable to government and farmers as clear evidence of a commitment to protect landscape and biodiversity, and to engage in a positive partnership for stewardship of the countryside. The costs of the schemes in relation to the possibly limited extent of the benefits have left a degree of scepticism amongst economists.

The author concludes that governments are likely to face difficulty with payment schemes that continue in the very long-term. Such commitments limit the flexibility to engage in new conservation initiatives as priorities change over time. He assumes a move to a more selective policy menu where incentive mechanisms will only be used at the margin and over the relative short-term. Bob Crabtree has some doubt whether taxpayers will be willing to pay the increasing cost of large-scale intervention to maintain historic practices and their associated landscapes for an indefinite period.

In Chapter 8, Jan Luijt and Carel van der Hamsvoort investigate the development of land prices in the Netherlands. This country has a high density of population, economic activities, and agricultural activities. Trends in land prices are relevant, since land is the main input in agricultural production. One of the most significant recent problems in the Netherlands is the use and organization of the limited land available. The high level of economic growth and the substantial increase in income in recent years has increased demand of land for housing, infrastructure, business premises, and nature and landscape. However, land is a limiting resource, and approximately 70 per cent of it is in use for agriculture. The growth in demand and the limited availability of land is being translated into developments in the real estate market.

The authors are convinced about the relevance of the different policy fields for the land market. Viewed separately, the environmental, nature and agricultural policies might be consistent with the goals they are supposed to achieve, but in interaction they are conflicting and preclude the simultaneous achievement of these very same objectives. The agricultural land market plays a pivotal role in this network of interactions. The authors conclude that high guaranteed prices in combination with technical development lead to an expansion of agricultural production and an increase of scale. Since increase of scale via expansion of acreage is only possible in dribs and drabs, due to the mainly demographically determined rationed supply of agricultural land and the massive non-agricultural claims on it, agricultural land use is becoming more and more intensive, although sometimes curbed by production restrictions such as quotas that give rise to costly production rights.

The authors also conclude that the EU market and price policy, with the exception of the milk quotas, caused the price of land to rise. In addition, land prices also increased due to environmental and nature policy. Finally, the recent growing economy has created many urban claims on agricultural land, causing the price of agricultural land to rise along with the general increase of real estate prices. For farmers, the dramatic high land price is reason to make even a more intensive use of agricultural land. The interaction between agricultural policy, nature policy, and town and country planning policy via the real estate market cannot be overlooked.

The final chapter of this part of the book examines the sectorial perspective on agricultural policy that is broadening in Greece. Chapter 9 by Leonidas Louloudis and Nikos Beopoulos provides clear evidence about the various countries of the EU facing different types of problems in agricultural policies. In Greece, for example, the government only recently became aware of the harmful effects of agriculture on the environment. Additionally, Greek farmers were not adequately prepared for the new significance ascribed in European agriculture to environmental protection. Despite these factors hampering the implementation of measures to integrate environmental requirements in farming, major changes have recently taken place in the pattern of rural development.

The authors examine changes which have taken place in the rural countryside of Greece during the past few decades. Geopolitical conditions, for example, the immigration since the end of the 1980s, have largely changed the demographic conditions of rural areas, as well as the structure of their economies and labour markets. In addition, social changes have also taken place.

The authors conclude that the programmatically multisectorial and complementary character of the policies implemented in Greece, was not designed adequately. If designed, as was the case with agri-environmental policy, they were not consistently adhered to during their implementation. The prevailing problems are the lack of political will at government level and the weakness of the 'Mediterranean' syndrome of public administration. Other relevant factors are the prevalence of economic interests of powerful lobbies related to the exercise of monosectorial agricultural policy, the lack of mechanisms for agricultural education and training, and, possibly, throughout the whole network of national rural policy planning. In addition, also relevant are factors such as a lack of a culture of creative adaptation to the new conditions of international competition, and of legitimization of the rural development policy.

Part three of the book identifies some major changes in market conditions and in the CAP that will also alter the future potential of interactions between nature and agriculture in the context of the European Union.

Chapter 10, by Maurizio Merlo, identifies a range of environmental recreational goods and services (ERGS) supplied by agriculture and forestry. Examples include attractive landscapes, maintenance of rural footpaths, habitats for various animals and plants, grounds for sport and other recreational activities. Additionally, agriculture and forestry produce substantial negative effects on nature and the environment: environmental bads and disservices (EBD). These ERGSs and EBDs influence the welfare position of many people. However, there is no market for them and therefore an optimal allocation of production factors cannot be assured in this case. Therefore, policy tools have been developed aimed at achieving sufficient provision of ERGSs and prevention of EBDs.

The author presents the results of a survey conducted in Austria, Germany, the Netherlands and Italy. He concludes that the various policy tools to promote ERGSs have both advantages and disadvantages. However, it is clear that they cannot be seen, and conceived, separately, and this is a common feature of environmental policies aimed at increasing the provision of ERGSs. Mandatory legally binding instruments, new and old ones, should be applied together with economic–financial and marketed tools. The sustainable provision of the various ERGSs and the prevention of EBDs, goes through jointly devised and applied policy tools integrated and permeated by the transparency of information, including measures of persuasion and communication. From the survey it becomes clear that it is also important that the policy mix should be devised area by area according to the subsidiarity principle, developing specific packages of policy measures and tools. The concept is not new, being for instance demanded by the Structural Fund.

Chapter 11, by Ingo Heinz focuses on the cost effectiveness of environmental policies. The traditional instruments of legislation and the implementation of economic instruments cannot take into account the special conditions in vulnerable areas. Since the impacts on the environment are typically diffuse due to the complex processes in water and soil, enforcement of legislation to comply with compulsory measures and ensuring the requirements for the application of economic instruments, such as charges on pollution, are very difficult. In particular, the level of water pollution resulting from the agricultural activities of a certain farmer is often very difficult to identify. As a consequence, in recent years voluntary approaches to influence the farming practices have been increasingly adopted in some EU member countries.

The author gives an overview of the principles of co-operative agreements in agriculture. Their linkages with other agri-environmental policy instruments are examined. Moreover, the occurrence and the reasons for establishing co-operative agreements in the EU member countries are discussed. Additionally, the author comes to the conclusion that legislation opens itself increasingly for voluntary approaches and that in some cases compulsory rules have been replaced by voluntary agreements. Here the authorities give priority to voluntary negotiations with farmers over a rigid enforcement of obligatory rules. The main argument for doing so is the observation made that voluntary approaches have some advantages in terms of environmental effectivity and economic efficiency.

While, initially, in Germany and the Netherlands co-operative agreements between farmers and water suppliers are practised, this instrument is not common in several EU member states, especially in the Mediterranean region. In some other member states such as Austria, Denmark and the United Kingdom, the first steps towards negotiations between water suppliers and farmers can be observed.

Chapter 12, by Markus Hofreither discusses the broader problem of rural development. He is of the opinion that agriculture is no longer the key factor of development in the rural countryside, as this was the case in the 1950s. Farm output has lost its regional focus, being mainly produced for international markets. Farmers remaining self-employed often have to enter new fields of non-agricultural activities and so gradually may turn into non-agricultural entrepreneurs. At the outset of this process traditional regional policies have supported these transformations in their attempts to enhance regional economic conditions via top-down measures, mainly in the form of providing support and adjustment subsidies.

The author compares the success and the failure of this transformation process in two Austrian mountain regions. He comes to the conclusion that, in general, the success of an integrated development strategy depends on three elements: the resource endowment of a region, the availability and activity of the actors and the actual measures realized. It is important that sufficient investment is realized in infrastructure and that a multi-sectoral approach is fundamental in new policies. Finally, the qualification of the labour force in the region and the presence and functioning of internal and external networks are preconditions for a successful rural development policy.

Markus Hofreither stresses that the increased emphasis on bottom-up factors does not imply that top-down policies are not relevant any more. Both the rules and the budgets of national and community level policies dedicated to support rural regions remain an important top-down element. Yet for the actual success of regional development processes an active and skilful bottom-up incentive is of indispensable importance in order to complement the top-down measures available. 'Integrated Rural Development' therefore must not be confined to improving the coherence and compatibility of community and national initiatives. It has to put at least the same weight on the endogenous ability and willingness of a region to act efficiently in favour of its own and new interests.

REFERENCES

Baldock, D., G. Beaufoy, F. Brouwer and F. Godeschalk (1996), *Farming at the margins: abandonment or redeployment of agricultural land in Europe*, London/ The Hague: Institute for European Environmental Policy (IEEP) and Agricultural Economics Research Institute (LEI-DLO).

European Commission (1998), *A partnership for integration: a strategy for integrating environment into EU policies*, Brussels: Commission of the European Communities, COM (98) 333.

European Commission and Eurostat (1999), *Agriculture, environment, rural development: facts and figures – a challenge for agriculture*, Brussels: DG VI, DG XI and Eurostat.

Gasc, J.-P. (ed.) (1997), *Atlas of Amphibians and Reptiles in Europe*, Paris: Musée National d'Histoire Naturelle.

Hagemeijer, W.J.M. and M. Blair (1997), *The EBCC Atlas of Europan Breeding Birds*, London: T. & A.D. Poyser.

Lowe, P. and D. Baldock (2000), 'Integration of environmental objectives into agricultural policy making', in F. Brouwer and P. Lowe (eds), *CAP regimes and the European Countryside: Prospects for Integration between Agricultural, Regional and Environmental Policies*, Wallingford: CABI Publishing, pp. 31–52.

Presser, H. (2000), *Die Orchideen Mitteleuropas und der Alpen*, Landsberg/Lech: Ecomed.

Tucker, G.M. and M.F. Heath (1994), *Birds in Europe, Their Conservation Status*, Cambridge: Bird Life International.

Varela-Ortega, C. and J. Sumpsi (1998), 'Spain', in F. Brouwer and P. Lowe (eds), *CAP and the rural environment in transition: A panorama of national perspectives*, Wageningen: Wageningen Pers, pp. 201–40.

Vos, W. and A. Stortelder (1992), *Vanishing Tuscan Landscapes*, Wageningen: Pudoc.

PART I

Methodology

2. Economics and the interface between agriculture and nature

François Bonnieux and Pierre Rainelli

INTRODUCTION

In a period of food scarcity agricultural policies have been designed to increase agricultural production and provide stable revenues to the farmers. More precisely, the aim of the former Common Agricultural Policy (CAP) was to stimulate an undercapitalized, peasant agriculture by increasing productivity. This objective has been reached but at the expense of nature, even if farmers remain important providers of public environmental goods. The dramatic increase of productivity has been obtained through the implementation of a highly coherent intensive model of farming aimed at maximizing a crop's potential for photosynthesis. This model is based on mechanization and more productive varieties sown earlier and with higher densities. All this requires more fertilizer use. But as these varieties are less resistant to disease and pests, they require more control. Irrigation gives another impetus to the yields' increase. In France, the fivefold increase in cereal yields over the past 40 years has only been possible through the massive use of fertilizers and phyto-pharmaceutical, of which France is the world's second largest consumer, and through the increase of the irrigated acreage.

This intensive model of farming results in a number of significant problems among which we can mention particularly:

- human health effects of pesticide and fertiliser residues in soil, water bodies and the food chain;
- Bovine Spongiform Encephalopathy (BSE), and the use of bone and meat meals, with potential consequences on human health;
- a shift from managing biodiversity spatially to managing it over time and consequently important losses of cultivars and an increase of pests resisting one or more pesticides;
- eutrophication of ground and surface waters leading to declines in the quality of aquatic resources, losses in recreational values and increased water supply costs;

19

● losses in landscape amenities due to the emergence of monocultures, the removal of hedges and the destruction of traditional farm buildings.

On the other hand, it can be argued that intensification can lead, all things being equal, to a better control of emissions of pollutants. For example, in the Dutch horticulture the introduction of artificial growing medium (that is substrate) under glass allowed an important reduction of consumption of nematicides (Brouwer and Van Berkum, 1998). For cereal farming, it has been shown that fewer chemicals are used for every unit of money generated from crop output when land is irrigated (Rainelli and Vermersch, 1999).

This chapter is organized as follows. The first section considers a series of interactions between agricultural policy and the environment, whereas the second analyses the nature of agricultural externalities from a social point of view. The third section focuses on possible policy strategy solutions to internalize them. The final section mainly emphasizes policy instruments which target the provision of environmental and rural amenities.

AGRICULTURAL POLICY AND ENVIRONMENTAL QUALITY

This section provides an overview on the mechanisms underlying agricultural policy which lead to an overuse, or a misuse, of natural resources. Basically, the detrimental environmental effects of support to agriculture are due to structural changes occurring in the pattern of resource allocation.

In a pure competitive market, technological change substitutes for factors unequally, and the theory of 'induced innovation' explains the rate and bias of technological change as an economic response to market forces by profit-maximizing entrepreneurs. Changes in factor ratios result from the cumulative effects of three elements: the simple factor substitution within the production function; the factor saving arising from technological change within the envelope of the isoquants available; and the factor saving arising from scientific knowledge. If the technological change is Hicks-neutral, the factor ratio is such that the relatively more expensive factor will be saved (Hayami and Ruttan, 1985). This general pattern is affected by two biases.

The first bias is related to scientific and technological developments leading to labour–saving technologies through sophisticated machinery, plant breeding advances, or new molecules of pesticides. This shift has been encouraged by the high level of the costs of hired labour comparative to the price of labour-saving capital goods. But another strong bias is introduced by agricultural policy and collective action by farmers. After the Second World War, the security of food production became the main objective of agricultural policy in all the European countries. In this context, a variety of measures including price support, input subsidies, direct payments, research and extension have been implemented. As a result the self-sufficiency rate is reached by the end of the seventies for EEC-10 (OECD, 1987, p. 15).

The combined result of these shifts is extensive substitution of capital for labour. For EEC-11 total factor productivity rises by 2.0 per cent a year from 1973 to 1994, and agricultural output in volume by 1.6 per cent a year in the same period. This result is obtained with a slight decrease of total inputs use (–0.4 per cent per year). But the volume of labour decreases by 2.9 per cent, whereas the volume of intermediate consumption and capital increases respectively by 1.5 per cent and 1.2 per cent (Bureau *et al.*, 1997). It is clear that the labour productivity gains are linked to the increasing capital-intensity, for example the labour–capital ratio.

High commodity prices have intensified competition for scarce resources, mainly for land, encouraging a more intensive use of this factor. For the period 1973–94 the volume of land has decreased for EEC-11 by 0.2 per cent a year (Bureau *et al.*, 1997). We have to mention the high price of land as a key driving force for introducing more intensive techniques, and the role of agricultural policy. Even if the system of direct payments issued from the 1992 CAP reform is less distorting, it nevertheless has an impact on the price of the land. In the short term, the direct support pushed down the real cost of land. But in the medium run this downward pressure has been cancelled out by its capitalization, in the form of rent, into the price of land. The recent trend in French land prices shows this effect of the direct support. As early as 1993, then 1994, the price of arable land began to rise in grain-growing *départements*: like Aube (up 4.6 per cent) and Marne (4.8 per cent). In 1995 for the first time since 1979, there was a rise of 0.4 per cent across the country as a whole, a rise which nowadays continues. The average national increase reached 4 per cent in 1999 (AGRESTE, 2000).

The process of agricultural intensification can be expressed by considering a simplified production function, involving just two factors: F, land, and an aggregate, G, representing all the other factors (labour, capital and intermediate consumption), and without economies of scale. Of course, land is no more a homogeneous production factor, but this simplified reasoning allows us to represent graphically the various ways of producing Y from different combinations of F and G, as illustrated by Figure 2.1 (Mahé and Rainelli, 1987).

If the price of agricultural products increases, either in absolute terms or in relative terms due to neutral technical progress, following Hicks' terminology, there will be a shift from isoquant Y_1 to isoquant Y_2. Point A on curve Y_1 represents the G–F price ratio w_1. However, if the shift from Y_1 to Y_2 is prevented by a shortage of land (constraint F), the relevant line will be OB,

Methodology

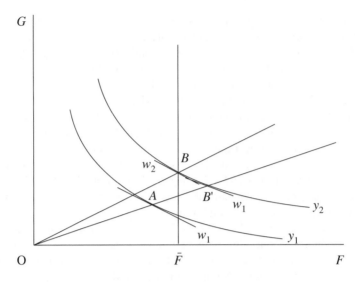

Figure 2.1   Land constraint and agricultural intensification

not *OA*, since the price of land will rise. It follows that the use of *G* per hectare will increase. What we have is a Ricardian type global process of intensification. Nevertheless, policy decisions also play a part. This is what happened when set-aside was introduced under the CAP reforms. The effect of this measure is to intensify constraint *F* for farmers.

For convenience, aggregate *G* is taken to include all factors of production other than land; all inputs are assumed to be strictly complementary and technical progress neutral. In fact, what happens is that there is a substitution between intermediate consumption and capital on the one hand and labour on the other due to a negative factor bias against labour. In addition, price ratio trends also favour the use of capital and chemical inputs at the expense of labour.

As a consequence of the above trends, there are more and more polluting inputs per unit of land. For instance, nitrogen pollution considered as a significant indicator, reaches alarming levels. Taking into account rate and spatial distribution of nitrogen application the nitrate leaching from the root zone of agricultural land in Europe has been estimated by modelling (Stanners and Bourdeau, 1995, p. 68). Over 85 per cent of the agricultural area exceeds the recommended level of 25 mg of nitrates per litre, and the maximum admissible concentration of 50 mg is exceeded at almost 20 per cent of the agricultural area. This proportion is higher in Belgium, Germany, England, the Netherlands, Denmark and the northern part of France. Another calculation based on the nitrogen balance, the difference between total inputs, including livestock manure, inorganic fertilizers, atmospheric deposition and nitrogen fixation, and the nitrogen removed with the harvested crops, shows that the surplus varies from 200 kg/ha/year in the Netherlands to less than 10 kg/ha/year in Portugal (European Environment Agency, 1998, p. 200).

Irrigation has played a key role in the intensification of the production process, thanks to direct and indirect support. According to the FAO data, irrigable surfaces in the European Union rose by 152 000 ha per year between 1961 and 1980, and by 146 000 ha per year between 1980 and 1996 (from 6.5 million ha in 1961 to 11.6 million ha in 1996). France shows the highest increase, the number of farms equipped for irrigation doubling between 1970 and 1995 while irrigated acreage multiplied fivefold over the same period (Strosser *et al.*, 1999). The 1992 CAP reform with the system of premia per hectare based on reference yields specific to irrigated areas has favoured this type of farming. This automatically generates heavier use of all kinds of polluting inputs, even if irrigated crop systems seem to be technically more efficient than non-irrigated ones. The scope for support to be capitalized into land reinforces this trend (Rainelli and Vermersch, 1999).

In parallel with intensification, price support for grains has resulted in a split between crop and livestock farming, leading to an important specialization within the farms and at the regional level. Moreover price support for cereals reduced the advantage of using European cereals in compound feed relative to raw material imported. The resulting separation of arable land and livestock farming has encouraged the trend towards a gradual intensification of animal rearing with bigger herds and a shift from the traditional upland and grassland areas of the European Union to the coastal areas to benefit from the attractive price of the imported material to produce compound feed. In addition, integrated farming systems preserve the genetic diversity and produce the aesthetic character of European landscapes.

In France, a country that accounts for 30 per cent of the European Union output of cereals, 37 per cent of the oilseed and 62 per cent of protein crops, arable farming is increasingly concentrated in fewer farms. Between 1988 and 1997 the number of cereal farms fell by 35 per cent, while the corresponding acreage rose slightly. Farm concentration has been more spectacular for oilseed rape with a 17 per cent increase in acreage over the same period, and a decline by 40 per cent in the number of farmers (AGRESTE, 1998). This specialization corresponds to a geographical specialization in two regions: the area around the Ile-de-France, accounting for 13.5 per cent of national cereal acreage, and in the Midi-Pyrénées region accounting for 7.8 per cent of total French cereal acreage.

From an economic standpoint, the past situation was characterized by economies of scope. According to the classical definition, these economies appear when the joint production cost of several goods is less than the production cost of these same goods produced separately. The system of guaranteed prices and the technological innovations have enhanced the agricultural production through intensification and specialization. This latter corresponds to the use of scale economies in a situation of land fixity (Vermersch, 1990). Moreover, a large part of traditional economic activities moved away from the farm to the profit of the market or upstream and downstream firms. In consequence, the level of internalization specific to the agricultural firm became smaller. This is consistent with the Coasean analysis of the firm, where the firm uses the market as soon as 'the organisation costs of additional transactions within the firm are equal to the costs produced by transactions on the market or to the costs of the organisation by another contractor' (Coase, 1937). This ranking of organization and transaction costs explains the respective role of size and scale economies. But in fact, there is no strict equivalence between scope economies versus scope diseconomies, and diversification versus specialization within the firm, because the entrepreneur thinks of scope economies in terms of private cost, whereas the decision maker measures them in terms of social cost.

AGRICULTURAL EXTERNALITIES: THE SOCIAL CHOICE PROBLEM

The intensification process due to price support and biased technological changes has given, as previously indicated, incentives to the overuse and degradation of natural resources including losses in species abundance and diversity and a decrease in landscape amenity and heritage. But in many areas specific types of agriculture have played, and continue to play an important role in creating the site-specific biodiversity and landscape amenities. Farming does not only impose harmful effects which decrease other people's welfare, but can also lead to positive externalities that benefit those affected. The underlying economic mechanism is illustrated by Figure 2.2. It displays the current situation in a specific area in which agriculture provides both positive and negative externalities: for high levels of intensification negative externalities dominate while for low levels of intensification positive externalities dominate.

The level of intensification is measured by a simple indicator Y which is the output per hectare. Agricultural supply is given by the marginal private cost C_{mp} whereas the second curve C_{ms} depicts marginal social cost, for example marginal private cost plus the marginal externalities stemming from farming activity. Point A_0 is the intersection of the two curves and is associated with the threshold Y_0 of intensification. If Y is smaller than Y_0, agriculture generates positive externalities, and for levels above Y_0 negative impacts

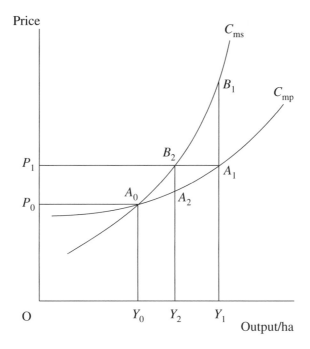

Figure 2.2   Intensification and externalities

progressively dominate the positive externalities. However, if the output per hectare becomes too low, marginalization and problems of abandonment might result.

The price support results in a price P_1 greater than P_0 leading to equilibrium point A_1 with output level per hectare Y_1. Output price being constant and equalled to P_1, a better possible environmental performance of agriculture is associated with point A_2 and output Y_2. This new equilibrium is obtained where marginal social cost equals the market price. The decrease in intensification from Y_1 to Y_2 leads to an increase in total welfare because the reduction in negative externalities ($A_1A_2B_2B_1$) is greater than the reduction in producer surplus ($A_1A_2B_2$). The conventional policy instrument to induce a shift from the private optimum A_1 to the social optimum A_2 is to implement a tax whose rate is A_2B_2. An additional decrease in intensification does not improve social welfare while Y is greater than the threshold Y_0. However, as intensification decreases under this threshold, positive externalities occur and are likely to compensate the loss in producer surplus. This can result in a new equilibrium which is socially better than the former one corresponding to Y_2. The overall welfare implications of a decrease in both the price support and the level of intensification are still ambiguous. In order to illustrate this point let us consider a simultaneous shift of the output per hectare from Y_1 to Y_0 and of the price from P_1 to P_0. This leads to a decrease in negative externalities given by $A_0A_1B_1$ and a decrease in producer surplus equal to $P_0A_0A_1P_1$. There is therefore an improvement in social welfare if and only if: $A_0A_1B_1 > P_0A_0A_1P_1$.

The policy issue is the reference level A_0 which determines when agricultural externalities are positive or negative, and the way to internalize, account for, and allocate the environmental costs and benefits. Reference levels are defined in relation to specific environmental targets, or standards for soil, water and air which are quality levels considered to be desirable for the ecosystems, including human health. For example, in the context of water pollution it applies to the concentration in a series of substances which are harmful for aquatic vegetation, fauna and humans. The fixation of reference levels is on the one hand crucial to defend environmental policies, but is on the other hand no easy task and certainly value based. Indeed reference levels integrate on environmental or ecological dimensions as well as on an economic and social one.

As the various linkages are very complex, a number of uncertainties remain. All economic activity, whether industrial or agricultural, operates in a constructed social context. In consequence reference levels take into account the current scientific knowledge as well as perceptions and views of scientists, policymakers and the general public with respect to risk and uncertainty. Environmental standards are defined along theses lines. They are the minimum levels for soil, water and air quality, which are considered acceptable for human health and living habitats. It is sometimes difficult to define what is positive and what is negative. Reference levels are indeed conditioned on social preferences and are to some extent historically contingent.

Once environmental targets are defined, farmers are explicitly obliged not to pollute beyond such levels. The Polluter Pays Principle implies that up to this level the polluter should bear expenses for carrying out measures decided by public authorities to ensure that the environment is in an acceptable state, according to the OECD definition. A symmetrically-opposite principle can be expressed when farmers are below A_0. In this case, farmers are viewed as generating external benefits for which they are not rewarded. The 'provider-gets' principle appears as the appropriate response (Blöchliger, 1994). The decision over whether an action constitutes a negative externality or whether it provides benefits to society relies on a clear definition of property rights. Paradoxically in our developed societies, agriculture maintains a profound political influence, the practical consequence of which is that agriculture has been somewhat indulged and favoured in comparison with other activities. Consequently, agriculture is characterized by presumptive property rights that have distorting effects (Bromley, 1997).

Changes in farming practices for producing agricultural commodities will at the same time contribute to improving or deteriorating ecological, habitat and amenity impacts. A focus on farm technology is therefore relevant to explore this relationship more deeply and to deal with the valuation of externalities. Despite the mentioned difficulties in delineating positive and negative externalities, let us suppose that reference levels are clearly established. First of all consider the case of positive externalities. Farming is assumed jointly to produce private goods X which are marketed and positive externalities Q which are public goods. Define social welfare U as a function of both vectors X and Q: $U = U(X,Q)$ and the product transformation curve that bounds the set of all technologically feasible combinations (X,Q): $G(X,Q) = 0$ where environmental and quasi-fixed private inputs are omitted.

The social choice problem is to find a feasible combination (X_0, Q_0) which maximizes social welfare U subject to available technology described by G. Graphically the solution of the problem is illustrated by point A_0 which lies at the tangency of the isosocial welfare curve U_0 and the production possibility frontier G (Figure 2.3). At the tangency, the marginal rate of social substitution between the private and public goods is set equal to marginal rate of technical transformation. For market goods, prices serve as signals to which consumption and production adjust to establish the conditions at point A_0. Where prices do not exist, there is no market mechanism that ensures social optimum is achieved. Indeed, farmers do not have incentives to internalize

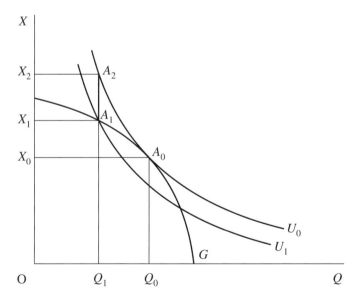

Figure 2.3   Valuation of an increase in positive externalities

the environmental benefits into their activities when decisions are made. The agri-environmental performance is likely to be sub-optimal. In such a case the outcome is given by the point A_1 and society only achieves a level of utility indicated by U_1. If there is no adequate scheme or regulatory framework, there is an under-supply of public goods and an over-supply of private goods: $U_1 < U_0$, $Q_1 < Q_0$, $X_1 > X_0$.

Suppose at point A_1 an increase in public goods is offered to consumers. Of interest is whether such an increase in the provision of public goods would be valued more highly by consumers than by the producers. Farmers must give up X to produce more Q at a rate defined by the slope of the production possibility frontier. In terms of profit foregone, a shift from A_1 to A_0 is valued in units of X by: $X_1 - X_0$.

The amount of X consumers who would be willing to pay (*WTP*) for the increase in Q is measured at the utility level U_0 achieved after the change in Q. The value of the shift in units of X equals: $WTP = X_2 - X_0$.

Indeed, as shift along U_0 from A_2 to A_0 involves an increase in Q from Q_1 to Q_0 it is compensated by a decrease in X from X_2 to X_0.

Under standard curvature properties shown in Figure 2.3, $WTP > X_1 - X_0$, which implies that consumers would be willing to pay more than farmers would have to pay to increase Q from Q_1 to Q_0.

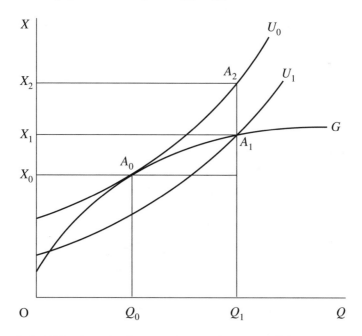

Figure 2.4   Valuation of a decrease in negative externalities

A similar argument applies to when Q denotes a public bad as described in Figure 2.4. Here agricultural commodities and negative externalities are complements as shown by the production possibility frontier G. The curvature of the utility function indicates a positive marginal rate of substitution between X and Q, because every increase in the public bad must be compensated by an increase in private goods in order to keep constant the level of utility. If there is no internalization scheme an over-supply of both categories of goods occurs as indicated by the point A_1. A reduction in negative externalities from Q_1 to Q_0 is needed in order to achieve the social optimum given by A_0. As before, consumers are willing to pay more than farmers for this change. Indeed, in units of X, WTP is given by $X_2 - X_0$ whereas profit foregone equals $X_1 - X_0$.

CONTROLLING NEGATIVE EXTERNALITIES

When a farmer does not bear all of the costs of producing commodities, his marginal private cost is less than his marginal social cost and he produces more than is socially optimal. The difference between marginal private cost and marginal social cost at each level of output is the marginal damage, and the corresponding misallocation of resources, that is the market failure, results in a loss of welfare (see, for example, Bonnieux and Guyomard, 1999). In the regulation of negative externalities there is a trade-off between the damage that people suffer from pollution and the resources required to reduce polluting emissions. Figure 2.5, where marginal abatement cost (MAC) and marginal damage (MD) functions are shown, may be used to illustrate this trade-off. The farmer's marginal abatement cost corresponds to the sum of all costs for achieving a one-unit decrease in emission levels or, alternatively, the costs saved if emissions are increased by one unit. The corresponding curve starts at the uncontrolled emission level E_0 and is upward sloping to the left. The marginal damage function corresponds to the sum of all the damage which stems from a unit change in emissions. The corresponding curve starts at the origin and is upward sloping to the right since marginal damage is assumed to increase with emission levels.

In the absence of government intervention, the farmer has no incentive to take into account the negative environmental externalities arising from his production, since damage and associated costs are incurred by others. Accordingly to his private interest, the farmer will decide to produce an output quantity which corresponds to uncontrolled emission levels E_0. Potential social costs are therefore completely ignored. Starting from point E_0, a decrease in emission levels leads to an increase in abatement costs which is more than offset by the induced decrease in damage costs. Marginal damage

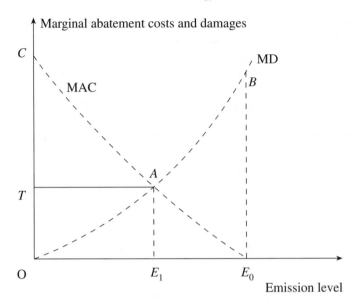

Figure 2.5   Tax on emissions versus emission standard

is greater than marginal abatement costs until point *A* where MD and MAC curves intersect. Accordingly, point *A* corresponds to emission levels E_1 which are optimal for the society. The optimal level of pollution for the society is thus always less than that which is optimal from the private perspective of the profit-maximizing farmer. Higher emissions expose society to greater costs stemming from increased environmental damage and lower emissions require society to pay for the costs in the form of resources devoted to abatement activities. The gap between the private optimum E_0 and the social optimum E_1 illustrates the failure of market mechanisms to maximize society's welfare in the presence of external effects when there is no government intervention.

A basic approach to correct the market failure due to a negative externality is to implement a taxation scheme to internalize the negative social costs resulting from an excessive level of polluting emissions. An emission tax whose rate equals OT, levied on each unit of emissions, clearly appears to be optimal. Its flat rate corresponds to marginal damage evaluated at social optimum point *A*. This tax gives the farmer the incentive to reduce his emissions from E_0 to E_1. Indeed, the equilibrium quantity of emissions is determined by the intersection of the tax line and the supply curve for abatement, that is MAC. Under such a tax fixed at optimal level OT, the total costs borne by the farmer are abatement costs (that is area E_0E_1A) and tax costs (that is area OE_1AT). He is forced to pay for the activities needed to reduce emissions until the socially optimal level is reached, as well as for the residual emissions. This corresponds to the implementation of the Polluter Pays Principle, which acknowledges that society holds the right to use the environment and hence, that farms must purchase this right in order to pollute. This involves a strict interpretation of the Polluter Pays Principle. As society commonly accepts a certain degree of pollution (below a defined threshold), a weak version of the Polluter Pays Principle will be enforced.

An alternative approach may be to rely on a command and control scheme to regulate directly the quantity of pollution that is permitted. The enforcement of an emission standard equal to E_1 also achieves the social optimum A. But, in that case, the costs borne by the farmer are restricted to abatement costs since he does not pay for the use of the environment. Both schemes are equivalent in terms of social optimality since the same level of negative externality is obtained. Nevertheless, they differ in terms of wealth distribution between the farm sector and the rest of the society.

Economic theory offers two basic strategies to control a negative externality, which are either to implement a tax on emissions or to enforce the equivalent standard. In the simple case of one polluting farm only, both strategies are optimal and lead to the same amount of abatement for the same resource cost. This is no longer the case with several polluting farms which have different marginal abatement costs. The tax strategy is more efficient than the standard approach in controlling multiple sources of emissions because it allows resource abatement costs to be minimized. If the same tax rate is applied to different farms with different marginal abatement cost functions, each farm will reduce its emissions until its marginal abatement cost equals the tax. Marginal abatement costs are then equalized across all the sources resulting in minimum overall abatement costs. This outcome can only be achieved by enforcing individually tailored standards which involve differences in marginal abatement costs among farms. Besides, the political feasibility of this individual approach is questionable. One possibility to achieve the lowest resource cost solution through emission control is to introduce a free market for discharge permits. The crucial decision is then related to the total number of discharge permits (emission credits) to be put into circulation, the permit price being the outcome of the market working.

The former discussion does not capture several important features of non-point pollution which complicate the management of negative externalities due to farming. The non-point source problem is characterized by specific features (Tomasi *et al.*, 1994) which rule out policy instruments based on emission control because it is not possible to observe the emissions of each farm. When many farms are contaminating in different ways it is no longer possible to attribute ambient pollution to the activities of any one. Consequently, it is impossible to define the individual liability of each farmer. In addition, the larger the number of farms, the more likely the free-rider behaviour is. Indeed, each farmer perceives his own pollution to be relatively small. Otherwise, environmental damages depend on the location of farms. This implies that the tax rate should be tailored in order to take into account all individual characteristics of farms. But the design and implementation of differentiated emission taxes is not feasible for practical and political reasons. Finally, the transport of pollutants and the magnitude of non-point source pollution are governed by stochastic processes. In consequence, for a given action by farmers, it is not possible to forecast exactly the resulting impact on the environment because of the occurrence of random natural events.

In this context it is not relevant to adopt a first best perspective. Indeed, as Lipsey and Lancaster (1956) stated in a classic paper, 'it is not true that a situation in which more, but not all, of the optimum conditions are fulfilled is necessarily, or is even likely, to be superior to a situation in which fewer are fulfilled'. This second-best-theorem has negative implications for welfare economics because intuitive ideas expressed by the Pareto conditions are not theoretically justified.

Public action to correct negative externalities has focused on the change in agricultural practices. In order to encourage the transition to alternative practices it may combine command-and-control with economic instruments as well as technical assistance and extension education. The EC Nitrate Directive is a typical example of the command-and-control approach. Its main objective is to reduce and prevent surface and groundwater pollution caused by nitrates from agricultural sources. It includes regulations on how to handle manure in zones particularly vulnerable to nitrate leaching and a maximum application rate of nutrients from animal manure. Manure may not be applied in amounts which exceed 170 kg N/ha (a maximum of 210 being allowed for the first four years). Cost-sharing to finance investments and subsidies are the most prevalent economic instruments whereas taxes are unusual. But, according to the Fifth Environmental Action Programme, the use of ecotaxes or tradable permits is likely to increase because these instruments provide an appropriate way to implement the Polluter Pays Principle and are in addition compatible with the World Trade Organization agreement.

A flat rate tax on chemical fertilizer would be in practice easy to implement and would lead to a reduction in fertilizer input. Its efficiency is, however, debatable because the demand for chemical fertilizer is inelastic as a number of studies indicate. Some use mathematical programming models (like linear programming) and others econometric techniques such as time series analysis and estimation of cost or profit functions on farm data. There are therefore significant differences among the estimators of the own-price elasticity of chemical fertilizer demand. Differences can be partly attributed to the assumptions made regarding the fixity of inputs such as land and labour. Based on earlier literature (Bonnieux and Rainelli, 1988) and recent studies (Bäckman, 1999) credible figures can be given. Short-run own-price elasticity of chemical fertilizer demand ranges from –0.2 to –0.3 and long-run own-price elasticity from –0.5 to –0.6. These values are consistent with empirical evidence in Austria, Sweden and Finland which have experienced a levy on chemical fertilizer. For Austria, Hofreither and Sinabell (1998) calculated a value of about –0.2, for Sweden, Drake (1991) estimated the elasticity to be between –0.17 and –0.25, and for Finland, Laurila (1992) found about –0.3. These values refer to short-run elasticity and confirm that the response to a nitrogen tax is moderate. However, a stronger response is expected in the long run as a new equilibrium involving a change in input and output mix is emerging.

Besides, the response to a levy would vary according to farm operators' efficiency. The least efficient farmers can be expected to decrease their demand for chemical fertilizers more than the most efficient ones (Vermersch *et al.*, 1993). In addition, a tax on chemical fertilizer would increase the opportunity cost of organic fertilizer and would result in a more efficient use of manure for crop production.

The overall response of chemical fertilizer demand to a flat rate tax on chemical fertilizer includes three different effects: (1) a direct decrease which is stronger in the long run than in the short run, (2) a decrease due to an improvement in farmers' efficiency and (3) a decrease resulting from a greater use of organic fertilizer. An additional levy can be considered on feed because it is an important source of nitrogen. Schemes based on a flat rate tax are easy to administer since the input price simply increases at the farm gate. However, they fail to recognize the importance of the interrelationships between farm practices and environmental impacts.

It is also possible to place a levy on the nitrogen surpluses produced by farms. This scheme clearly operates at the farm level and thus takes into account the farm individual characteristics. But it is more costly to implement, monitor and enforce since the drawing up of a nitrogen balance is required. A similar mineral accounting scheme, called MINAS, was introduced in the Netherlands in 1998. Farmers have to register the nitrogen input (in manure, fertilizer and feed) and output (in products) on a nutrient form and calculate nutrient losses. They have to pay a levy per kg of nitrogen and per kg of phosphorus above a levy-free surplus. The scheme started in 1998 for livestock farms with animal density over 2.5 livestock units per ha and should be extended to all farms by 2001.

Whatever instrument is applied, public policies are likely to lead farmers to reduce polluting emission. Abatement includes a wide array of means: dimi-

nution in output, changes in production technology, input switching, recy-
cling of residuals, treatment, abandonment of land. In all cases, abatement
involves the use of resources and expenditures which will affect production
costs for the farmer. The final outcome in terms of supply, farm income and
environmental impact will depend on a vast array of farm-specific factors
among which type of farming and location play an important role.

POLITICAL ISSUES AND PERSPECTIVES

The internalization of negative externalities should be based on the Polluter
Pays Principle which states that the polluter should bear expenses to carry out
the measures decided by the public authorities to ensure that the environment
is in an acceptable state. Nevertheless implementation of the Polluter Pays
Principle raises a number of technical difficulties due to the characteristics of
non-point pollution. But there is also a problem of political feasibility stemming from a lack of clear definition of property rights. This leads farmers to
be very reluctant to accept the principle itself and to pay a tax on polluting
inputs.

The absence of a market leads to an under-supply of environmental and
rural amenities associated with farming. This involves a recent emphasis put
on the multifunctional role of agriculture whose goals include reduced water
pollution, soil erosion control, flood protection, wildlife habitat and landscape preservation, and rural development. Most developed countries pursue
a similar set of environmental objectives but there is no general agreement
about the relevant policy to implement.

Quality products are valued in the market place and a labelling system is
enough to encourage their production. Wildlife and landscape quality support
a number of recreational activities such as hunting, fishing, walking and
green tourism which can be marketed. The use of hunting and fishing licences is very common to deal with such benefits. Otherwise the development
of green tourism mainly relies on the creation and growth of new markets for
specific types of accommodation and recreational activities. There are, however, a number of environmental benefits and rural amenities which could not
be marketed easily. In many areas, the wildlife, landscape and historical
interest of the countryside depend upon the maintenance of specific farming
practices. In this context, several policy instruments, among which zoning,
agri-environmental schemes and cross-compliance deserve more attention.

Many land use issues concern the human use of land that substantially
reduces its environmental value. Zoning is a command and control instrument which is sought to eliminate incompatible uses by designating particular
zones for particular types of uses. Land with specific problems such as

susceptibility to soil erosion, or land that has certain characteristics, such as wildlife habitat or landscape beauty are targeted. With this mechanism farming is strongly restricted as farmers must comply with a series of prescriptions. In some cases, there is no farming activity at all because every economic activity is banned.

Voluntary compensatory environmental programmes have been boosted by the accompanying measures of the 1992 CAP reform. Regulation 2078/92 proposes measures to 'compensate farmers for any income losses caused by reductions in output and/or increases in costs and for the part they play in improving the environment'. Under Agenda 2000 this policy orientation is reinforced (see also Chapter 4 and Chapter 12). The implementation of agri-environmental programmes widely varies among EU members, its scope is very limited in Belgium, for example, whereas about 85 per cent of total acreage are covered in Austria (Van Huylenbroeck and Whitby, 1999). In terms of policy appraisal, the multiple-objective nature of many programmes raises a classic issue which is the question of 'targets and instruments'. Since Tinbergen (1952), it is recognized that each policy target merits a separate instrument. It is therefore questionable that a single scheme may achieve multiple environmental objectives at minimum costs to society. This should favour a more diverse targeting strategy to increase positive externalities related to quality of rural landscape, species abundance and diversity. Programmes restricted to a limited area, such as a Site of Special Scientific Interest (SSSI) in the United Kingdom are likely to provide a high level of benefits per hectare, but they also involve relatively high transaction costs (Whitby and Saunders, 1996). In contrast, the French grassland premium scheme ('prime à l'herbe'), which consists in greening Less Favoured Areas (LFA) payments, operates on a very large scale but does not introduce strong restrictions on farming. This results in limited compensation and transaction costs per hectare. Local programmes, such as the Environmentally Sensitive Area (ESA) schemes in the United Kingdom, are between these two extreme cases. Agreements are available to all farmers within areas which are designated on the basis of broad objectives concerning landscape, habitat or water protection. Participants have to opt for one of a limited number of standard agreements. There is thus considerably less individual negotiation, and less monitoring and enforcement effort than in the former case, but conservation value per hectare is also smaller.

Data suggest the existence of size economies with regard to the number of agreements made in any one ESA, and a significant effect of scheme experience in exerting downwards-pressure on administrative costs (Falconer *et al.*, 2001).

The option also exists to link the right of farmers to price and income support to conditions ensuring beneficial public goods outcomes. Environmental cross-compliance can be defined as 'attachment of environmental conditions to agricultural support payments' (Baldock and Mitchell, 1995). This type of policy linkage emerged in the United States where, following the 1985 Farm Bill, the right of arable farmers to various forms of federal support was linked to set-aside of erodible land. The 1992 CAP reform defined cross-compliance as a policy instrument. Up to now cross-compliance has been applied on a very limited scale in the EU. Under Agenda 2000, this approach is in fact one out of three options to meeting environmental standards. Direct payments under the market organizations could be conditioned upon compliance with more environmentally sensitive farming practice. Cross-compliance strategy has considerable political appeal in that it can provide an efficient means to integrate environmental requirements into agricultural policy.

Agri-environmental payments are the price for purchasing or renting property rights which are implicitly acknowledged by the rest of society as belonging to farmers. When these payments are related to a positive contribution which is not already valued in the market place, this is compatible with general policy principles and especially the World Trade Organization Green Box (Ervin, 1999). When payments are conditional upon the reduction of negative externality such as nitrate contamination of water bodies, compatibility with principles and mainly the Polluter Pays Principle is an issue. A link between market mechanisms and Good Agricultural Practices can be established sometimes when the environmental quality of a system of production is remunerated through a price premium received from the commodity markets. This is the case of organic farming where extra private costs due to the non-use of chemicals are offset by higher market prices. The fact that organically grown commodities allow society to make savings on environmental expenditures is an argument to warrant special support measures.

CONCLUSIONS

From an economic point of view, the restoration of the positive association between agriculture and nature supposes two types of measures: the least possible distorting agricultural policies, and systematic use of economic incentives at the farm level.

Among the objectives of agricultural policy there is the reduction of farm income fluctuations due to large price changes, or to natural disasters. To achieve domestic price stability, and thereby to reduce domestic income fluctuations, border protection measures and stabilization mechanisms have been implemented. The insulation of the world markets, through the Common Market Organizations, had distorting effects, since market signals were impeded. Production controls and input restrictions created rigidities that slow down the re-allocation of production between regions or farms. In the case of non-tradable quotas, such as milk quotas in France, the value of income support is capitalized into the land. In addition, to the extent that farmers are risk-averse, when agricultural prices are wholly determined by the market, crop and livestock diversification is the best means to reduce the variability of the agricultural income. Conversely, when agricultural producers are operating in a framework of security the incentives to adopt risk-reducing management practices are lessened and therefore more specialized farming systems are adopted more easily.

By abandoning commodity-based market support policies in favour of direct payments based on acreage or headage (the decoupling), a series of advantages is obtained, mainly through a more efficient allocation of resources. However, agricultural policy reform, which lessens intensification, is a necessary but insufficient step to remedy all environmental impacts originating from agriculture. Decoupling cannot solve every problem occurring from production shifts, and economic incentives must be used to internalize costs and benefits.

At the farm level, in spite of the non-point source problem, which complicates the management of negative externalities, it is recognized that economic incentives are more efficient than command-and-control measures, even if only second-best measures are possible. The fertilizer taxation is a good example. As the internalization of negative externalities relies on the Polluter Pays Principle, the internalization of positive externalities provided by farmers supposes the use of the symmetric principle: the provider-gets-principle. But such an internalization is hindered by the difficulties involved in determining the optimal level of provision in the absence of a market when an amenity has public-good characteristics. In practice, the measures need to be targeted to local situations and to specific farm conditions. But this requires individual negotiated agreements implying high transaction costs. The challenge is to find the optimal mix of the policy variables: zoning, eligibility criteria, prescriptions and monitoring, control and penalties for non-compliance in order to minimize social cost, however, without forgetting the social benefits.

REFERENCES

AGRESTE (1998), *Les Cahiers,* Revue trimestrielle du SCEES, 36, Paris: Ministère de l'Agriculture.

AGRESTE (2000), *Les Cahiers, Chiffres et Données. Le Prix des Terres Agricoles en 1999*, 126, Paris: Ministère de l'Agriculture.

Bäckman, S. (1999), 'Literature review on levies and permits', in H. van Zeijts (ed.), *Economic Instruments for Nitrogen Control in European Agriculture*, Utrecht: Centre for Agriculture and Environment, pp. 41–61.

Baldock, D. and K. Mitchell (1995), *Cross-compliance within the Common Agricultural Policy: a Review of Options for Landscape and Nature Conservation*, London: Institute for European Environmental Policy.

Blöchliger, H.J. (1994), *The Contribution of Amenities to Rural Development*, Paris: Organization for Economic Co-operation and Development.

Bonnieux, F. and H. Guyomard (1999), 'Public policies, markets, and externalities', in F.B. Golley and J. Bellot (eds), *Rural Planning from an Environmental System Perspective*, New York: Springer, pp. 267–86.

Bonnieux, F. and P. Rainelli (1988), 'Agricultural policy and environment in developed countries', *European Review of Agricultural Economics*, **15**, 263–81.

Bromley, D.W. (1997), 'Environmental benefits of agriculture: Concepts', in OECD, *Environmental Benefits from Agriculture: Issues and Policy. The Helsinki Seminar*, Paris: Organization for Economic Co-operation and Development, pp. 35–53.

Brouwer, F. and S. van Berkum (1998), 'The Netherlands', in F. Brouwer and P. Lowe (eds), *CAP and the Rural Environment in Transition: A Panorama of National Perspectives*, Wageningen: Wageningen Pers, pp. 167–84.

Bureau, J.C., J.P. Butault and J.M. Rousselle (1997), 'Analyse spatiale et temporelle de la productivité des agricultures européennes entre 1973 et 1994', *INSEE Synthèses*, **10**, May 1997, 17–23.

Coase, R. (1937), 'The nature of the firm', *Economica*, **4**, 386–405.

Drake, L. (1991), quoted in Bäckman (1999).

Ervin, D.E. (1999), 'Toward GATT-proofing environmental programmes for agriculture', *Journal of World Trade*, **33**(2), 63–82.

European Environment Agency (1998), *Europe's Environment: The Second Assessment*, Luxembourg: Office for Official Publications of the European Communities.

Falconer, K., P. Dupraz and M. Whitby (2001), 'An investigation of policy administrative costs using panel data for the English Environmentally Sensitive Areas', *Journal of Agricultural Economics*, **52**, 83–103.

Hayami, Y. and V. Ruttan (1985), *Agricultural Development: An International Perspective*, Baltimore: Johns Hopkins University Press.

Hofreither, M. and F. Sinabell (1998), quoted in Bäckman (1999).

Laurila, I. (1992), quoted in Bäckman (1999).

Lipsey, R.G. and K.J. Lancaster (1956), 'The general theory of second best', *Review of Economic Studies*, **24**, 11–32.

Mahé, L.-P. and P. Rainelli (1987), 'Impact des pratiques et des politiques agricoles sur l'environnement', *Cahiers d'Economie et de Sociologie Rurales*, **4**, 9–31.

OECD (1987), *National Policies and Agricultural Trade*, Paris: Organization for Economic Co-operation and Development.

Rainelli, P. and D. Vermersch (1999), 'Environmental impacts and agricultural support: cereal irrigation in France', in OECD, *Improving the Environment through Reducing Subsidies. Part III, Case Studies*, Paris: Organization for Economic Co-operation and Development, pp. 47–78.

Stanners, D. and P. Bourdeau (eds) (1995), *Europe's Environment: The Dobříš Assessment*, Copenhagen: European Environment Agency.

Strosser, P., M. Pau Val and V. Plötscher (1999), 'Water and agriculture: contribution to an analysis of a critical but difficult relationship', in: European Commission and Eurostat, *Agriculture, Environment and Rural Development: Facts and Figures – A*

Challenge for Agriculture, Brussels: DG VI, DG XI and Eurostat of the European Commission (http://europa.eu.int/comm/dg06/envir/report/en/eau-en/report.html).

Tinbergen, J. (1952), *On the Theory of Economic Policy*, Amsterdam: North-Holland.

Tomasi, T., K. Segerson and J. Braden (1994), 'Issues in the design of incentive schemes for nonpoint source pollution control' in C. Dosi and T. Tomasi (eds), *Nonpoint Source Pollution Regulation: Issues and Analysis*, Fondazione Eni Entico Mattei, Dordrecht: Kluwer Academic Publishers, pp. 1–37.

Van Huylenbroeck, G. and M. Whitby (eds) (1999), *Countryside Stewardship: Farmers, Policies and Markets*, Amsterdam: Elsevier Science.

Vermersch, D. (1990), 'Une mesure des économies d'échelle locales de court terme: application au secteur céréalier', *Revue d'Economie Politique,* **100**(3), 439–53.

Vermersch, D., F. Bonnieux and P. Rainelli (1993), 'Abatement of agricultural pollution and economic incentives: The case of intensive livestock farming in France', *Environmental and Resource Economics*, **3**, 59–70.

Whitby, M. and C. Saunders (1996), 'Estimating the supply of conservation goods in Britain: a comparison of the financial efficiency of two policy instruments', *Land Economics*, **72**, 313–25.

Zeijts, H. van (ed.) (1999), *Economic Instruments for Nitrogen Control in European Agriculture*, Utrecht: Centre for Agriculture and Environment.

3. Ecology and the interface between agriculture and nature

William M. Stigliani

INTRODUCTION

Whereas the other chapters in this book focus on nature and agricultural policies in the European Union (EU), the current chapter provides a perspective from the USA. Emphasis is given to pollution problems arising from crop and livestock production, which are very much related to the external environmental effects resulting from agricultural production. The chapter provides a wider geographical perspective, giving evidence that nutrient control measures are also critical factors in agricultural production in parts of the world other than the EU.

Specifically, this chapter discusses the Iowa agricultural system from the aspects of economy, environment, and energy (the so-called 'three E's'). Ideally, these aspects should work in unison, but currently in Iowa they do not. There is strong emphasis on maximizing crop yields and livestock production for increasing profit, but this comes at the expense of the state, continental, and global environments, and at a great waste of energy. This analysis focuses on the mass flows of two important components of the agricultural system, the input of synthetic nitrogen fertilizer (N-fertilizer), and the output of hog manure. The analysis shows the impacts of too much N-fertilizer application and too little appropriate use of manure. A hypothetical, alternative ecological system is discussed that reduces greenhouse gas emissions and water pollution, improves the energy efficiency of the agricultural enterprise, saves money from reduced inputs of N-fertilizer, and gives added value to manure when managed as an energy and nutrient rich resource rather than as a nuisance waste.

IOWA'S AGRICULTURAL ECONOMY

Iowa, nestled between the Missouri River on the west and the Mississippi River on the east, is a farm state in the American Midwest, possessing soils that are among the most fertile in the world. A century and a half ago nearly all of the Iowa landscape was covered by tall grass prairie, but today only 0.1 per cent of remnant prairie remains, most of the rest having been ploughed under and converted to agricultural land. Of Iowa's total land area of 145 830 km², about 74 per cent is cropland. Whereas relatively small, diversified farms were typical one generation ago, today the farms are, on average, much larger and mainly dedicated to two crops, maize (corn), and soybean. In 1998, about 4.9 million hectares (comprising 34 per cent of all the land in Iowa) was planted in maize, and about 4.4 million hectares (comprising 30 per cent of total Iowa land) was planted in soybean.

Iowa, with a population of only 2.7 million, is the largest producer of maize, soybean, and hogs in the US. Table 3.1 shows the production and income from these three commodities. Including income from cattle and dairy products (a combined $2.18 billion per year), Iowa earns over $12 billion per year from its top five agricultural and livestock enterprises, making it second only to California in total farm income.

Table 3.1   Iowa statistics for the three largest farm commodities

Production/Profit	Maize (corn)	Soybean	Swine
Annual production	45.83[a]	13.36[a]	15.30[b]
(per cent of US total)	(17.3%)	(18.0%)	(24.6%)
Annual income[c]	$3.78 billion	$3.29 billion	$ 2.96 billion

Notes:
a   In units of thousands of tons (1999).
b   In units of millions of head of hog (1998).
c   Income is for 1997.

Sources: USDA (1999 a,b,c)

ENVIRONMENTAL COSTS OF AGRICULTURE IN IOWA: IN-STATE IMPACTS

The enormous wealth generated by farming in Iowa is accompanied by huge environmental costs, most of which are considered as externalities. A recent comprehensive assessment of the state's environmental problems (IDNR, 1999) indicated that the three issues of most concern are 1) water quality, 2) soil erosion, and 3) animal production. These issues are inextricably linked to current agricultural practices.

Water Quality

Table 3.2 presents an overview of sources affecting water quality in Iowa. Altogether, after adjusting for double counting, 46 per cent of all stream kilometres are impaired, as well as 34 per cent of lake hectares and 59 per cent of wetland hectares. One may readily observe that the major cause of water impairment comes from non-point sources, and that agriculture is clearly the dominant component. The mechanisms by which agriculture impacts on the aqueous environment are soil erosion and runoff.

Erosion by wind and rainfall affects water in three ways. First, eroded soil particles wash into lakes, ponds, rivers, and streams causing siltation. Siltation results in water turbidity and enhanced rates of sedimentation. Second, fertilizers in agricultural soils (particularly nitrogen and phosphorus) are generally applied in quantities in excess of the nutritional needs of crops. In this case, excess fertilizer enters water bodies adhered to eroded soil particles, or dissolved in runoff water during storms. The fertilizer inputs increase biological productivity in aquatic ecosystems that under high nutrient loads result in increased rates of eutrophication. Thus, heavily silted, shallow and eutrophied waters with depleted levels of oxygen and frequent algal blooms are common to many parts of the state.

A third way that erosion affects water is as a transporter of pesticides adhering to soil particles. The most common contaminants are the insecticides chlordane, dieldrin, heptachlor epoxide, DDE, DDT, and the herbicide trifluralin. The pesticides accumulate in aquatic biota, including game fish, which when caught and eaten pose risks of cancer and other diseases.

Soil Erosion

Soil is Iowa's most important resource, but current agricultural practices are depleting it through massive losses caused by erosion. As noted by Dennis Keeney, Director of the Leopold Center for Sustainable Agriculture in Ames, Iowa, as much as 50 per cent of the original topsoil has been lost to erosion over the last 150 years, and most of the loss has occurred in the last half century. Thus, soil erosion is not only a major source of impairment to aqueous ecosystems; it also depletes a precious, non-renewable, natural resource of critical importance to Iowa's economy.

Significant progress in reducing soil erosion has been achieved since the early 1980s. Between 1982 and 1992, soil erosion by water decreased by an overall 28 per cent (Figure 3.1). In 1982, on average 16.8 tons/hectare/year were lost to water erosion, while in 1992 these losses declined to 12.1 tons/hectare/year. Soil erosion by wind also declined significantly in the same period. In 1982, 6.5 tons/hectare/year were lost, while in 1992 only 2.9 tons/hectare/year were lost.

Table 3.2   Sources of impairment of Iowa's water bodies

Source of impairment[a]	Streams[b] (kilometres) (% of total)[c]	Lakes[b] (hectares) (% of total)[c]	Reservoirs[b] (hectares) (% of total)[c]	Wetlands[b] (hectares) (% of total)[c]
Non-point sources				
Agricultural runoff	5,285[d] (56.3%)	5,705[e] (34.2%)	4,209[f] (32.8%)	6,228[g] (59%)
Hydrological/habitat modifications	4,329 (47.0%)	–	–	1,621 (15.4%)
Urban runoff	77 (<1%)	654 (3.9%)	–	231 (2.2%)
Resource extraction	42 (<1%)			
Point sources				
Municipal	775 (8.4%)	78 (0.3%)	–	–
Industrial	227 (2.4%)	–	–	–
Combined sewer flows	68 (<1%)	–	–	–
Other sources				
Natural	24 (<1%)	6,021 (36.1%)	–	–
Unknown	69 (<1%)	–	–	–
Miscellaneous	68 (<1%)	45 (0.3%)	–	–

Notes:

a   Impairment is defined as a condition in which the water body is not fully supporting its designated use.

b   Kilometres and hectares impaired include major impacts plus moderate/minor impacts.

c   Some percentages add up to more than 100 per cent because a given water body may be impaired by more than one source.

d   Agricultural runoff causes major impacts on 1758 kilometres of streams, and moderate/minor impacts on 3424 kilometres.

e   Forty-six lakes are affected by agricultural runoff, which causes major impairment in 27 lakes and moderate/minor impairment in 19 lakes.

f   One of Iowa's four flood control reservoirs (the Red Rock Reservoir) only partially supports its uses for aquatic life as a result of agricultural runoff.

g   Agricultural runoff has major impacts on 45 wetlands, nearly 60 per cent of the wetland acres assessed.

Source: IDNR (1994)

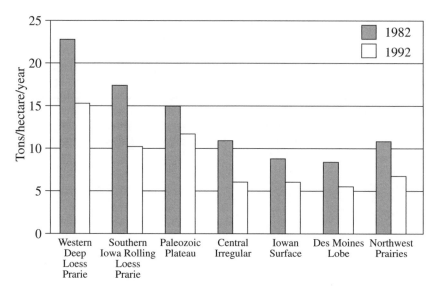

Source: Soil Conservation Service (1995)

Figure 3.1   Water erosion in Iowa ecosystems

The reason for the decrease in soil erosion has been the adoption of agricultural conservation measures such as conservation tillage, and the Conservation Reserve Program (CRP).[1] By practising 'no-till' farming, farmers have reduced soil erosion and increased soil moisture. Despite improvements, the state's farmlands still lost 177 million tons of fertile topsoil in 1994. Moreover as of 1992, out of 10.1 million hectares of total cropland, 5.3 million (52 per cent) suffered average annual soil losses that exceeded the soil replacement rates (SCORP, 1995). Further, the reduction in erosion has not been achieved without environmental costs. Much of the improvement realized by the practice of no-till cropping was accompanied by high inputs of herbicides such as atrazine.

Although it is difficult to measure the economic value of systems damaged by soil erosion, the costs are undoubtedly high. No detailed studies on this topic have been conducted for Iowa in recent years. In 1987, Rosenberry *et al.* published a comprehensive assessment of the 'off-site' costs of erosion in five areas of activity: (1) transportation; (2) urban water quality; (3) fish, wildlife and recreation; (4) water management; and (5) on-farm costs. The cost to recreation (category 3), valued at nearly $30 million annually, was the highest among the five categories.

Three cost indices were examined for recreational areas: (1) damages to fish, wildlife and recreation; (2) expenditures to date for erosion control; and

Table 3.3   *Annual projected costs of off-site erosion to fish, wildlife and recreation in Iowa*

Cost category	Costs (million $)
(1) Recreational damage	7.3
(2) Measures committed for erosion control	3.1
(3) Additional measures needed for erosion control	18.8
Total costs	29.2

Source: Rosenberry *et al.* (1987)

(3) expenditures needed for maximum protection of the lakes. The total costs are shown in Table 3.3. Damages (category 1) were determined by estimating activity days lost, and multiplying the number of days lost by the daily expenditure rates. Six activities were included: fishing; swimming; boating; camping; picnicking; and hunting.[2]

The estimated monetary value of recreational damage presented in the table appears to be rather conservative. The authors assumed expenditures for fishing and hunting to be only $3.70/day, and all other activities (swimming, boating, camping, and picnicking) to be $3.50/day. Other data suggest, however, that those participating in fishing and hunting spend close to $50/day. Just considering fishing alone, for which the authors estimate that erosion causes 1.1 million days lost, damages would total slightly more than $50 million. If this estimate is more reflective of the actual damages, it suggests that expenditures lost from recreational damages (cost category 1) are substantially larger than funds required to implement measures to control erosion (cost categories 2 and 3).

Animal Production

In recent years, the growth of large-scale hog confinements in Iowa has become a contentious issue with regard to its impacts on quality of life, human health, and ecosystems. Manure generated by these animals is estimated to be more than 2.5 million tons per year (as volatile solids) (Ney *et al.*, 1996). The strong stench from confinement lots can diminish the aesthetic value of downwind communities, and significantly devalue real estate (Dahlquist Associates, Inc., 1996). Odours that affect a community can be generated from a feedlot far upwind, where no local mechanism exists for regulating the emissions to air or water. In previous decades the scale of animal production was such that it tended to be a strictly rural issue, for which neighbours could work out solutions among themselves. With the rise of larger hog lot facilities, however, the potential for large-scale contamination of recreational waters, and the transport of putrid odours have threatened the sense of communities, both large and small.

Most of the large hog facilities are financed by companies that are not owned locally or in state. Communities may perceive this as a threat from the outside, which leads to a loss of trust. The loss of jobs from smaller hog operations against the gain in jobs in large-scale hog production pits neighbour against neighbour and community against community. This situation may lead to loss of traditional social values such as mutual respect and willingness to solve problems together.

The sheer magnitude of the hog production enterprise in Iowa, and its potential for environmental destruction, particularly in the aquatic environment, is illustrated by the number of fish kills attributed to confinement lots that occur around the state. In 1996, over 730 000 fish were killed in Iowa streams and rivers from ten reported accidental spills over a five-month period (Figure 3.2). The source of three of these spills was manure from hog confinements. In just one spill into Little Buffalo Creek in Winnebago and Kossuth counties, nearly 587 000 fish were killed. Combined kills from hog manure alone accounted for 87 per cent of the total fish-kill from the ten spills. Three spills of cattle manure killed over 32 000 fish, about 4 per cent of the total. Three spills of ammonia from industrial facilities killed nearly 64 000 fish (9 per cent of total). Two of the three facilities are agro-industrial plants that manufacture nitrogen fertilizer, of which ammonia is a major feedstock.

ENVIRONMENTAL COSTS OF AGRICULTURE IN IOWA: CONTINENTAL AND GLOBAL SCALE IMPACTS

Effects in the Gulf of Mexico

It is important to understand that the impacts of Iowa agricultural activities affect not only the state's environment, but also the continental and global environments. The most prominent continental scale problem is the so-called 'dead zone' in the Gulf of Mexico, located about 1200 kilometres to the south of Iowa (Figure 3.3). This zone encompasses about 18 000 km^2, and is so named because in the spring and summer the concentrations of oxygen are too low to support aquatic life that would otherwise thrive in these waters.

It has been established that the main cause of this phenomenon is the inflow of excess nitrogen (and to a lesser extent phosphorus) to the Gulf from the Mississippi River (Rabalais *et al.*, 1996, 1991). These nutrients 'fertilize'

47

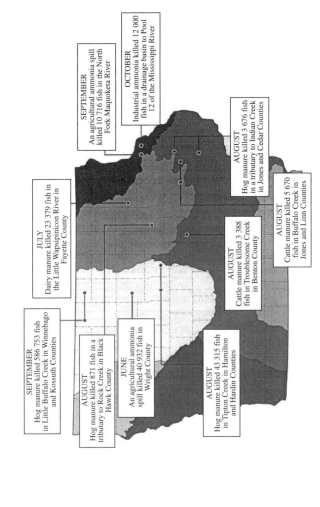

SEPTEMBER
An agricultural ammonia spill killed 10 716 fish in the North Fork Maquoketa River

OCTOBER
Industrial ammonia killed 12 000 fish in a drainage basin to Pool 12 of the Mississippi River

AUGUST
Hog manure killed 3 676 fish in a tributary to Indian Creek in Jones and Cedar Counties

JULY
Dairy manure killed 23 379 fish in the Little Wapsipinicon River in Fayette County

AUGUST
Cattle manure killed 5 670 fish in Buffalo Creek in Jones and Linn Counties

AUGUST
Cattle manure killed 3 388 fish in Troublesome Creek in Benton County

SEPTEMBER
Hog manure killed 586 753 fish in Little Buffalo Creek in Winnebago and Kossuth Counties

AUGUST
Hog manure killed 871 fish in a tributary to Rock Creek in Black Hawk County

JUNE
An agricultural ammonia spill killed 40 932 fish in Wright County

AUGUST
Hog manure killed 43 315 fish in Tipton Creek in Hamilton and Hardin Counties

Source: Iowa Fish and Wildlife News (1997)

Figure 3.2 Ten fish kills and their sources over period from June to October 1996

Figure 3.3   The Mississippi River drainage basin and the 'dead zone' in the
Gulf of Mexico

the Gulf waters near the outflow, creating an explosion of biological activity
with a concomitant reduction in oxygen (a phenomenon called hypoxia).

With a drainage basin of 7.8 million km^2 (comprising about 40 per cent of
the land area of the contiguous US) the Mississippi is one of the ten largest
rivers in the world. Each year it delivers to the Gulf about 580 km^3 of water
containing 1.5 million tons of nitrogen. Nitrogen input today is three times
larger than it was in 1960, and phosphorus input has doubled over the same
period.

The largest source of nitrogen use in the Basin, estimated at around 6.5
million tons per year (by weight N), is synthetic nitrogen fertilizer (N-fertilizer)
applied on agricultural lands. In Iowa alone, farmers apply on the order of 800
to 900 thousand tons per year. The second largest source of nitrogen is animal
manure, some of which is spread on the land as a supplement to N-fertilizer.
Also, as noted above (see Figure 3.2), significant amounts of manure are added
directly to surface waters during accidental spills of containment vessels at
large feedlots. A third, though less important source of nitrogen delivered to the
Gulf is from municipalities and industries, estimated to release 270 thousand
tons to rivers and streams feeding into the Mississippi.

The US Geological Survey estimates that 56 per cent of the nitrogen that
drains into the Mississippi River (840 thousand tons) is runoff of N-fertilizer

from farmland, and another 25 per cent (375 thousand tons) comes from animal manure. In contrast, municipal and domestic wastes account for only 6 per cent (90 thousand tons) of the nitrogen reaching the river.[3]

More than 40 per cent of US commercial fisheries are located in the Gulf of Mexico. The suffocating, hypoxic waters drive away or kill fish and most bottom dwellers such as shrimp and crabs. The catch of fishermen and shrimpers has declined in recent years, and they have blamed the hypoxic zone for the decreased yields.

Several strategies are available for reducing nitrogen inputs to the Gulf. One obvious way is to reduce N-fertilizer inputs on croplands. Scientists estimate that reducing nitrogen flowing to the Gulf by 20 to 25 per cent would significantly reduce the hypoxia problem. This might be accomplished if farmers would reduce their inputs of N-fertilizer. Equally as important would be the restoring or building of wetlands and riparian buffer zones along the stretch of the Mississippi. Both serve as filtering systems that can strip nitrogen out of the runoff water before it washes into the river.

Emissions of Greenhouse Gases

Certain atmospheric gases, the so-called 'greenhouse' gases, possess the ability to trap infra-red radiation emitted from earth, thus increasing the earth's surface temperature. Human activities are increasing the atmospheric concentrations of most of the greenhouse gases. As a result, there is general consensus among climatologists that if present trends continue, there will be significant changes in the earth's global climate within the timeframe of 50 to 100 years (IPCC, 1995).

Though not widely recognized, conventional agricultural practices are significant sources of greenhouse gas emissions. The particular gases of concern in agriculture are methane (CH_4) and nitrous oxide (N_2O). Although these are considered to be less important than carbon dioxide (CO_2), a crucial distinction needs to be made between *concentration* and *potency*. While it is certainly true that the atmospheric concentration of CO_2 (370 parts per million) dwarfs those of CH_4 (1.7 parts per million) and N_2O (0.3 parts per million), the latter two are much stronger greenhouse gases than CO_2 on a *per molecule* basis. One molecule of CH_4 exerts the same greenhouse effect as 22 molecules of CO_2, and one molecule of N_2O has the same effect as 270 molecules of CO_2. As a result, the current contribution of CH_4 to the global greenhouse effect is around 15 per cent of the total, and the contribution of N_2O is about 6 per cent.

N_2O is increasing in the atmosphere at a rate of about 0.8 per cent per year, and a major cause of the increase is the ever-increasing global use of N-fertilizers. Excess nitrogen, in the form of ammonia (NH_3) or nitrate (NO_3^-), not taken up by crops is eventually converted by bacteria to N_2, its original atmospheric form, thus completing the global nitrogen cycle. However, in the conversion of NO_3^- to N_2, a small fraction (5 or less per cent) goes to N_2O; for example,

$$N_2O \ (\leq 5\%)$$
$$\nearrow$$
$$NH_3 \rightarrow NO_3^- \rightarrow N_2 \ (\geq 95\%)$$

Under natural conditions, nitrogen is often a limiting nutrient, and the amounts of excess NH_3 and NO_3^- are generally minimal. The introduction of synthetic N-fertilizer has caused a large perturbation in the global nitrogen cycle,[4] with the result that bacteria are processing much more NH_3/NNO_3^- with a concomitant increase in emission of N_2O. In the case of Iowa, it has been estimated that the excess nitrogen resulting from the overuse of synthetic N-fertilizer causes the emission of 15 050 tons of N_2O (Ney *et al.*, 1996).

The global atmospheric concentration of CH_4 is increasing at a rate of about 0.9 per cent per year. There are numerous sources causing this increase, and one of them is the way livestock manure is managed. Animal manure is rich in organic carbon (CH_2O) as well as in the nutrients nitrogen (N), phosphorus (P), and potassium (K). The fate of CH_2O in microbial decomposition depends on the availability of oxygen (O_2). In aerobic environments the reaction is:

$$CH_2O + O_2 \rightarrow CO_2 + H_2O$$

In anaerobic environments it is:

$$2\ CH_2O \rightarrow CH_4 + CO_2$$

In Iowa, hog manure in particular is managed (or perhaps it is better to say 'mismanaged') in ways that create anaerobic conditions leading to copious generation of CH_4. Table 3.4 shows the various routes of manure disposal, and the resulting emissions of CH_4.

The information above provides an estimate of greenhouse gas emissions from the overuse of N-fertilizer, and the current management of hog manure. Using the potency factors of 22 and 270 for CH_4 and N_2O, respectively, the emissions can be expressed in terms of 'CO_2 equivalents.' The results are shown in Table 3.5.

To put these numbers into perspective, the total annual CO_2 equivalent of 6.1 million tons from these two agricultural practices in Iowa alone equals

Table 3.4   Annual routes of disposal of hog manure and resulting emissions of methane (tons in 1990)

	Anaerobic lagoons	Drylot	Pit storage < 1 month	Pit storage > 1 month	Other	Totals
Manure	79,122	791,214	290,112	1,028,577	342,859	2,531,884
Methane	20,294	2,480	8,557	60,679	879	92,889
Methane (per ton manure)	0.256	0.003	0.029	0.059	0.003	0.037

Note: 'Manure' refers only to the volatile solid component, and emission factors refer to the Iowa case study, and are lower than 'maximum methane potential' generation.

Source: Ney *et al.* (1996)

Table 3.5   Annual greenhouse gas emissions expressed as CO_2 equivalents from N-fertilizer application and hog manure management in Iowa

Source	Gas	Emissions (tons)	Emissions (tons, CO_2 equivalents)
Manure management	CH_4	92,889	2,043,558
Fertiliser use	N_2O	15,053	4,064,310
Total			6,107,868

the amount of CO_2 that would be emitted from burning 3.0 billion litres of gasoline per year. This constitutes the equivalent of about 36 per cent of total gasoline use in the state per year.

ENERGY BALANCE IN IOWA'S AGRICULTURAL SYSTEM

In addition to economic and environmental factors, analysis of energy balance offers a third way of characterizing Iowa's agricultural system. Energy balance is more than merely the question of how much fossil fuel is used in growing, harvesting, processing, and transporting food. A rigorous analysis requires that we also look at the 'embodied' energy of the agrochemical inputs as well as outputs from the system including wastes. In this section, we continue the focus on N-fertilizer and hog manure, both of which play a large role in Iowa's on-farm energy balance.

N-fertilizer

Table 3.6 shows the energy inputs for producing 7.85 tons of maize per hectare of Iowa farmland in units of *litres of gasoline equivalents (lge)*. As shown, the input energy of N-fertilizer is 2.5 times greater than on-farm fuel use, and more than 40 per cent of the total energy requirements. The reason for this large value is that the synthesis of N-fertilizer (typically in the form of NH_4NO_3) from N_2 requires a large expenditure of energy. Producing just 1 kilogram (by weight N) of N-fertilizer takes an energy input of 3.1 lge.

Table 3.6   Input energy per hectare in maize production (yield = 7.85 tons/ hectare)

Type of input	Energy input (litres of gasoline equivalents)	Energy input (per cent of total)
Labour	0.9	0.1
Machinery	212.3	19.0
Fuel	179.6	16.1
Fertilizer-N	457.3	41.0
Fertilizer-P	67.3	6.0
Fertilizer-K	25.3	2.3
Lime	19.6	1.8
Corn seed	74.8	6.7
Insecticide	21.5	1.9
Herbicide	29.0	2.6
Electricity	14.0	1.3
Transport	13.1	1.2
Total inputs	1114.8	100.0

Source: Pimentel (1992)

In 1995, farmers added 756 675 tons of N-fertilizer to Iowa farmland (Ney *et al.*, 1996). The energy needed to produce the fertilizer was about 2.35 billion lge, corresponding to about 28 per cent of the total gasoline Iowans consumed for transportation in 1995.

Beginning in 1982, when a state-supported programme for reducing soil erosion was established (see Figure 3.1) there has been a concerted effort between Iowa farmers and state agencies to use N-fertilizer more efficiently. As shown in Table 3.7, rates of N-fertilizer inputs for corn declined by 15–20 per cent over the period from 1985 to 1995. The primary factors behind this

Table 3.7   *N-fertilizer inputs compared to maize crop yields*

Year	N-fertilizer input (kilograms N/hectare)	Maize yield (kilograms/hectare)	Ratio (yield/kg N)
1985	163	7,914	48.7
1986	147	8,480	57.7
1987	148	8,166	55.2
1988	156	5,276	33.8
1989	144	7,412	51.6
1990	142	7,914	55.6
1991	135	7,349	54.6
1992	132	9,233	69.8
1993	128	5,025	39.3
1994	136	9,548	70.3
1995	135	7,726	57.4

Source: Ney *et al.* (1996)

trend had been concern about nitrogen's negative impact on aquatic systems, and the increased propensity for soil to erode when subjected to intensive, high-tech practices aimed at increasing yield at all costs. In fact, the table shows the important additional result that despite reduced N-fertilizer inputs, there was no discernible reduction in crop yield. Rather, climatic conditions appear to have had the biggest influence. The years 1988 and 1993 were years of drought and flood, respectively; 1992 and 1994 were years of ideal weather during the growing season.

The overall benefits gained from this fertilizer reduction programme illustrate how *energy, economy*, and *environment* can work in unison when wise choices are made that optimize all three aspects. Over the documented 11-year period, consumption of N-fertilizer was approximately 1.9 million tons *less* than it would have been without the reduction management plan in place (Ney *et al.*, 1996). Four major benefits have accrued from these measures: (1) the management plan cost the state $26 million, but farmers saved over $360 million in avoided N-fertilizer costs, with no apparent change in crop yield; (2) nitrogen pollution in Iowa's aquatic environments, while still severe, did not worsen as it would have had there been no reduced nitrogen inputs; (3) the N-fertilizer input energy was reduced by about 5.8 billion lge, an amount equal to about 70 per cent of Iowa's transportation-energy consumption in one year; (4) emissions of the greenhouse gases were reduced by 17 to 22 million tons of equivalent CO_2 (an amount that would be released by burning 9 to 11 billion litres of gasoline).

The latter benefit is particularly significant for N-fertilizer, because large amounts of greenhouse gases are emitted during both its production and its microbial degradation. As illustrated in the following sequence, CO_2 is emitted in the production stage and N_2O is released during degradation.

$$CO_2 \text{ (4 to 7 kg/kg NH}_3\text{)} \quad N_2O \text{ (0.018 kg/kg NH}_3\text{)}$$
$$\nearrow \qquad\qquad\qquad \nearrow$$
$$N_2 + H_2 + \text{energy} \rightarrow NH_3 \rightarrow NO_3^- \rightarrow N_2$$
$$\text{(production)} \qquad\quad \text{(use)} \quad \text{(degradation)}$$

The emission of 0.018 kilograms of N_2O per kilogram of synthesized NH_3 is, in terms of greenhouse potency, equivalent to 4.9 kg of CO_2. Thus, the emissions from production and degradation are comparable. This calculation suggests that reductions of N-fertilizer use are particularly effective in reducing greenhouse gas emissions in Iowa.

Hog Manure

Hog manure is potentially a rich source of energy and plant nutrient, particularly in a farm state such as Iowa where millions of tons are generated annually. Manure can be dried and then combusted as a fuel, or alternatively, it can undergo anaerobic fermentation in a biogas digester to produce CH_4. The latter process appears to be the more practical option for Iowa. CH_4 is a high quality energy source: on a per kilogram basis, it has 24 per cent more embodied energy than coal, and 16 per cent more than gasoline. Also, for a given amount of energy produced, combustion of CH_4 emits 40 per cent less CO_2 than coal and 25 per cent less CO_2 than gasoline.

As was noted in Table 3.4, production of hog manure in Iowa in 1990 was 2.5 million tons, from which the emission of CH_4 to the atmosphere was 92.9 thousand tons (2.0 million tons of CO_2 equivalents). It is important to note, however, that the management of hog manure shown in the table reflects the current system in Iowa in which manure is treated as an unwanted waste, rather than as an important resource. Ideally, CH_4 produced from anaerobic digestion should be collected and applied as a fuel either for on-farm uses such as crop drying or space heating for animals, or sold for uses off-farm. When CH_4 is burned as a fuel, it releases the greenhouse gas CO_2, but as noted above, CO_2 is 22 times less potent per molecule than CH_4. Moreover, there are two additional benefits, that is, there is a reduction in stench, and the residue from the anaerobic digester is a rich fertilizer.

Table 3.4 also indicates that for a given ton of manure, anaerobic lagoons are the largest emitters of CH_4, releasing about 4.3 times as much as pit storage (> 1 month) and 85 times as much as drylot storage. Clearly, from an environmental perspective, anaerobic lagoons should be banned. They not only vent copious amounts of the greenhouse gas CH_4 to the atmosphere, they also release foul odours, threaten nearby water bodies, and waste a valuable energy resource. There would be substantial environmental improvement if energy in the form of CH_4 were harvested from the manure.

From Table 3.4 one may observe that anaerobic lagoons and pit storage (> 1 month) are the largest current sources of CH_4 vented to the atmosphere (20.3 thousand and 60.7 thousand tons, respectively). If Iowa hog producers were to send most of this manure to anaerobic digesters, energy would be produced while overall CH_4 emissions would decline. A state-of-the-art biogas digester can produce about 0.91 tons of CH_4 per 10 tons of manure (weighed as volatile solids). Table 3.8 shows the benefits from an ecological management system in which all of the manure currently sent to anaerobic lagoons, and one-half of the manure currently sent to pit storage (> 1 month) was rerouted to anaerobic digesters. This step would reduce the venting of atmospheric CH_4 by over 50 thousand tons, and produce nearly 60 thousand tons of CH_4 as fuel. At the consumer price of $266 per ton CH_4, the total value of the fuel would be $15.8 million.

CH_4 emissions would decline even further if substantial amounts of manure were judiciously applied to farmland as fertilizer. When manure is spread thinly enough to ensure its direct exposure to the atmosphere, aerobic conditions prevail. In this case, as discussed earlier, the organic carbon is oxidized to CO_2 rather than reduced to CH_4.

Let us assume, as shown in Table 3.9, that our hypothetical ecological system includes the added component of manure application as a fertilizer. In this system all the residue from the biogas digester, and one-half of the manure from the other routes of disposal are applied as fertilizer.

Manure used as fertilizer has other benefits in addition to reducing CH_4 emissions. One is that it improves soil quality. It enhances soil tilth, augments water-holding capacity, reduces wind and water erosion, increases aeration, and promotes beneficial organisms in the soil.

Second, manure application reduces the amount of N-fertilizer that needs to be applied. It thus reduces the energy input and greenhouse gas emissions inherent in the production of N-fertilizer. For the 61 thousand tons of N-fertilizer that could be replaced by manure, the energy savings would be the equivalent of about 189 million lge, and CO_2 emissions would be decreased by 244 to 428 thousand tons.

Third, manure is rich in the three macronutrients, nitrogen (N), phosphorus (P) and potassium (K). Their market values per kilogram are $0.44, $0.77, and $0.40 for N, P, and K, respectively. Also to be considered is the avoided expense (about $330 per ton) of the N-fertilizer replaced by manure. The

Table 3.8 Potential for reducing CH_4 vented to the atmosphere and harvesting CH_4 as an energy source (tons per year)

	Biogas digestion	Anaerobic lagoons	Drylot	Pit storage < 1 month	Pit storage > 1 month	Other	Totals
Current system: CH_4 vented to atmosphere	0	20,294	2,480	8,557	60,679	879	92,889
Ecological system: CH_4 vented to atmosphere	0	0	2,480	8,557	30,340	879	42,256
Ecological system: CH_4 harvested for energy	59,390[a]	0	0	0	0	0	59,390

Note: a Tonnage based on the conversion factor in the biogas digester of 0.91 tons CH_4 per 10 tons of manure.

Table 3.9 Potential for reducing CH_4 vented to the atmosphere by applying manure as a fertilizer (tons per year)

	Biogas digestion	Drylot	Pit storage < 1 month	Pit storage > 1 month	Other	Totals
Ecological system: Manure distribution	593,411	791,214	290,112	514,289	342,859	2,531,884
Ecological system: Manure to fertilizer	415,388[a]	395,607	145,056	257,145	171,430	1,384,626
Ecological system: CH_4 vented to atmosphere	0	1,240	4,279	15,170	440	21,129

Note: a This amount refers to the output from the digester, which is a liquid slurry reduced in volume by about 30 per cent relative to the input manure to the digester. Fertilizer nutrients are not affected, however, because the slurry is enriched in N, P, and K by about 30 per cent.

Table 3.10 *Ecological system: nutrients delivered annually to cropland from manure and their value*

	Biogas digestion	Drylot	Pit storage < 1 month	Pit storage > 1 month	Other	Total
Fertilizer collected (tons)	415,388	395,607	145,056	257,145	171,430	1,384,626
N content[a] (tons)	33,231	22,114	8,109	14,374	9,583	87,411
N content[b] (tons after losses)	24,923	11,500	6,487	11,500	6,708	61,117
N value[c]	$10,966,243	$5,059,782	$2,854,238	$5,059,791	$2,951,545	$26,891,598
P content[a] (tons)	10,842	7,240	2,655	4,706	3,137	28,579
P content[d] (tons after losses)	8,131	5,068	2,655	4,706	2,572	23,132
P value[c]	$6,261,039	$3,902,149	$2,043,984	$3,623,430	$1,980,809	$17,811,411
K content[a] (tons)	21,351	14,242	5,222	9,257	6,171	56,244
K content[e] (tons after losses)	16,013	8,545	5,222	9,257	4,814	43,851

K value[c]	$6,405,283	$3,418,044	$2,088,806	$3,702,888	$1,925,502	$17,540,524
Total value (N+P+K)	$23,632,566	$12,379,975	$6,987,028	$12,386,109	$6,857,855	$62,243,533

Notes:

a. The contents of N, P, and K in manure from the digester are 8.0 per cent, 2.6 per cent, and 5.1 per cent, respectively; the contents from the other sources of manure are 5.59 per cent, 1.83 per cent, and 3.60 per cent respectively.

b. The losses of N during handling and storage are assumed to be 25 per cent, 48 per cent, 20 per cent, and 30 per cent for biogas digester, drylot, pit storage (both < 1 month and > 1 month), and other, respectively.

c. The values per kilogram of N, P, and K are $0.44, $0.77, and $0.40, respectively.

d. The losses of P during handling and storage are 25 per cent, 30 per cent, 0 per cent, and 18 per cent for biogas digester, drylot, pit storage (both < 1 month and > 1 month), and other, respectively.

e. The losses of K during handling and storage are 25 per cent, 40 per cent, 0 per cent, and 22 per cent for biogas digester, drylot, pit storage (both < 1 month and > 1 month), and other, respectively.

amounts of nutrients present in the manure, and their values are summarized in Table 3.10.

PROSPECTS FOR IMPLEMENTATION OF A MORE ECOLOGICAL SYSTEM OF MANAGEMENT IN IOWA

The current way that N-fertilizer and hog manure are used and managed in Iowa can only be justified when short-term economic interests are the over-riding consideration. Table 3.11 compares this system with the alternative, more ecological system described herein. It illustrates the kind of benefits that might accrue if there were a common goal of harmonizing economic, environmental, and energy concerns. Local impacts such as water pollution, soil erosion, and hog manure stench are reduced, as is Iowa's contribution to the 'dead zone' in the Gulf of Mexico.

Moreover, instead of venting over 90 thousand tons of the greenhouse gas CH_4 to the atmosphere, nearly 60 thousand tons (107 million lge) can be captured and utilized as a fuel with an overall value of about $15 million. Manure is an excellent fertilizer as well. Its application could replace over 60 thousand tons of N-fertilizer, with an added value of $27 million, and a reduction in CO_2 emissions of approximately of 240 to 420 million tons.

The actual situation is, of course, much more complex than can be captured in Table 3.11. Several factors act as barriers to implementing a more ecological system for growing crops and producing hogs in Iowa. One is the 'inertia' factor. The normal way of operating a farm or feedlot will tend to persist until conditions prevail that affect profits or other motivations in a substantial way. Currently, there are no strong market or regulatory incentives to fundamentally change agricultural practices.

Another factor is education. Experience in Iowa has shown that even when farmers apply manure to their fields, they tend to add just as much N-fertilizer as they would without the manure. This is the case because they are sceptical or uninformed about the manure's nutrient content, and thus do not view it as a substitute for N-fertilizer. Moreover, there is no infrastructure in the state for processing, marketing and distributing hog manure as a fertilizer. As noted in the previous discussion, the manure must be judiciously applied, rather than 'dumped' on agricultural lands in excessive amounts. The projected 1.4 million tons of hog manure (containing over 60 thousand tons of nitrogen) that could be applied as fertilizer would have to be spread widely over Iowa's agricultural landscape. At an average application rate of 145 kg per hectare for maize, the manure would have to be spread over at least 420 thousand hectares. The area would be considerably more if the manure is added as a supplement to N-fertilizer (as is likely to be the case). Building this infrastructure is certainly

Table 3.11   *Comparison of current use and management of N-fertilizer and hog manure with a more ecological system of management*

	Current system	Proposed ecological system
	Environment	
In-state	Severe pollution of rivers and lakes from excessive applications of N-fertilizer, and spills of manure from large hog confinement lots; loss of topsoil through erosion caused by unsustainable farming practices; stench from hog confinements degrading quality of life in downwind communities.	Reductions in water pollution from reduced inputs of N-fertilizers, and better management of hog manure; improvement in soil quality by replacing N-fertilizer with hog manure; reduced stench by minimizing the stockpiling of manure as a waste, and maximizing its use as an energy and fertilizer resource.
Continental	Contributes the 'dead zone' in the Gulf of Mexico by excessive use of N-fertilizer and manure waste spills.	Reduces probability of manure waste spills; lowers soil erosion by improving soil tilth, water holding capacity, aeration, and beneficial soil organisms.
Global	N-fertilizer use and manure management contribute to global warming through emissions of CO_2, N_2O, and CH_4; amounts emitted are equivalent to more than 6.1 million tons of CO_2 emissions.	Harvesting CH_4 from hog manure as a high-quality fuel, and substituting N-fertilizer with hog manure will lower equivalent CO_2 emissions by nearly one third to about 4.2 million tons.
	Energy	
Expended/ saved per year (in units of lge)	N-fertilizer applied to cropland in Iowa has 'embodied energy' equal to about 2.79 million lge; negligible amounts of CH_4 as a fuel are harvested from hog manure.	Energy saving from substitution of N-fertilizer by hog manure equals about 0.27 million lge; CH_4 energy harvested from hog manure is nearly 60 thousand tons (equivalent to 107 million lge).
	Economy	
Costs/value added per year	Cost of N-fertilizer used in Iowa is about $270 million per year; (environmental and energy costs not included).	Value added to manure is about $26.9 million for N content; value added for harvesting CH_4 is about $15.8 million for a combined $42.7 million (does not count value of P and K content in manure).

feasible from a technical point of view, but its cost would be undoubtedly high and there are no substantial funds to date appropriated for such an initiative.

There is a similar problem with respect to harvesting and utilizing CH_4 as a fuel. The required biogas digesters are expensive, and once the CH_4 is generated it needs to be distributed. On-farm uses are undoubtedly the most effective way of using the fuel. Working against the development of a manure-to-methane industry is the low cost of energy in Iowa and the nation as a whole. Even though it is estimated that CH_4 from manure is an energy source worth $15 million per year, the tendency is to view savings on energy as marginal and not worth a major investment.

On the other hand, there is a hopeful sign on the horizon. The low priority given to reducing greenhouse gas emissions in the agricultural sector could change significantly if the 1997 Kyoto Protocol on Climate Change were to come into force in the US. It would require the US to cut its emissions of greenhouse gases (including N_2O and CH_4) by at least 7 per cent for the five-year budget period of 2008–12. Such a development could substantially increase the economic value of reducing greenhouse gas emissions, particularly if farmers could earn emission reduction credits for their efforts. Because N_2O and CH_4 are such potent greenhouse gases, reductions in their emissions are worth much more than comparable reductions in CO_2 on a per ton basis. Our calculations show that, when expressed as equivalents of CO_2, reductions of 1.9 million tons per year are possible. Adding value to emission reductions, for which there is no current remuneration, could change the economics of on-farm handling of N-fertilizer and manure. From this perspective, the manure-to-methane option seems particularly attractive. CH_4 emissions are reduced by over 50 thousand tons (1.1 million tons of CO_2 equivalents), and nearly 60 thousand tons of CH_4 fuel is generated. Similarly, reductions in N-fertilizer use and its substitution by manure avoid considerable emissions of CO_2 from production of N-fertilizer (240 to 430 thousand tons per year), as well as decreases in CH_4 emissions from manure by an additional 20,000 tons, as less of it is stockpiled under anaerobic conditions at large hog confinements.

It seems that a combination of factors can help to guide Iowa toward a more sustainable agricultural future. One step forward would be a true accounting of the environmental costs including state, continental, and global impacts, and measures taken to reduce those impacts. The Kyoto Protocol is but one example of how such an accountability could be realized.

Advanced technology may also play a role. For example, GPS (Global Positioning System) is being applied to gauge more precisely how much fertilizer a crop actually needs. If successfully implemented, this innovation may substantially reduce the excessive use of fertilizer that is the root cause of so many problems.

Prudent policies are needed that encourage investment in infrastructure required to 'jump start' green agricultural industries such as manure-to-methane or manure-to-fertilizer operations. A comparable model already exists for the promotion of renewable energies in Iowa. Iowa has over 250 operating state-of-the-art 750–kW wind turbines that provide electricity to about 100 000 Iowa families, making it the second leading state in wind energy generation. Most of the turbines are located on farmland, and farmers supplement their income with revenues from utilities for rent of their land. The notion that farmers can harvest energy as well as crops is an attractive idea. It provides added value to rural agricultural regions, opens up new markets, and may greatly benefit the environment as well.

IMPACTS OF LONG-TERM ACCUMULATION OF PERSISTENT CHEMICALS IN AGRICULTURAL SOILS

Over the long term, all agricultural soils are vulnerable to accumulation of heavy metals and other persistent pollutants. Iowa (Tanaka, 1999) and the EU (Stigliani and Anderberg, 1994) are no exceptions. In the case of heavy metals, soil water pH is a critical factor; the soil's capacity for accumulation increases as the pH increases and vice versa.

One special quality of agricultural soils is that they are buffered against acidification through application of lime, which maintains the soil at artificially high pH values of 6 or more. At these pH levels the storage capacity of the soils is correspondingly high, allowing them to store heavy metals via adsorption on the surfaces of soil particles. If for any number of reasons the pH of the soil were to decline, its metal holding capacity would decline as well, with the concomitant release of soluble heavy metals to the soil water. This may lead to increased uptake of heavy metals by crops or vegetation, and increased concentration of the metals in groundwater.

The cadmium (Cd) concentrations in agricultural soils of the Rhine Basin are estimated to have doubled between 1950 and the 1990s to an average value of about 720 g/ha (to a depth of 20 cm) (Stigliani, 1995). Calculations suggest that if soil pH were, on average, to decline by 0.5 pH units, the average estimated increase in crop uptake of Cd would be 120 per cent; if the pH dropped 1.0 pH units, crop uptake of Cd would increase by 360 per cent (Stigliani *et al.*, 1993). If the pH were to decline from 6.0 to 4.5 (which could happen, for example, if agricultural lands are converted to forests), it is estimated that the dissolved phase Cd concentration would increase more than 10–fold, from 0.0005 mg/L to 0.006 mg/L (Stigliani *et al.*, 1993). This could lead to increased plant uptake and/or increased concentrations of Cd in groundwater.

Such increased mobilization of toxic metals to the environment due to changes in land use as well as other perturbations has been studied extensively in Europe within the so-called 'chemical time bomb,' programme[5] (see Salomons and Stigliani, 1995; ter Meulen *et al.*, 1993; Stigliani *et al.*, 1991; Stigliani, 1988).

CONCLUSIONS

Similar pressures on the environment and nature are observed in the US and the EU. Legislation and command-and-control measures are relatively widely used in the EU to protect physical resources, whereas regulation is currently used selectively in the US to control water pollution. There are similar concerns with respect to nitrate pollution of water for example. Responses to harmful effects of agricultural practices on the environment have been reactive in the sense that measures were introduced in response to emerging or documented problems. This is applicable to most policies to internalize external effects from agricultural practice, irrespective of differences in cultures and preferences in the EU and the US.

This chapter provides evidence that meeting ecological objectives in agriculture also creates additional benefits for the farm economy and energy conservation. Reduced use of synthetic fertilizer, particularly nitrogen, is good for the environment, saves farmers' money, and lowers the high energy demand required for its production. Likewise, use of manure either as a fertilizer or an energy source can reduce water pollution, provide income, lower the stench, and improve the on-farm energy balance.

NOTES

1. The CRP provides money to farmers in the most marginal and erodible agricultural lands to take land out of crop production and plant prairie grasses or other vegetative cover for a prescribed period of time.
2. Of the total days lost for all six activities, fishing accounted for 53% of the total, followed in decreasing order by camping (17%), picnicking (12%), swimming (9%), boating (8%), and hunting (3%).
3. Only a fraction of the nitrogen consumed in the Basin actually reaches the Mississippi River and is transported to the Gulf. For example, the 840 000 ton input to the river from N-fertilizer is about 13% of total N-fertilizer use in the Basin.
4. The natural, annual preindustrial flow of 'fixed' nitrogen is estimated to have been about 100 million tons globally. This is comparable in amount to the nitrogen fixed annually in N-fertilizer. Counting other anthropogenic sources of fixed nitrogen, current annual nitrogen flows are about 250 million tons, thus amounting to two and a half times the natural, preindustrial flow.
5. The Program on Delayed Effects of Chemicals in Soils and Sediments (also known as the 'Chemical Time Bomb Project') was a collaborative effort from 1989 to 1994 between the

Foundation for Ecodevelopment 'Stichting Mondiaal Alternatief', Hoofddorp, The Nether-
lands, the International Institute for Applied Systems Analysis, Laxenburg, Austria, and the
National Institute of Public Health and Environmental Protection (RIVM), Bilthoven, The
Netherlands. Financial support for the programme was provided by The Netherlands Minis-
try of Housing, Physical Planning and Environment (VROM), and the Commission of the
European Communities, DG XI.

REFERENCES

Dahlquist Associates, Inc. (1996), *Choices for Iowa's Environment: Iowa Town Meetings Report (Phase I)*, Final Report to the Iowa Comparative Risk Project, Des
Moines, Iowa: Energy Bureau, Iowa Department of Natural Resources.

IDNR (1994), *Water Quality in Iowa During 1992 and 1993*, Des Moines, Iowa: Iowa
Department of Natural Resources.

IDNR (1999), *Comparative Risk Project,* Final Report to Energy Bureau, Iowa Department of Natural Resources, Des Moines, Iowa.

Iowa Fish and Wildlife News (1997), *Fish Kills Cause Loss of More than 730 000 fish
during 1996*, Des Moines, Iowa: Fisheries Bureau, Iowa Department of Natural
Resources.

IPCC (1995), *IPCC Second Assessment, Climate Change 1995*, Report of the Inter-
governmental Panel on Climate Change, Geneva: World Meteorological Organization
and the United Nations Environment Programme.

Ney, R.A., J.L. Schnoor, N.S.J. Foster and D.J. Forkenbrock (1996), *Iowa Greenhouse Gas Action Plan*, Report to the Energy Bureau, Iowa Department of Natural
Resources, Des Moines, Iowa City, Iowa: Center for Global and Regional Environmental Research and Public Policy Center, University of Iowa.

Pimentel, D. (1992), 'Environmental and economic benefits of sustainable agriculture', in: *Neue Partnerschaften in der Marktwirtschaft oder Ökologische
Selbstzerstörung,* sponsored by Bundesministerium für Land- und Forstwirtschaft,
der Österreichischen Gesellschaft für Biotechnologie, and Österreichischen
Vereinigung für Agrarwissenschaftliche Forschung, Vienna, Austria.

Rabalais, N.N., R.E. Turner, W.J. Wiseman Jr. and D.F. Boesch (1991), 'A brief
summary of hypoxia on the northern Gulf of Mexico continental shelf: 1985–
1988', in R.V. Tyson and T.H. Pearson (eds), *Modern and Ancient Continental
Shelf Anoxia*, Geological Society special publication no. 58, London: The Geological Society, pp. 35–46.

Rabalais, N.N., R.E. Turner, D. Justic, Q. Dortch, W.J. Wiseman Jr. and B.K. Sen
Gupta (1996), 'Nutrient changes in the Mississippi River and system responses on
the adjacent continental shelf', *Estuaries, 19*, 386–407.

Rosenberry, P.E., B.C. English, S.R. Johnson, M.L. Siemers and V.H. Temeyer (1987),
Offsite Costs of Erosion Damage in Iowa, Final Report to Southern Iowa Ag
Boosters, Ames, Iowa: Center for Agricultural and Rural Development, Iowa State
University.

Salomons, W. and W.M. Stigliani (eds) (1995), *Biodynamics of Pollutants in Soils
and Sediments, Risk Assessment of Delayed and Non-linear Responses*, Berlin:
Springer-Verlag.

SCORP (1995), *1995 Iowa SCORP, State Comprehensive Outdoor Recreation Plan,*
Des Moines, Iowa: Division of Parks, Recreation and Preserves, Iowa Department
of Natural Resources.

Soil Conservation Service (1995), *Natural Resources Inventory Data,* Washington, DC: US Department of Agriculture.

Stigliani, W.M. (1988), 'Changes in valued capacities of soils and sediments as indicators of nonlinear and time-delayed environmental effects', *International Journal of Environmental Monitoring and Assessment,* **10**, 245–307.

Stigliani, W.M. (1995), 'Global perspectives and risk assessment', in W. Salomons and W.M. Stigliani (eds), *Biogeodynamics of Pollutants in Soils and Sediments: Risk Assessment of Delayed and Non-Linear Responses,* Berlin: Springer-Verlag, pp. 331–43.

Stigliani, W.M. and S. Anderberg (1994), 'Industrial metabolism at the regional level: The Rhine Basin', in R.U. Ayres and U.E. Simonis (eds), *Industrial Metabolism – Restructuring for Sustainable Development,* Tokyo: United Nations University Press, pp. 119–62.

Stigliani, W.M., P.R. Jaffe and S. Anderberg (1993), 'Heavy metal pollution in the Rhine Basin', *Environmental Science and Technology,* **27**, 786–93.

Stigliani, W.M., P. Doelman, W. Salomons, R. Schulin, G.R.B. Smidt and S.E.A.T. van der Zee (1991), 'Chemical time bombs: predicting the unpredictable', *Environment,* **33**(4–9), 26–30.

Tanaka, M. (1999), *Inputs of Cadmium and Other Toxic Heavy Metals in Iowa Agriculture: Possible Risks and Environmental Consequences,* Masters Thesis, Cedar Falls, Iowa: Environmental Programs, University of Northern Iowa.

ter Meulen, G.R.B., W.M. Stigliani, W. Salomons, E.M. Bridges and A.C. Imeson (eds) (1993), *Proceedings of the European State-of-the-Art Conference on Delayed Effects of Chemicals in Soils and Sediments, 2–5 September 1992, Veldhoven, The Netherlands,* Hoofddorp, The Netherlands: The Foundation for Ecodevelopment 'Stichting Mondiaal Alternatief'.

USDA (1999a), *Production and Acreage Charts for Corn and Soybean (1999),* Washington, DC: National Agricultural Statistical Service, US Department of Agriculture. (http://www.usda.gov/nass/aggraphs).

USDA (1999b), *Meat Animals Production, Disposition, and Income – 1998 Summary*, Washington, DC: National Agricultural Statistical Service, US Department of Agriculture (http://usda.mannlib.cornell.edu/re).

USDA (1999c), *Statistical Highlights 1998–99: Farm Economics,* Washington, DC: National Agricultural Statistical Service, US Department of Agriculture (http://www.usda.gov/nass/pubs/stathigh/1999/ec-cr-05.htm).

4. Agri-environmental policy development in the European Union

Clive Potter

INTRODUCTION

It is inevitable that any analysis of European rural policy will be dominated by the Common Agricultural Policy (CAP). As an agricultural support system it has been around now for over 40 years, shaping the pattern of farming and dictating policy choices, not only in the agricultural, but also in the agri-environmental and rural development fields. The unintended environmental consequences of the CAP are large and, until recently, have eclipsed efforts to manage rural environments more deliberately through the agency of agri-environmental policy. Some commentators believe that the CAP has been so influential in shaping the pattern of rural land use that it is not inappropriate to talk about a 'productivist countryside', moulded by the commodity regimes and wedded to intensive, environmentally destructive systems of agricultural production. According to the policy mind set which gave rise to this state of affairs, agricultural output and productivity are the ultimate benchmarks of success, the primary purpose of rural policy being to raise the living standards of farmers through modernization. Re-balancing policy and reforming institutions in order to give greater priority to environmental protection and less agri-centric forms of rural development, has been a slow process. There has been a complicated co-evolution of public attitudes and policy approaches, in which mounting criticism of agriculture's environmental impact has been met with a series of policy adaptations and adjustments. The result is that today we have a wide range of policy instruments being used to tackle environmental problems in agriculture which can only be understood if they are analysed within the broader agricultural policy context.

This chapter begins by describing how current agri-environmental policy approaches came into existence. It starts by analysing how policymakers have traditionally viewed the relationship between agriculture and the environment and the way in which the environment has been treated within the productivist policy model. By recognizing farmers as producers of public

environmental goods, policymakers were able to justify from an early stage
an essentially voluntaristic strategy of subsidizing them for the environmental services they provided. Under this policy model, the use of environmental
contracts based on the 'Provider Gets Principle', complements other approaches such as the use of environmental regulations based on the 'Polluter
Pays Principle'. It has been well said that policymakers find it easier to add
than to subtract. In the agri-environmental policy field measures have tended
to be bolted on to a CAP which is basically productivist in its design and
operation. Nevertheless, the outlines of a more sustainable and better integrated rural policy which will eventually come to replace the existing CAP
are now apparent. The chapter discusses the achievements of agri-environmental policy to date and identifies the constraints on its further expansion. It
concludes by looking forward to a new era of European rural policy, in which
a much broader and more integrated range of policy measures is deployed to
achieve environmental protection and rural development policy goals.

THE PRODUCTIVIST COUNTRYSIDE

Consider first the traditional policy model that has prevailed until very recently (see Figure 4.1). As can be seen, this views the countryside as a
pyramid, split between a nominally protected 'conservation estate' made up
of designated conservation sites and protected landscapes, Less Favoured
Areas (LFAs) eligible for special income aids and a wider farmed countryside

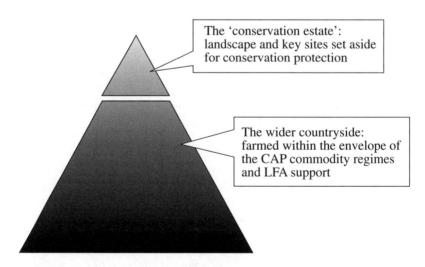

Figure 4.1   The productivist countryside

largely managed according to the dictates of the market and the commodity regimes. The underlying policy assumption is that the best way to manage the rural environment is to farm it. Indeed, in the early days of the CAP the greatest threat to the character and biodiversity of the countryside was thought not to be farming intensification but rather agricultural decline and desertification in marginal locations (Potter, 1998).

When it was first set up in 1958 the CAP was primarily regarded as a mechanism for raising living standards in agriculture at a time when those employed in or connected with the industry accounted for a quarter of the civilian population in the six founder states of France, West Germany, The Netherlands, Belgium, Italy and Luxembourg. According to the much quoted formulation given by the European Commission, 'sufficient farmers must be kept on the land. There is no other way to preserve the natural environment, traditional landscapes and a model of agriculture based on the family farm as favoured by society generally' (Commission of the European Communities, 1991, p. 9). For many Europeans, this idea connects with a long-standing debate about the undesirable social and environmental consequences of agricultural decline and land abandonment, which in France goes under the heading of 'desertification'. Delorme (1987) has pointed out that one important aspect of this is the threat of agricultural decline to the accepted idea of landscape as a cultivated area shaped by agricultural work.

In effect, policymakers were implicitly adopting what Hodge (1999, p. 265) has called a 'public goods' model of the relationship between agriculture and the environment, 'premised on agricultural systems that have often co-evolved with the environment over substantial periods of time to the extent that there is a close interrelationship between the valued characteristics of the environment and certain attributes of the agricultural systems that are associated with them'. By comparison, nature conservation policy has for a long time been an enterprise of selecting and designating nature reserves and other categories of conservation sites to sample biodiversity and to protect the most special or threatened species, habitats and landscapes at the top of the pyramid. Rarely extending to more than 3 per cent of the utilized agricultural area of the European Union (Bischoff and Jongman, 1993), this conservation estate has often been set apart, managerially and psychologically, from the rest of the farmed countryside. As Felton (1993) points out, the luxury of being able to present nature conservation as a scientific and educational project centred on the selection, management and protection of key sites, was only possible because a prescribed form of countryside management was not thought to be required elsewhere – the wider countryside, in other words, could safely be left to the farmers' care.

Unfortunately, by choosing to support farming incomes through blanket price support and, in the case of LFAs, headage payments, linked or 'coupled' up to the production decisions of farmers, it can be argued that policymakers accelerated intensification, endangered site protection and began to undermine the rationale for this public goods model of agricultural support. The CAP came into existence just as a revolution in agricultural techniques was getting into its stride and the effect of the policy was to give an irresistible incentive for farmers to expand production by adopting high input farming systems and abandoning high natural value agricultural techniques. Over the three decades after 1950 agricultural output was to expand by over 3 per cent annually, with the almost wholesale replacement of one mode of production dependent on horsepower and manpower being replaced by one based on tractors, chemicals and oil. A reflection of this is the fact that manpower was cut by two thirds after 1950 and the land under cultivation by 10 per cent, but output multiplied by two thirds (Duchene *et al.*, 1985). The effect has been widespread environmental change and the creation of a situation in which conservation sites are increasingly divorced from the expanse of intensively managed countryside which surrounds them.

Beginning in the 1960s, farmers in north west Europe began to abandon the mixed farming systems which were largely responsible for the joint production of food and landscape that informed the public goods model of agriculture. Economies of scale in the use of the specialized machinery and equipment that were rapidly becoming indispensable in farming operations could only be achieved with high rates of throughput. A perverse effect of the CAP, however, was that opportunities for amalgamation to increase the scale of operations on individual farms were relatively few because despite the steady decline in the number of holdings, the high price regime had the effect of keeping more farmers on the land than would otherwise be the case (Colman and Traill, 1984). The result was that farmers reduced the number of enterprises on their farms in an effort to realize what Bowers and Cheshire (1983) have called 'economies of specialization'. Monocultural cereal production now began to spread throughout the countryside of north-western Europe, displacing the traditional mixed farming centred on bocage-type landscapes of small fields, hedgerows and woodland. There was at the same time an accelerating loss of farmland habitat like wetland, semi-natural grassland and heathland as farmers reclaimed land in order to maximize their receipts of price support.

This was accompanied by a general intensification of farming, creating, for the first time, an externality problem in agriculture. By the late 1970s, the pollution impact of intensive livestock production in the Netherlands was attracting government attention and by the end of the decade less than half of the animal waste produced annually could be disposed of safely on the farms concerned (in 1996 total manure production stood at 80 million tonnes, with an excess of 18 million tonnes, mainly from pigs and poultry farms: Brouwer,

2000). Elsewhere, arable farming emerged as the greatest non-point source of water pollution in the EU. Nitrate pollution of groundwater has been a particularly important issue for Germany and France, where it moved rapidly up the political agenda during the 1980s once the public health implications became clear. By 1990 it was estimated by the World Health Organization (WHO) that 25 per cent of EU groundwater supplies exceeded the recommended limit safe for human health (Conrad, 1990). In large parts of the EU the growth in dairy herd sizes and the trend towards housing stock in cubicles rather than bedding them on straw, greatly increased the volume of liquid slurry to be disposed of, and with it, the risk of serious pollution of surface water.

ENVIRONMENTAL IMPACTS VERSUS COUNTRYSIDE PROTECTION

All of this led to the adoption of a new 'impacts model' of agriculture and the environment in public debate, particularly in northern member states like the Netherlands, France and Germany. According to this conceptualization of the relationship between agriculture and the environment, 'the environmental impacts or negative externalities are directly associated with input use. The model assumes an agriculture operating in opposition to the environment. Therefore a reduction in intensity of production will automatically lead to an improvement in environmental quality' (Hodge, 1999, p. 7). It was within this paradigm that the Dutch government began setting targets in the late 1970s for the control of manures, imposing legally binding restrictions on the timing and rate of applications and setting standards for safe storage on farms. In France, the water quality issue more than any other pushed agri-environmental problems up the political agenda, leading to new legislation covering the control and management of water sources. The initial focus of concern was localized, linked mainly to the use of inorganic fertilizers and pesticides in the Paris basin. Boisson and Buller (1996) chart the slow emergence of the water pollution issue in France and the symbolic challenge this posed to the traditional view of agricultural production as a public good.

Eventually, new legislation at Community level through a series of directives and regulations accelerated the process of regulating agriculture in the interests of pollution control. The Fourth Environmental Action Plan expressed the Community's intention to protect water from pollution caused by the spreading of manure and the excessive use of fertilizers, opening the way for legislation to control some of the more controversial side effects of intensive agriculture such as the leaching of nitrates into surface and groundwater. The Drinking Water Directive of 1980 was the first piece of

Community legislation in this vein. It defined upper limits on concentrations of nitrate and pesticides in drinking water and imposed on member states mandatory sampling and reporting procedures. Following amendment in 1991, the Directive further required Member States to define Nitrate Vulnerable Zones within which restrictions on nitrogen fertilizer use and manure applications will be imposed. In another policy innovation, member states were required to establish Codes of Good Agricultural Practice which refer to fertilizer application rates, storage of livestock effluent and the establishment of fertilizer records and plans.

At the same time, the public goods model was in the process of being reinvented to justify the use of environmental subsidies on an increasingly large scale and to accommodate these externality problems in ways which preserved farmers' property rights. The story begins in the mid-1980s, when Member States like the UK and the Netherlands began setting up voluntary schemes which offered farmers environmental payments to subsidize the observation or adoption of environmental management practices. For the UK, the landscape and nature conservation consequences of agricultural change were always more important than the polluting effects of intensification, the narrative of countryside conflict traditionally having been expressed associatively in terms of the loss of landscape values and wildlife, rather than instrumentally as a threat to health from agricultural pollution. Agri-environmental policies were needed to safeguard the character and biodiversity of the wider countryside outside key sites and to ensure that habitats and landscape features were properly managed and effectively conserved. The Environmentally Sensitive Areas (ESA) programme, first set up in 1986, offered farmers in landscapes threatened by farming intensification or decline the chance to sign up to management agreements with agriculture departments in return for an annual hectarage payment. The concept of 'paid stewardship' was first given prominence in Community law in 1985 following passage of a regulation which permitted Member States to provide funding from their own resources for such agri-environmental schemes. As the preamble to the regulation points out, farmers in certain environmentally sensitive areas 'are in a position to perform a valuable service to society as a whole (and so) the introduction of specific measures may encourage them to introduce or retain agricultural production practices that are compatible with the increased need to protect or preserve the countryside'.

This is a perfect consummation of the public goods model, justifying government support in terms of the public good benefits farmers, by dint of their ownership or occupancy of land, are in a special position to provide. As Hanley *et al.* (1999) observe, it implies that farmers have the right to carry out the most profit-maximizing activity on their land but that if farming in a more environmentally sensitive manner imposes costs, then society must compensate them for these costs. In fact, under the agri-environmental policy schemes which now began to be introduced, farmers could be paid both to secure an improvement in quality or quantity terms above the current baseline and to prevent a deterioration below the baseline due to possible abandonment and extensification (this latter would mean that state support for farmers, particularly in Less Favoured Areas (LFAs), could be explicitly justified as a means of preventing depopulation and preserving an occupied countryside).

It subsequently became possible to address the problems posed by intensification within this broad policy framework by emphasizing the environmental benefits of extensification. In the UK, farmers inside Nitrate Sensitive Areas are offered payments in return for accepting limits on the use of fertilizers for winter wheat and oilseed rape and limits on the application of manure. Additional payments are available to farmers who convert arable land to low intensity grassland. The Ministry of Agriculture, Fisheries and Food (MAFF)'s position on the Nitrates Directive is that farmers who find themselves in a Nitrate Sensitive Area and thus subject to constraints on their farming practice, deserve to be compensated because of an accident of geography. In effect, MAFF is prepared to pay farmers for not applying fertilizer up to a level that would be regarded as 'good agricultural practice'. Significantly, the Commission had already conceded that farmers could be compensated under the Directive for reducing nitrogen use and making any necessary adjustments to farming practice (Reeve, 1993). The Polluter Pays Principle should not apply, it was argued, because the geographically specific nature of the problem would mean penalizing farmers who happened to farm land overlying vulnerable aquifers. Even in the Netherlands, where the Government had gone furthest in regulating agriculture, farmers within groundwater protection zones are eligible for compensation (though such payments have gradually been scaled down in recent years), while in most other member states agriculture departments have already agreed to defray some of the costs to farmers through various grant aid schemes and to pay compensation to achieve necessary changes in land use and farming practice. In 1987 the European Commission succeeded in adding extensification to countryside management as an activity for which farmers could receive agri-environmental payments. By arguing that the environmental problems associated with intensive agriculture are 'just as destructive' as those resulting from rural desertification, and, moreover, should qualify farmers for subsidies from the public purse, it managed to blur the boundary between regulation and subsidization and establish the basis for the next round of agri-environmental reforms.

THE DOMINANT MODEL

Paid stewardship has now become the dominant mode of agri-environmental policy intervention throughout the EU. In 1992 Regulation 2078/92 effectively made agri-environmental policy a mandatory requirement for all Member States under EU law. According to this important regulation, Member States are required to set up rolling programmes designed to subsidize extensification and countryside management. Schemes may be 'narrow and deep' (targeted at particular locations, landscapes or types of farmland) or 'broad and shallow' (requiring larger numbers of farmers throughout the countryside to abide by simpler environmental conditions), but they should all address pressing environmental problems in agriculture. The regulation sets out the conditions to be attached to the payment of aid, referring to the need to take into account 'the undertaking given by the beneficiary and the net loss of income and the need to provide an incentive'. Co-financing by the EU was increased to 75 per cent in Objective 1 regions (defined as areas lagging behind the rest of the EU and where at least 25 per cent of the population have a Gross Domestic Product (GDP) per capita of less than 75 per cent of the EU average) and to 50 per cent elsewhere. Importantly, ministers agreed that agri-environmental policy should henceforth be financed from the guarantee section of the CAP, creating the possibility – for that was all it was at this stage – of transferring much larger sums of money from price support into these environmental schemes.

Within three years all Member States had agri-environmental schemes in operation or on stream. These comprised:

- schemes to reduce nitrate and pesticide pollution;
- measures to extensify arable farming by reducing inputs, and livestock farming by reducing stocking densities;
- conversion and maintenance payments for organic farming;
- schemes to encourage conversion of arable land to grassland, wetland, coastal marsh and river marshes;
- schemes to conserve habitat and landscape features in environmentally sensitive areas;
- measures for maintaining and improving cereal steppelands;
- schemes to protect perennial crops of cultural, landscape and wildlife value such as olive groves in Greece, Portugal and Spain and traditional orchards in Germany and the UK.

By October 1999 the EU was spending 4 per cent of total farm support to co-finance these measures (Commission of the European Communities, 1999a). Estimates of total expenditure, including the national contributions, are not

Table 4.1   *Distribution of expenditure under Regulation 2078 by Member States*

State	Total co-financeable expenditure (1993–1997) (mecu)	EAGGF contribution (mecu)	Assumed Member State contribution (mecu)	Proportion of total EU-15 EAGGF agri-environmental budget (%)
Austria	1 553	806	746	21.30
Belgium	6	3	3	0.08
Denmark	38	19	19	0.50
Finland	798	399	399	10.54
France	1 018	509	509	13.44
Germany	1 294	918	376	24.24
Greece	15	11	4	0.29
Italy	714	432	282	11.43
Ireland	217	163	54	4.30
Luxembourg	9	4	4	0.11
Netherlands	49	25	24	0.66
Portugal	197	148	49	3.92
Spain	167	125	42	3.30
Sweden	252	126	126	3.33
UK	192	98	94	2.59
TOTAL	6 519	3 787	2 458	100

Source: Buller *et al.* (2000)

published, but it has been calculated that this latter probably amounts to double the EU contribution on average (House of Commons, 1997). As Table 4.1 shows, some Member States have invested more heavily in agri-environmental policy than others. The UK strategy for implementing 2078 can be characterized as narrow and deep, orientated as it is towards the management of landscapes and habitats in ESAs through often quite complicated tiered management agreements (60 per cent of the total UK agri-environmental budget was spent on the ESA scheme in 1998). This targeted approach to policy, also found in Sweden and Denmark, results in a lower total spend but arguably produces better environmental returns on each euro spent. The alternative approach of offering simpler schemes on a broader front characteristic of the approach in France, Austria and Germany is justified from a perspective which sees agri-environmental policy as less significant in solving specific environmental problems than in acting as a channel for redirecting resources and in playing a pivotal role in the reorientation of the CAP towards broader policy goals. There is a clear north–south divide in the uptake of 2078, with the northern bias of the policy predisposing a more successful implementation in northern than in southern Member States. From their analysis of implementation patterns across the EU, Buller *et al.* (2000) comment on the very uneven distribution of negotiated contracts viewed in these terms. Germany for instance accounts for 41 per cent of all current contracts in the EU-15, with Austria, France and Germany combined accounting for 67 per cent of the total number. At the other extreme are the four southern states of Spain, Portugal, Greece and Italy, accounting for just 16 per cent of all negotiated contracts. As Buller *et al.* (2000, p. 243) comment, 'the disparity is all the more striking when one considers that these (latter) four states account for 68 per cent of all farms in the EU'.

Leaving these different implementation strategies aside, it has become clear that environmental contracting exhibits common drawbacks as a mechanism for agri-environmental policy. One of the most widely recognized problems is that of 'adverse selection', where schemes are found to have most appeal to farmers who have to make the smallest adjustments to their farming practice to qualify for payment. Given the uniform payments on offer, and the voluntary nature of participation, those farmers who can meet the conditions of a management agreement with the lowest opportunity cost will inevitably enrol in schemes first. In particular, someone who has already been using a low input technology, for example, will tend to have a greater incentive to sign up for extensification payments than a farmer using a high input technology because the former will have to make fewer and less severe changes to current farming practice. This may compromise the environmental value for money of schemes because the result is few additional environmental benefits and over-compensation of participating farmers. The quandary for policy assessors, as Hanley *et al.* (1999, p. 73) observe, is that, while 'ensuring that environmental outputs pass (the) additionality test is clearly important, since otherwise farmers are being paid for a zero environmental gain, this does involve identifying what would have happened in the absence of the policy being appraised. This alternative state of the world may be quite different to the current situation, due to the dynamic nature of the system'.

A further problem is 'moral hazard', where participants in schemes find they have an incentive to default on aspects of a contract which *do* incur a net cost. Economic theory predicts that if effort is costly and compliance monitoring imperfect, participants will have an incentive to engage in a non-compliance gamble. In practice, most studies suggest that moral hazard is not widespread in the agri-environmental field – a recent study in the UK, for instance, found that only a minority of farmers participating in the (often demanding) Countryside Stewardship Scheme were in violation of their agreements. Nevertheless, ministries will come under increasing pressure to spend more money on monitoring and assessment if moral hazard is not to become a problem in future. A recent study of the transaction costs of agri-environmental policy discovered that these were often already very high in some Member States (Falconer and Whitby, 1999).

Agri-environmental schemes are on average more costly to administer relative to other types of policy such as the commodity regimes for farm income support because they involve more direct interaction with farmers and often complicated negotiations to ensure participation. Average annual administrative costs per participant ranged from 140 to 2446 ECU, with average levels typically of 200–300 ECU per participant. The UK and France exhibit the highest administrative costs, devoting much higher proportions of their total agri-environmental budgets to this purpose compared to the average (see Table 4.2). While there is also some evidence that these costs will fall as operating procedures become more established, there remains a basic question about how tightly administered and monitored agri-environmental schemes should be. Too free a rein may increase the risk of moral hazard, too tight and Member States could find they are charged with spending too much on administration and not enough on stewardship. It seems likely that the former will be the most likely scenario, especially in southern Member States, where there is evidence that the development of administrative structures is

Table 4.2   Average annual administration costs of agri-environmental schemes, 1998

	ECU per hectare[a]	ECU per contract[b]	ECU per 100 ECU paid as compensation[c]
Austria	20.5	216.9	8.8
Belgium	58.6	388.6	63.4
France	75.6	1522.0	87.1
Germany	10.2	177.5	12.3
Greece	59.7	470.1	8.6
Italy	13.1	140.0	6.6
Sweden	9.1	190.4	11.3
UK	48.0	2445.5	47.9

Notes:
a.   area-weighted.
b.   participant-weighted.
c.   expenditure-weighted.

Source: Falconer and Whitby (1999)

not keeping pace with the rapidly increasing scope, scale and complexity of agri-environmental schemes. The poorer members of the EU may find they cannot mobilize the resources necessary to cut the transaction costs of such policies.

AGENDA 2000 – EVOLUTION OR REFORM?

For the moment, however, the most important constraint on the future expansion of agri-environmental policy is budgetary. Critics point out that, despite the injection of new funds, expenditure on agri-environmental programmes is still dwarfed by expenditure on producer aids and compensation payments under the CAP. A consequence of the same package of CAP reforms which set up the Agri-environmental Regulation in 1992 was a series of reductions in price support that have been offset by a huge expansion in compensatory aid schemes. There has thus been a continuing tension between the large direct and indirect payments being channelled to farmers under these MacSharry reforms and the small conservation dividend trickling through Regulation 2078. At a farm level, the result is that incentives for environmental management on farms are still outweighed by continuing price and production support. Low take-up by farmers in some locations is blamed on the conflict between the payments offered and the financial rewards under other aspects of the CAP. Examples include the competition in hill and upland areas between agri-environmental payments and headage payments available under the Hill Livestock Compensatory Allowance (HLCA) scheme and other livestock subsidies in LFAs. In lowland areas the balance is usually even more skewed in favour of production, with the benefits of converting grassland to arable, for instance, easily outweighing the payments available under agri-environmental schemes.

The Agenda 2000 CAP reforms, agreed in Berlin in March 1999, were expected to improve this state of affairs by the applying the principle of *degressivity* to agricultural support. Such a reform would have meant reducing expenditure on compensation payments over time and, according to the surprisingly radical formulations circulating in Brussels preceding the agreement, redirecting the money saved to support the so-called 'second rural development pillar' of the CAP. In the event, degressivity proved a step too far for conservative-minded policymakers and while environmentalists won the technical argument they effectively lost the political battle. Indeed, critics have remarked on the rather regressive nature of the agricultural elements of reform package which was finally agreed: expenditure on compensation for the further price reductions agreed in Berlin has actually been increased, inflating the proportion of the farm budget given over to compensation measures. Total farm spending will increase from €42 to 48 billion between 2000 and 2006, adding up to €323 billion over these seven years. Meanwhile, Agenda 2000 commits few additional resources for environmental supports. Agri-environmental expenditure within the envelope of the new Rural Development Regulation 1257/1999 may even be frozen until 2006. On the other hand, the reform agreement opens the way to some green recoupling of support by exploiting the scope for modulation and cross-compliance contained in the agreement.

The Rural Development Regulation lays the basis for a Community rural development policy as the second pillar of the CAP. It gives discretion to Member States to combine rural development, early retirement, agri-environmental and forestry schemes together within seven year rural development programmes tailored to fit the circumstances of different rural regions (the Regulation also reforms and re-targets the Structural Funds, allocating €183 billion to this purpose over the planning period). Agri-environmental policy is the only compulsory element of the Rural Development Programmes which will have to be implemented throughout the territories of all Member States. Significantly, the Regulation redefines the funds from which rural development actions can be financed, allowing all rural development funding to come from the European Agricultural Guidance and Guarantee Fund (EAGGF) Guarantee Fund. This creates the possibility of very large flows of funds into rural development in future if Member States are minded to set up the programmes to achieve this. As Buckwell (1999) comments, it also signals victory for Agriculture Directorate-General in maintaining its control of the rural development portfolio. For the moment, the European Commission estimates that the funds available from the Guarantee budget for rural development and the new accompanying measures will rise slightly, in line with inflation, from just under €4.4 billion in 2000 to just over €5 billion in 2006. Total expenditure will be over €33 billion over the seven years, representing about 10 per cent of total CAP spending.

An important detail is the reform of LFA support which Member States will now be able to make inside the envelope of the rural development programmes. First, headage payments are to be converted into hectarage payments, breaking the link for the first time between the receipt of payments and the number of livestock. Receipt of the subsidy will be conditional on farmers agreeing 'to apply good farming practices compatible with the need to safeguard the environment and maintain the countryside, in particular by sustainable farming practices' (Commission of the European Communities, 1999b). Member States may also now make more inventive use of LFA payments to support farmers in locations where farming is restricted because of environmental regulations or specific handicaps. This should enable the inclusion of land with high natural value where continuation of farming is required to maintain the environmental interest.

Increased discretion is to be given to Member States in deciding how to rebalance their agricultural support. In particular, Member States have been provided with other mechanisms for increasing the rural development and agri-environmental spend. Modulation is the term that has been coined to describe the discretion to be given to Member States to reduce the rate of compensation paid to farmers in different sectors. Under the agreement, Member States may reduce compensation payments to farmers by up to 20 per cent. The resources saved may then be used as co-financing for additional spending under the accompanying measures, including agri-environmental programmes. Unlike the compensation measures, however, accompanying measures are funded on the basis of matched European and national finance, so domestic funds would have to be available to draw down the modulated savings. Even so, the increased resources made available for agri-environmental schemes via this route could be significant. In the UK, the MAFF has announced its intention to allocate an additional 600 000 euros for this purpose (effectively a doubling of current agri-environmental expenditure) by modulating the Arable Area Payment Scheme. In France, an even more substantial reallocation of funds is promised by applying the maximum rate of modulation to payments received by larger arable farmers.

Meanwhile, the new provision for applying environmental conditions to the compensation and producer aids which the majority of farmers continue to receive through the mechanism of cross-compliance, may significantly increase the environmental leverage policymakers can exert on farmers outside agri-environmental policy itself. At its most basic, cross-compliance refers to the linking of environmental conditions to agricultural support payments (Baldock and Mitchell, 1995). Farmers who chose not to comply with a set of pre-determined environmental guidelines risk forgoing payments (under the Agenda 2000 reforms agriculture departments can recycle any savings made back into agri-environmental schemes, though compared to modulation, the likely boost to overall spending from this source is likely to be small). Cross-compliance has gained much ground since the 1992 Maastricht Treaty, Article 130r of which requires Member States to integrate 'environmental protection requirements into the definition and implementation of other community policies'. In policy design terms, cross-compliance is something of a hybrid between the regulation based approach and the environmental payments model that have been discussed so far. It contains elements of regulation, in that certain prescriptions need to be followed to remain eligible for CAP support, yet there is no coercion since farmers are free to opt out and voluntarily forgo part of all of their CAP support payments. There seems to be a broad understanding across the EU that cross-compliance should not go as far as to impose onerous or costly obligations on farmers (Baldock and Mitchell, 1995), implying that only moderate cross-compliance conditions will be imposed, requiring the farmer to observe codes of good practice and to maintain existing landscape and habitat features. At present it looks unlikely that all Member States will implement this provision. Germany, for instance, is insisting that its agri-environmental laws and regulations are among the most stringent in the EU, thus obviating the need for compliance conditions.

THE AGENDA 2000 COUNTRYSIDE

After more than a decade and a half of agri-environmental policy development, there have been important changes to the pattern and extent of Member State intervention in the countryside. As Figure 4.2 shows, the productivist assumption of a demarcated countryside split between conservation sites, LFAs and the remaining agricultural area, has given way to a more complicated picture in which regulation, environmental standard setting and paid stewardship are being combined in different ways to promote environmental management on a much broader front. Site protection is still at the apex of the pyramid, though now increasingly informed by new thinking from landscape ecology and co-ordinated at an EU level through the Natura 2000 network. Meanwhile, at the base of the pyramid there is a clear trend towards

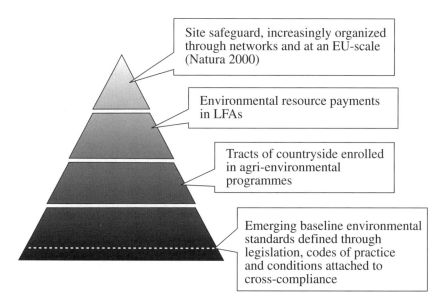

Figure 4.2   The Agenda 2000 countryside

establishing baseline environmental standards for all farmers, both implicitly through legislation and explicitly via the setting up of codes of good environmental conduct. Cross-compliance is an earnest of this trend, defining standards of practice which may at some future date stand alone to define a regulatory floor below which no farmer will be allowed to fall without incurring a legal penalty. Operating in between these two approaches, agri-environmental policy and the new 'greened' LFA policy, the first increasingly geared to rewarding farmers throughout the countryside for contributions to environmental quality and quantity above the baseline; the latter operating as an environmental resource payment which underwrites traditional systems of farming where large tracts of countryside have to be farmed if their characteristic landscapes and biodiversity are to be maintained.

EUROPEAN AGRI-ENVIRONMENTAL POLICY – THE WAY AHEAD

The future development of the EU's agri-environmental policy must be seen in the context of the CAP as a whole and the likely future trajectory of reform. There are two sets of forces which are now driving CAP reform: the prospect of further enlargement of the EU to the east and the impact of moves towards the liberalization of agricultural trade under the auspices of the World Trade Organization (WTO). A first round enlargement involving Poland, Hungary, Czech Republic, Slovenia and Estonia will increase the utilized agricultural area of the EU by 23 per cent and the farming population by 55 per cent (Tangermann and Swinnen, 2000). With its fragmented farm structures, over-manning and low living standards, agriculture in these Central and Eastern European Countries (CEECs) will make huge demands on the CAP budget if policy entitlements are extended to farmers in their current form. Leaving aside the macroeconomic impact of accession, the main contention is whether direct payments presently available to farmers in the EU-15 should be offered to farmers in the Visegrad countries. As many commentators have pointed out, it is hard to argue on grounds of natural justice for compensation payments to be given to farmers who have never been beneficiaries of price support. Moreover, tackling problems of over capacity and depressed incomes through price support risks repeating the mistakes of the past. As Buckwell (1999, p. 264) contends:

> We have much experience now of the outcome of such a policy. It will simply encourage an over expansion of production focusing the bulk of any benefits on the largest farms. It is plain that there will have to be a large shift of labour out of agriculture in most applicant countries. The way to facilitate this with least distor-

tion is through appropriate rural development actions, not by subsidising agricultural production.

Part of the rationale for the Agenda 2000 reforms was to adjust the CAP in advance of accession in order to make this possible. The failure of policymakers in Berlin to make significant inroads into price support and their reluctance to dismantle compensation payments had led many commentators to expect a further round of reforms within the next three to five years.

This will likely coincide with the conclusion of the Millennium Round of international trade talks, partly dedicated to the liberalization of agricultural trade. Under the Uruguay Round Agriculture Agreement (URAA) signed in 1993, members have already committed themselves to further agricultural policy reform in order to eliminate non-tariff barriers to trade, phase out export subsidies and to decouple domestic support. According to the 'built in agenda' from this Round, and under pressure from the Cairns Group and the United States, all WTO members must now make further progress on these issues. As far as agri-environmental policy is concerned, a question mark hangs over the legitimacy of payments to farmers which are not strictly production neutral. In order to qualify for the 'Green Box' of measures that will be exempted from further reductions, environmental payments must be part of a 'clearly defined government agri-environmental programme and be dependant on the fulfilment of specific conditions' (Paragraph 12 of Annex 2 of the URAA). At the same time, however, payments must cover the costs incurred and give rise to measurable environmental outputs.

These disciplines, enshrined in the URAA and used as a point of reference by the Americans and members of the Cairns Group, pose a serious intellectual and political challenge to European agri-environmental policy as it is currently constituted. First, and most obviously, it suggests that cross-compliance has a limited shelf life given that the compensation payments to which conditions are to be attached will come under heavy scrutiny in the WTO and may be rendered illegal at some point after the conclusion of the next round. Presently classified as 'blue box' measures which enjoy temporary exemption from the reduction requirement under the 'Peace Clause' that is due to expire in 2003, their disappearance will remove the lever through which compliance can be required. More significant, however, is the implicit challenge to the green box compatibility of reformed LFA payments and to 'broad but shallow' agri-environmental payments, both of which undoubtedly have production effects, albeit indirect ones. Paragraph 1 of annex 2 of the URAA states that all green box measures must not be, or must be minimally, trade distorting. A strict interpretation of this paragraph could invalidate some environmental payments that are currently given to farmers to continue with traditional farming practices. As Burney (2000) points out, it is often difficult to deliver

European agri-environmental programmes in a totally decoupled way, chiefly because we are interested in maintaining the farming processes associated with a landscape or piece of habitat rather than specifying particular environmental management tasks which need to be undertaken in return for payment. An environmental resource payment available to farmers in LFAs, for instance, may fail to pass the green box test because they seek to maintain stocking levels in order to ensure that heather moorland is adequately grazed. Fraser and Russell (1997) observe that even when the payment itself is decoupled, there may be production effects, for instance in the case of a hill sheep farmer who receives an agri-environmental payment and uses this to stay in business as a sheep producer.

The European defence of these arrangements, meanwhile – that they help protect a multifunctional agriculture in which food and environment are produced as joint outputs – is regarded with scepticism by American and Australian negotiators. 'Multi-functionality' is an important concept which will be used by the Europeans and other countries such as Japan, Norway, Korea and Switzerland, to justify retaining measures which may not be completely production neutral in some of their effects.

At the time of writing it is hard to assess how seriously this challenge will be progressed within the WTO. At root is a clash of explanations about how agri-environmental problems arise and can best be addressed. The supporters of multi-functionality are approaching agri-environmental issues from a predominantly public goods perspective which emphasizes the importance of maintaining extensive systems of farming over large tracts of countryside in order to ensure that landscape and wildlife are jointly produced with agricultural outputs like beef, sheepmeat and olive oil. Under this analysis, environmental quality will be damaged where traditional farming systems disappear, as might happen following the withdrawal of agricultural support under a scenario of extreme liberalization (Potter *et al.*, 1999). The result could be undermanagement and environmental decline. In other words, trade liberalization, without adequate flanking measures, will not deliver the win–win scenario (in terms of greater economic wealth and better environmental quality) which free traders suppose. All of this contrasts with the American position, which is that liberalization should be environmentally beneficial because it will encourage a reduction in the inputs such as fertilizer and pesticides as well as stocking densities which give rise to the only agri-environmental problems of any significance – that of overexploitation and pollution. According to their understanding of agri-environmental relationships, if there is a case for paying farmers to produce public goods, this should be through tailored payments which are designed to achieve specific environmental outcomes.

Reconciling these opposing views will be a major challenge for the next round of trade talks. In reality, there is likely to be scope for a re-negotiation of the green box in order to enable appropriate forms of agri-environmental support to be retained by those members committed to a multifunctional agriculture. For this to be possible, however, it will have to be conceded that some types of environmental payment will have production effects, albeit ones that arise as unintended consequences of programmes with legitimate and transparent environmental policy objectives. Stricter tests of legitimacy will almost certainly be required and these could be modelled on the WTO's existing Sanitary and Phyto Sanitary (SPS) agreement. Ervin (1999) suggests these could include:

- whether the actions of farmers are regarded as generating an external benefit, such that the Provider Gets Principle applies;
- whether, in the absence of the payment, the environmental value would fall below the level demanded;
- whether there is a demonstrable link between the action that is being subsidized and specific external benefits;
- whether the policy mechanism is targeted on the most appropriate indicator.

CONCLUSIONS

Agri-environmental policy, defined in its broadest sense to include regulation, incentives and site safeguard, is now well established as an important mechanism for stewardship in the EU. Its incremental development as an accompanying measure to the CAP, however, means that there are still many imperfections in the system. Even so, land managers today have far more incentive to reduce pollution and to manage habitats than they did ten years ago. Coming years will see further evolution towards a more integrated application of policy instruments within a broad EU framework setting down standard operating procedures and basic principles. With increasing amounts of public money presently spent on farm support being recoupled to agri-environmental incentive schemes, pressure will grow for improved monitoring and enforcement. Better ways of delivering schemes to farmers and a broader client base of land managers will need to be found, as well as mechanisms for bringing in groups of managers in order to conserve entire landscapes and watersheds. At the same time the traditional reluctance to regulate farmers and their actions in order to protect the environment will likely give way to a readiness to combine regulation and incentives. As time goes on, this debate will more and more be conducted in an international setting, the WTO coming to occupy a more central role in the conduct of agri-environmental policy. The next round of trade talks will be a critical testing ground for many of the assumptions and principles underlying European policy.

REFERENCES

Baldock, D. and K. Mitchell (1995), *Cross-compliance within the Common Agricultural Policy: A Review of Options for Landscape and Nature Conservation*, London: Institute for European Environmental Policy.

Bischoff, N. and R. Jongman (1993), *Development of Rural Areas in Europe: the Claim for Nature*, The Hague: Netherlands Scientific Council for Government Policy.

Boisson, J-M. and H. Buller (1996), 'France', in M. Whitby (ed.), *The European Environment and CAP Reform: Policies and Prospects for Conservation*, Wallingford: CAB International, pp. 105–30.

Bowers, J.K. and P.C. Cheshire (1983), *Agriculture, the Countryside and Land Use: An Economic Critique*, London: Methuen.

Brouwer, F. (2000), Personal Communication.

Buckwell, A. (1999), *Agenda 2000 and Beyond: Towards a new Common Agricultural and Rural Policy for Europe*, Florence: Accademia Dei Georgofili.

Buller, H., G.A. Wilson and A. Höll (eds) (2000), *Agri-environmental Policy in the European Union*, Perspectives on Europe, Contemporary Interdisciplinary Research, Aldershot: Ashgate.

Burney, J. (2000), 'Agriculture, Trade Negotiations and the Environment', Paper to the Royal Institute of International Affairs Conference on Sustainability in the WTO Millennium Round and Beyond, 27 March 2000.

Colman, D. and B. Traill (1984), 'Economic pressures on the environment', in A. Korbey (ed.), *Investing in Rural Harmony: A Critique*, Reading: Centre for Agricultural Strategy, pp. 30–41.

Commission of the European Communities (1991), 'The Development and Future of the CAP', COM 91(100), Luxembourg: Office for Official Publications of the European Communities.

Commission of the European Communities (1999a), *Agriculture, Environment and Rural Development: Facts and Figures*, Luxembourg: Office for Official Publications of the European Communities.

Commission of the European Communities (1999b), *Agenda 2000 Explanatory Memorandum: The Future of European Agriculture, Nine Regulations and their Financial Impact,* Brussels: DGVI.

Conrad, J. (1990), *Nitrate Pollution and Agriculture*, Aldershot: Avebury.

Delorme, H. (1987), 'An outline of French views on land conversion programmes', in D. Conder and D. Baldock (eds), *Removing Land from Agriculture, the Implications for Farming and the Environment*, London: Council for the Protection of Rural England/ Institute for European Environmental Policy.

Duchene, F., E. Szczepanik and W. Legg (1985), *New Limits on European Agriculture: Politics and the Common Agricultural Policy*, London: Croom Helm.

Ervin, D. (1999), 'Toward GATT-proofing environmental programmes for agriculture', *Journal of World Trade*, **33**(2), 63–82.

Falconer, K. and M. Whitby (1999), 'The invisible costs of scheme implementation and administration', in G. Van Huylenbroeck and M. Whitby (eds), *Countryside Stewardship: Farmers, Policies and Markets*, Oxford: Elsevier Science, pp. 67–88.

Felton, M. (1993), 'Achieving nature conservation objectives: problems and opportunities with economics', *Journal of Environmental Planning and Management*, **36**(1), 23–31.

Fraser, I. and N. Russell (1997), 'The economics of agri-environmental policy: present and future developments', *Economic Issues*, **2**(1), 67–84.

Hanley, N., M. Whitby and I. Simpson (1999), 'Assessing the success of agri-environmental policy in the UK', *Land Use Policy*, **16**, 67–80.

Hodge, I. (1999), 'Agri-environmental relationships and the choice of policy mechanism', *The World Economy* **23**(2), 257–73.

House of Commons (1997), *Environmentally Sensitive Areas and Other Schemes under the Agri-environmental Regulation*, Vol 1, Report and Proceedings, Select Committee on Agriculture, Second Report, Session 1996–97, London: HMSO.

Potter, C. (1998), *Against the Grain: Agri-environmental Reform in the United States and the European Union*, Wallingford: CAB International.

Potter, C., M. Lobley and R. Bull (1999), *Agricultural Liberalisation and its Environmental Effects*, English Nature Research Report, Peterborough: English Nature.

Reeve, R. (1993), 'Making environmental policy: Britain, the Netherlands and the new EC Nitrates Directive', in E. Bolsius, G. Clark and J. Groenendijk (eds), *The Retreat: Rural Land Use and European Agriculture*, Utrecht: Royal Dutch Geographical Society, pp. 61–81.

Tangermann, S. and J. Swinnen (2000), 'Conclusions and implications for food and agriculture in the process of accession to the EU', in S. Tangermann and M. Banse (eds), *Central and Eastern European Agriculture in an Expanding European Union*, Wallingford: CAB International, pp. 185–200.

5. Environmental valuation methods in rural resource management

Clive L. Spash and Claudia Carter

INTRODUCTION

Economic valuation methods have been employed to assess whether policy costs are justified in terms of their benefits. In the rural environment, land use changes from wildlife habitat to agriculture (including the change from extensive to intensive farming), woodland to agriculture or housing, or introduction of minerals/aggregates extraction or waste disposal have been common. While conversion to agriculture has dominated land use changes, some reversal is occurring in the form of reintroduction of wildlife habitats (for example hedgerows, woodland) and less intensive practices of farming and floodplain management (see for example Bromley and Hodge, 1990; Beaufoy, 1994; Pruckner, 1995; Bonnieux and Le Goffe, 1997). Examples include restoration projects along the Rhine floodplains, UK marshland projects and the introduction of grants for environmentally sensitive management to increase wildlife habitat area and quality. Similarly, the trend towards monoculture is being challenged by mixed and organic farming and land use practices. Simultaneously, the drive for continued scientific and technocentric approaches to agricultural production and environmental management continues, for example genetically modified crops. In all these issues concerns arise over the extent to which potential (ex ante) and actual (ex post) environmental damages or improvements can be taken into account in economic decisions. This has raised the idea that farmers should be 'compensated' for improving the environment in contrast to a Polluter Pays Principle in other sectors of the economy. An incentive for policy to be developed in this direction comes from the need to reduce market and price support measures to crop and livestock production under the Common Agricultural Policy (CAP), and the idea that an alternative is to support the supply of a range of rural goods and services, including species and ecosystems. The amount of any such 'compensation' and how it should be calculated is then of direct policy concern.

This chapter provides a survey of methods of environmental valuation which have been proclaimed as relevant to answering such rural resource management issues. In doing so, the chapter will: (a) outline a range of values associated with agricultural production and rural land use change; (b) set out the methods of cost–benefit analysis (CBA) appropriate for assessing rural land use activities while referring to empirical work; (c) explain the main problems associated with those methods; and (d) recommend the most appropriate method(s) for empirical work to evaluate the monetary benefits and costs of land use change. The second section provides an overview of the environmental values related to rural land use and divides these into market, non-market and non-economic values. Non-market values include a range of the environmental side-effects which might be associated with managing the countryside such as wildlife habitat conservation. The following section summarizes the principal methods for generating estimates of the non-market values and major problems in their application. The techniques discussed are the travel cost method (TCM), the production function approach (PFA), hedonic pricing (HP) and stated preference techniques, mainly the contingent valuation method (CVM). The final section summarizes the extent to which these valuation methods can be used in the European context to inform the decision-making process and stimulate better co-ordination of policy on agriculture and nature, especially with regard to accounting for the effects of modern agricultural production on the environment. Emphasis throughout this chapter is placed upon awareness of the limitations of these methods, which therefore demand prudent use in any policy context. Some overall conclusions and tentative recommendations are given in the final section.

THE RANGE OF RELEVANT ENVIRONMENTAL VALUES

Economic assessment, associated with evaluating externalities, can differ from impact assessment under a natural science or engineering approach where physical impacts are central. That is, under the economic approach, emphasis is placed upon the physical impacts only to the extent that they follow a path to specific targets which affect human welfare. Environmental change is then linked to human welfare via characterizing the environment as goods and services, which may be broadly defined. Thus, changes in the provision of environmental goods and services, such as the number and range of common bird species, form the focus of attention. This means economic value categories relate to what are regarded as relevant welfare generating aspects of the environment in terms of the environmental goods and services provided, rather than the source of physical changes, for example loss of ecosystems, such as meadow or floodplain habitat, or biodiversity. Another difference between economic values and physical changes is that the expectation of an impact and its psychological effect can be important in terms of economic welfare, even if there is no physical change, as, for example, in the case of some 'food scares'. Economic valuation techniques appeal to human preferences and as a result are influenced by impacts upon those preferences and ignore whatever those preferences fail to take into account.

The next three sections sketch the range of potential values which could be affected by rural resource management and how they relate to economic activities. The type and characteristics of agricultural and recreational uses associated with the impacts are largely left unspecified and no attempt is made to specify the importance of different impacts. At this stage the aim is to show where economic valuation techniques are regarded as being operative.

Potential Impacts on Existing Markets

Goods and services sold directly to consumers or to firms as inputs to production may be impacted by certain rural land use changes or practices. For example, dust from aggregates extraction may impact agricultural crops raising production costs; large scale monoculture may reduce tourist trade in farm holidays, or organic food production may be valued for its environmental benefits by consumers and gain a higher price. In such cases a market exists where goods and services are traded so that standard economic models of supply and demand in that market can be employed to estimate the economic impacts. Some of the markets which could be impacted by intensive agricultural land uses, intensive forestry, mineral/aggregates extraction and waste disposal include those for: water supply, freshwater and coastal products, and recreation and tourism.

Water supply
Both ground- and surface water may be adversely affected by intensive farming practices, largely from application of fertilizers and pesticides. Where this affects the water supply industry the costs of supply may rise accordingly and will reflect the cost of additional treatment of water to potable standards in accordance with governmental or international standards, or the cost of paying farmers to change their practices. Where water quality is reduced, industry reassurances may be insufficient to prevent consumer substitution away from the supplier, thereby reducing demand. In order to capture these effects a model of the water supply market would be required which allowed both consumer and producer welfare surpluses to be estimated.

Freshwater and coastal products

The quantity and quality of freshwater and coastal life also provide direct benefits as a source of food. In the bio-economic literature the term 'fish' is used to cover all living freshwater, estuarine and marine resources including fish, mammals, crustaceans and molluscs (for example Clark, 1976; Hartwick and Olewiler, 1986). The water environment provides a nursery for young fish, as well as providing food and habitat. The life-cycle and thus productivity, quality and quantity of fish for consumption as well as for by-products is related to the quality of the water environment. Soil deposition and pollution runoff from farmland or forestry can influence fish stock recruitment and distribution.

Marine plant sea food is harvested but currently in small amounts in Europe; for example seaweed sold by the Findhorn community in Scotland. Non-food products include primary goods, for example shells, star fish, fertilizers, and by-products such as fish oils. Pollution from intensive agricultural practices may also reduce the option for exploiting or harvesting marine products which are currently regarded as non-commercial.

Recreation and tourism

Recreational and tourist opportunities may be temporarily or permanently lost due to intensification of land use. Some uses allow for a site to be restored ameliorating these impacts and restricting them to the duration of the land use conversion, for example some mineral extraction. The impact of lost demand for recreation and tourism would be felt in the local economy if no alternative (perfect) substitute site were available in the area for the activities involved, and a regional substitution effect might occur. Alternatively, the site may have unique characteristics with no opportunities for substitution. For example, ornithologists might be prevented from viewing a rare species associated with one specific habitat destroyed by intensive farming or conversion to forestry.

Some recreational activities may have close market substitutes. Thus, non-commercial harvesting of food can be related to the markets for the commercial substitutes to estimate the value of the product loss. However, in general, recreational activities involve an experience related to the quality of the environment which depends not only upon site characteristics and the availability of substitutes, but also the value gained from participation in the activity. Thus, recreational and tourist activities can involve values beside those costs associated with related markets or identifiable physical aspects of ecosystems. For example, gathering flowers, wild berries or mushrooms may be related to market substitutes but the experience of harvesting is of more central concern to the welfare gained. This means that people may incur travel costs in excess of the value of the harvest gathered, as measured by the equivalent commercial product costs, because the experience is valued in itself. If markets are directly related to an activity such as travel costs, entry fees and equipment costs, the opportunity cost can be approximated, but not the welfare gained which is the consumer surplus. The welfare in terms of surplus would require using a technique which would derive a surrogate demand function for the site's non-market values such as CVM, or TCM as discussed below.

Non-market Values

The activities outlined above tend to result in either direct markets being set up to buy and sell services or goods related to the environment, or in impacts upon uses which are directly related to market activities. In this section the focus is upon non-market aspects and non-marketable values associated with the impacts of rural land use changes. These values include a range of goods and services from cultural heritage to biodiversity.

Aesthetics

Several attempts have been made to value aesthetics. For a review of literature see Graves (1991). The aesthetic appeal of a given environment or site involves the subjective perception of what is beautiful or what stimulates the emotions. The relationships between a person and their physical environment can form an important part of their identity affecting their feelings of personal and/or social worth, self-efficacy, distinctiveness or uniqueness (see for example Twigger-Ross and Uzzell, 1996). Hence, the concept of 'landscape' and the particular characteristics of different landscapes such as rugged hills, a gently rolling lowland valley, a river plain or birdsong and 'natural' sounds associated with different landscapes, can form an important aspect of people's identification with, or reaction to, a place and their perception of any changes to the status quo. Such aesthetic/landscape appeal could be partially reflected as a characteristic of the local housing market. Thus, sites of great natural beauty may be associated with specialized markets, for example retirement homes, tourism and holiday sites. Where such aesthetic qualities are regarded as rare or unique, a lack of aesthetic substitutes can mean enjoyment of a location produces a premium in terms of local property values (which might then be assessed via an HP approach). Studies which attempted to assess aesthetic values by direct questioning of the public (for example CVM) have tended to estimate an individual's preference for a specific aspect of aesthetic quality, such as improved visibility due to better air quality or the introduction of specific tree species. Following this reasoning, aesthetic quality would then need to be identified with specific site characteristics by visitors or local residents. Such reductionism may be difficult or impossible to achieve, for example relating aesthetics to the type and quantity of individual landscape features. Questions can also be raised as to the relevance of a current aesthetic preference. That is, some landscapes may be regarded as worthy of preservation for the values they encapsulate and therefore should be removed from the vagaries of consumer choice, fashions and fads. This is certainly one of the principles underlying the foundation and spread of national parks.

Cultural and historical values

Cultural, historical and archaeological sites can be disturbed or destroyed by rural land use practices. Cultural values may be associated with geological features, ecosystems (for example an ancient woodland) as well as buildings or ruins. The site-specific nature of these values can, in theory, allow estimation of their economic benefits (using for example HP, TCM or CVM), although in practice defining and measuring what is meant by the concepts of culture and history would prove difficult. The importance of a site in public perception can vary greatly from that of an expert, say an archaeologist or historian. Local or regional perception of a site's cultural and historical features may also diverge strongly from national or international opinion, for example World Heritage Sites versus local economic interests.

Health and safety

There are several potential or perceived influences from agriculture, forestry, minerals/aggregates extraction and waste disposal operations on health and safety. These include:

- reductions in water quality;
- reductions in food quality and variety;
- allergies, asthmatic attacks and skin irritations (from crops and/or pesticides);
- toxic side effects from chemicals used in production;
- genetic side effects from chemical applications or genetic manipulation in food production;
- fallout from dust and/or chemical spraying; and
- increased traffic (for example heavy goods vehicles and cars on the road; barges and ships on waterways) making public transport routes more dangerous.

In terms of preference-based measures of economic welfare loss, the risk perception of individuals is all-important, rather than the judgement of scientists, engineers or other experts. As long as the aim is to learn about the individual's preferences and willingness to pay or accept then knowledge is required of the individual's view of the trade-off, including subjective risk assessment (see Freeman 1993, Chapter 8). Thus, the fact that health and safety hazards have been largely eliminated through tighter regulation of the agriculture, waste disposal and aggregates industries may be irrelevant in terms of the value of the impact that the public perceives. Of course, public preferences based on mistaken beliefs or poor information may be deemed an inappropriate point of reference for policy.

Peace and quiet

Noise from activities such as large agricultural machinery, landfilling, quarrying and transport of waste or aggregates by lorry will reduce the enjoyment of peace and quiet. Such noise pollution can be a substantive impact. The reaction may be to take ameliorative steps such as installing double glazing in nearby houses and these protection costs could then be used to estimate the damages resulting from noise pollution. However, unless the protection is a perfect substitute for the benefits foregone, this approach will be an underestimate of the loss. For example, double glazing is only effective as a sound barrier inside a house with the doors and windows closed. A fuller range of economic loss may be reflected in the value of houses and land in the vicinity which could be depressed by the presence of a busy road or a modern heavily machine-intensive farm so that the externality is capitalized. (In this case HP models might be employed to estimate the damage.)

Water and air quality

Reduced water quality can affect the ability of populations and varieties of flora and fauna to live in a particular water, marsh or coastal habitat. It also can affect human health directly, for example a disease may be contracted when water is accidentally swallowed, or indirectly when food grown in polluted waters is ingested. Human health impacts from air quality reductions have been a major concern for policy leading to local air quality improvements, for example the transformation of local domestic pollution from coal and wood burning, through central power generation, to internationally transported pollutants and acidic deposition. Reductions in air quality can affect a range of activities besides health. Dust and particulates, depending upon quantities and composition, can cause increased costs for households and firms resulting from, for example, an increased need for washing of clothes, cars or windows, damage to materials left in the open (such as paint work) and impacts on the growth of garden plants.

Ecosystems functions and biodiversity

The functions which ecosystems perform are many and varied. Only a minority of these fall within the framework where they can be bought and sold on markets subject to private ownership. Amongst the most important functions performed by ecosystems are maintenance of climatic stability and nutrient cycles. In terms of rural land uses, avoiding the loss of species and their habitats will help maintain biodiversity. Biodiversity of ecosystems, genes and species is seen as an important aspect of natural capital and a key to sustainable development. However, valuation of biodiversity is complicated by a poorly informed general public and the extent to which people reject market valuation in this area (Spash and Hanley, 1995). Direct questioning of the public, for example via CVM, may be able to provide some aspects of species value or even ecosystem diversity but is unable to address many of the concerns raised by the need to maintain ecosystems functions and protect biodiversity. Where an identifiable output or service can be related to an ecosystem function and this output or service is connected to a market product the economic value of changes in ecosystem functions may be assessed (that is, using PFA). Impacts of rural land use practices in this area can be complex, highly uncertain or unknown, such as the loss of a site-specific species which has never been classified.

Intrinsic Value in Nature

This category of values is by definition outside the economic calculus to evaluate. The category is mentioned here in order to qualify the discussion over the extent to which economic techniques can achieve a comprehensive valuation of the benefits of the environment. Intrinsic values are related to non-consequentialist and therefore non-utilitarian aspects of the environment. For example, a species may be valued as a food source and because it is beautiful and because of its potential to benefit science, but it may also be valued separately from all these uses or aspects of its nature which create good consequences for humans.

Individuals who regard the world from a non-teleological perspective will express absolute values beyond any possible trade. Teleological ethical theories place the ultimate criterion of morality in some non-moral value (for example welfare, utility, happiness) that results from acts. Such theories see only instrumental value in such acts, but intrinsic value in the consequences of these acts. In contrast, deontological ethical theories attribute intrinsic value to features of the act, themselves. This could be apparent as an expression of the rights of animals to welfare or the rights of humans to life.

Intrinsic values may be regarded as rights or non-compensatory choices. Freeman (1986) has suggested that lexicographic preferences may be taken as a belief in such rights. When preferences are lexicographic, the individual cannot be compensated for the loss of a quantity of one good by increases in the quantity of one or more other goods, no matter how small the former or how large the latter. However, this approach reduces the difference between payment offered and compensation demanded to an anomaly within utilitarianism rather than a fundamental difference in philosophical outlook. The refusal to trade becomes particularly relevant when disruption of the environment affects such things as human health, animal welfare and ecosystems' functioning and structure. In such cases intrinsic values in non-human animals, plants or ecosystems are recognized by individuals as a serious constraint on economic trade-offs. Studies show that a significant proportion of respondents to valuation surveys on biodiversity and wildlife show rights-based beliefs (Stevens *et al.*, 1991; Spash, 1998a, 1998b, 2000).

METHODS FOR ENVIRONMENTAL CBA

This section turns to a discussion of the specific methods for monetary valuation of the environment which have been mentioned above. In doing so, the main problems associated with applying these methods to different aspects of the environment are raised. This shows how the idea that environmental damages and improvements might be reflected in monetary terms confronts both theoretical limitations and practical problems.

Travel Cost Method

Travel cost method (TCM) is the oldest of the non-market valuation techniques predominantly used in outdoor recreation modelling (see Hanley and Spash, 1993, Chapter 5). The basic method is to place a value on non-market environmental goods by using the costs of consumption behaviour in related markets. For example, to evaluate recreational fishing, a TCM survey would typically gather information on travel costs, access/fish licence fees, on-site expenses, and capital expenditure on fishing equipment. Varying such costs and predicting fishing activity changes can then be used to derive surrogate demand functions for fishing at a specific location.

TCM is normally applied to site-specific locations and the cost of travel tends to be road based, via cars. The basic problems are: whether to use zonal or individual visits, how to treat visits to other sites, deciding the treatment of costs, and statistical problems. Randall (1994) has suggested the subjective treatment of costs means that TCM must be calibrated using information generated from fundamentally different methods so that TCM is no longer an independent tool. This might follow the example of Cameron (1992) who combined TCM with CVM, an approach successfully followed by Kling (1997).

Zonal or individual visits?

A choice is required between measuring visits from a given geographical zone or the number of visits made on an individual basis. Individual visits are usually measured by visits per annum for each respondent. Zonal visits are usually measured by visits per capita. The option chosen determines the dependent variable. On theoretical grounds neither option ranks above the other. Unfortunately, consumers' surplus estimates for a given site or class of sites have been shown to vary substantially with the choice of measure.

Non-site benefits

A visit to a specific site may be only part of the purpose for an individual's journey. This is problematic because the full travel costs cannot be attributed to the site in question. There are several options for handling this problem. However, Mendelsohn *et al.* (1992) regard most TCM studies as having either ignored multiple destination trips or arbitrarily allocating trip costs across visited sites. They suggest treating combinations of multiple destinations as unique sites and incorporating them into a demand system. A related problem concerns people who have travelled from temporary holiday accommodation to the site. Their daily travel costs reflect only part of their cost of attending the site and some of their travel costs from their permanent residence to the holiday residence should be included.

Judgements on costs

Calculating the cost of distance travelled involves setting a price per kilometre. This requires either using petrol costs only, as an estimate of marginal cost, or allowing for all the costs of motoring by including an allowance for sunk costs such as depreciation and insurance. Individuals, in maximizing utility, are assumed to compare the marginal utility with the marginal costs of consumption to achieve an economically efficient outcome. This process implies marginal costs should be used, since including all costs will result in a measure of price per mile using average costs. The choice will influence the consumers' surplus figures.

Time is expended both in travelling to a site and whilst enjoying the site itself. As a scarce commodity, time clearly has an implicit or shadow price. If individuals are giving up working time, in order to visit a site, the wage rate is the correct opportunity cost; if a site visit occurs while on holiday leave, the opportunity cost will be measured with reference to the value, at the margin, of other recreation activities foregone. Ideally, a separate value would be calculated for each individual to reflect their set of leisure activities and valuations. In practice, such data is too difficult and expensive to collect. Debate on the appropriate approach continues.

The general conclusion would seem to be that TCM researchers are forced to assign their own subjective estimation of visit costs. Randall (1994) has argued that visit costs are inherently subjective, but give an ordinal measure if the cost increases with distance travelled. Thus, the traditional TCM yields an ordinal measure of welfare. However, TCM cannot then serve as an independent technique for estimating recreation benefits; rather, it must be calibrated using information from other methods.

Another more general problem is the extent to which aggregating preferences reflects the type and range of values of concern. For example, the presence and size of human settlements in areas bordering a site or national park may play a decisive role in determining attributed monetary values. The closer an ecosystem is to large human settlements the more there are likely to be frequent visitors and hence a larger aggregate monetary value may be calculated as being associated with the site. Those coming from further away to a remote site will have a higher willingness to pay which can counter this impact on total site value, but a green space in the city may easily prove to have a higher monetary value on the basis of low cost but frequent visits. In the extreme a wilderness area which restricted all access would be regarded as having no value under the TCM. Thus, contrary to a criterion of environmental prioritization based upon the pristine or virgin status or biodiversity of an ecosystem, an altered and ecologically degraded site can appear socially preferable and of more value under the TCM. Using TCM in Europe to indicate which ecosystems should be protected as rare habitats may therefore lead to the loss of ecosystems in remote regions, regardless of their ecological quality or significance.

Statistical problems

As part of the process of calculating welfare changes via TCM a regression analysis will be undertaken to predict visits, for example visits per capita are a function of travel costs. Loomis (1995) has argued that regional economic effects associated with the improvement of a recreation site will be underestimated unless all aspects of the decisions to undertake recreation are included. He identifies four recreation aspects of choices: participation in a given recreation activity; the site(s) to visit; the frequency of trips to a given site; and the length of stay. He goes on to explain recent advances in statistical techniques for modelling each recreational choice, and illustrates (using deer hunting) how linking two of the four recreation choices yields more complete estimates of the change in number of trips, income and employment.

TCM and rural resource management

The extent to which TCM might help assess the environmental externalities associated with changing rural land use to agriculture or other intensive use is summarized here. Recreation and tourism cover several activities such as hiking, painting, photography and bird watching. TCM was developed with the site-specific recreational visitor in mind and is therefore well suited to assessing these values, but the qualifications mentioned above (for example non-site benefits) must be taken into account. The extent to which TCM can address other aspects of environmental value is often limited.

- Aesthetic changes, such as 'wilderness' aspects, are only likely to be discernible in TCMs where the site has special features creating a recreational demand, and even then they may be difficult to define or measure;
- cultural and historical values would only be part of TCM estimate of demand where they are associated with site specific features, and require site visits for enjoyment or evaluation;
- peace and quiet, as part of a site's recreational experience, might be included under TCM, but the impact on the wider community of noise pollution, for example from farming machinery or aggregates extraction, would be excluded;
- health and safety concerns associated with certain rural land uses would fall beyond the scope of TCM to evaluate.

In general, the site characteristics valued by TCM are only those recognized by visitors as important. That is, the values are implicit in the preferences of the visitors. This means, if visitors fail to recognize the importance or even existence of a characteristic of a site (for example biodiversity) then this characteristic will be absent from the valuation via TCM. In particular, genetic diversity and ecosystem functions are unlikely to form part of site values obtained under TCM.

Production Function Approach

The production function approach (PFA) generally uses scientific knowledge on cause–effect or dose–response relationships, that is the relationship between environmental quality variables and the output level of a marketed commodity. The PFA has been popular in studying air pollution impacts on agricultural crops (reviewed by Spash, 1997), but has also been applied elsewhere, such as to pollution impacts on fisheries, for example Kahn (1991) and Silvander and Drake (1991). The PFA requires a quantifiable definition of the environmental change of concern, linking this change to a receptor response function, and then applying the results to an economic model for a related market good. Thus, applications have been determined by the availability of existing scientific information on dose–response functions.

The cause–effect relationship
To assess the gain or loss of benefits resulting from an environmental quality change requires the analysis of biological processes, technical possibilities, their interactions with producer decisions and the effect of resulting production changes on consumer and producer welfare. Biological or production response data provide a link between an environmental variable, such as water or air quality, and the performance parameters of an ecosystem. The response relationship may be quantified directly from biological experimentation, indirectly from observed producer output and behavioural data (secondary data) or from some combination of data sources.

Procedures based upon producer data (for example production or cost functions) are preferable from the viewpoint of economic analysis (Adams, 1983) and can avoid the need for explicit cause–effect functions. However, data and statistical difficulties have restricted their applicability. At present scientifically derived cause–effect functions are most commonly applied in economic assessments. Cause–effect models offer a means of measuring the economic costs of several important environmental quality changes. However, controversies over the appropriate way in which to model responses mean that widely varying estimates of economic damages can emerge. In addition, the model must be linked to data on the physical environment (for example water or air quality) in order to make accurate impact predictions. Such data needs to be locally or regionally disaggregated and is normally unavailable.

Choosing the economic model
The choice of the economic model brings its own set of problems. Three main categories of economic approach can be defined: traditional models, optimization models and econometric models (see Spash, 1997). The traditional approach takes given market prices and multiplies these by losses in output. Thus, the latter two approaches are to be preferred as they avoid this crude approximation of economic impacts in an oversimplified market structure. The main requirement for easy assessment of consumer and producer welfare is the existence of well established economic models. In their absence the analyst must construct a model and test its validity.

PFA and rural resource management
In the case of the environmental externalities from land use changes the main areas in which a PFA could operate would be in looking at impacts on water supply, agricultural and freshwater/coastal products, but also on health effects as these can be related to labour markets. The PFA is unsuitable for estimating the benefits from wildlife conservation, recreation and tourism unless there is an associated market good or service with which to link dose–

response functions. For example, if wildlife conservation increased or reduced production costs, or increased or reduced marketed output, then a link could be feasible with the impacts on existing product supply, cost and/or profit functions. Cultural and historical values which might be lost due to land use practices could only be assessed via physical impacts on materials (for example the rate at which chemical applications might cause erosion) which would relate only to maintenance costs rather than the socio-economic aspects of culture.

Ecosystems functions are commonly ignored by consumers and producers and therefore difficult to value in economic terms. The PFA is the only method which seems appropriate here because of its basis in scientific knowledge which can then be linked into economic processes, although the values it will be able to assess would still be limited. A more general problem is the lack of suitable scientific information on many rural land use activities. For example, assessing the water quality impacts of intensively farmed land would require disaggregated monitoring of the ambient surface and groundwater quality levels in the affected area. Water quality would need to be related to receptors such as human beings, animals or plants. Neither the environmental quality data nor these dose–response functions are available.

Hedonic Pricing

In this section reference is made to house prices as an example of how hedonic pricing (HP) could be applied to rural land use change, although similar models have been applied in labour markets where environmental risks are internalized in the wage rate. Aspects of the environment can be valued via their impact on the price of housing by being one of the characteristics which contribute to the definition of the commodity which a particular house and location represent. Thus, proximity to clean water and air, recreational opportunities, peace and quiet can all be expected to be factors increasing prices of housing in certain markets. Conversely, the existence of intensive land use may reduce the price of housing in the vicinity. The problems with implementing the HP approach include choosing the variables to include and the functional form.

Constructing the model
The analyst must decide which factors to include as explanatory variables in the HP equation and the demand curve. Excluding a variable which has a significant effect on house prices, and which is correlated with some or all of the other variables in the model, will influence the estimation of coefficients. This leads to biased estimates for these coefficients and for the implicit prices (see Atkinson and Crocker, 1992).

Several of the independent variables included in the HP equation may be closely correlated with each other. For example, if a house is sited in the vicinity of a rural business which causes habitat loss, affecting local wildlife, and air, soil and water quality to decline, affecting health and safety, the variables measuring these various externalities are liable to be correlated. This is the problem of multi-collinearity.

The HP equation is non-linear so as to allow derivation of a demand equation. However, there is no universally preferred functional form. Criteria which might be used to select the functional form include: restricting the number of parameters, selecting parameters justified by economic theory, choosing the form which economizes on computing time, finding a form which provides a good explanation of the observed data and gives correct predictions, for example house prices falling with increased pollution (see Garrod and Allinson, 1991).

Housing markets are often segmented on grounds such as ethnic composition, rental versus owner-occupied, and price bracket. This can bias coefficients in the price function because segmentation implies that demand parameters vary across sectors. The HP analyst must then estimate separate price equations for each segment of the market. In a study of Boston, Michaels and Smith (1990) asked estate agents to segment the housing market and so identified four distinct sub-markets. Separate HP equations were then estimated for each segment in order to value the disutility of living close to hazardous waste sites.

Estate agent surveys
Estate agents can be used more specifically than above to substitute for the estimation of variables in an HP equation. Estate agents' local knowledge is then used to control for market differences which would normally be derived from the set of independent variables in a regression equation. For example, estate agents could be asked to compare the prices of similar houses in areas affected by surface mineral extraction with those unaffected by such extraction. Such an approach has for example been employed by the consultancy firm London Economics to estimate the benefits from the New National Forest and Central Scotland Forest.

Forecasting environmental quality
HP assumes that current levels of environmental quality are the main influence on house prices, but they can also be influenced by expected changes in environmental quality. For example, the prospect of strict dust and noise regulations relating to quarries can keep prices higher in zones near such sites than in the absence of such expectations. The implicit price would fail to measure the valuation of current noise and air quality levels alone. Similarly,

the expectation that a quarry will close in the near future, and the site will be restored, can raise prices where they had been depressed by the quarrying activities.

HP and rural land use changes

The HP approach is related to regional or site-specific characteristics but can be used to gain aggregate estimates of demand on the basis of site data. Where recreation and tourism are recognized components of the housing market HP could be used to value changes in their quality, subject to the qualifications above. Aesthetics, or aspects thereof, have been subject to benefit estimation using HP, although CVM, which is discussed below, is seen to have several advantages. The extent to which the aesthetic concept is seen to be captured will depend upon how it is defined, for example beauty versus water quality. Providing a disaggregation of aesthetic values seems unlikely due to the difficulty of finding and agreeing upon any measure of aesthetic variation. On a more practical level, Graves (1991) points out that data is severely limited, not only due to a lack of measurement but also because many important aesthetic features are located away from well developed markets. Cultural and historical values could also, in theory, be derived from HP where the characteristics associated with these values are identifiable, for example a particular geographical location or building. However, the extent to which such values are capitalized into land or house prices is questionable; for example, house location can be unrelated to the enjoyment of cultural and historical sites. In general, HP would be useless due to the inability to provide data measuring quantity or quality variations of these concepts by location. Health and safety, noise and air pollution may be assessed via HP. For example, Hughes and Sirmans (1992) have used a standard HP model to show a substantial negative effect of traffic externalities on single-family house prices. Similarly, house prices have been shown to be influenced by the positive externalities from urban forests which include benefits derived from pleasant landscape, clean air, peace and quiet and screening, as well as recreation (Tyrvainen, 1997). However, HP studies do not generally disaggregate these estimates but rather tend to assess the total (positive or negative) externality.

The theoretical assumptions underlying HP mean it will give inaccurate estimates of environmental externalities if buyers lack perfect information about relevant environmental quality variables, if buyers are unable to attain their utility maximizing position, or if the housing market is in disequilibrium. Furthermore, HP requires weak complementarity which means only those environmental externalities of rural land uses that have an impact on the property market will be measured. Finding suitable variables to measure environmental quality attributes can be problematic.

Stated Preference Methods

Stated preference methods directly survey individuals to obtain their preferences rather than analysing their actual behaviour as revealed in the market place. This has led to some criticism from those economists who prefer to use secondary data collected by government agencies but which is related to actual behaviour. Research collecting primary data on intended behaviour is common in other social sciences and the conditions for convergence with actual behaviour have been studied extensively (for a principal source see Fishbein and Ajzen, 1975). In terms of the CVM there have also been tests comparing actual with stated willingness to pay. The apparent advantage attributed to methods such as TCM and HP is that they relate to actual behaviour, but as has been explained above the links being drawn between observational data and the underlying motives are often weak or purely speculative. This suggests the need for economists to pay far more attention to motives for behaviour, whether intended or actual.

CVM is the principal stated preference method although both conjoint analysis and choice experiments have received some recent attention and so are discussed near the end of this section. In contrast to the other three methods reviewed above, CVM has received considerable and increasing attention in the literature with academic journal articles on the subject in excess of 1000 studies world-wide. The main advantage attracting this attention is the ability of CVM to estimate what are termed option, 'existence' and bequest values in addition to direct use values. The combination of these indirect or passive use values can be large compared to the direct use values associated with non-market goods to which the other methods are solely restricted.

Contingent valuation method
There are several stages to conducting a CVM study: survey design, pretesting, carrying out the main survey, estimating willingness to pay (WTP) and/or willingness to accept (WTA), bid curve analysis, data aggregation, and final assessment. In particular, application of the technique requires careful survey design, awareness of potential biases and a decision on whether to use WTP or WTA.

Survey design and conduct The design of a CVM study includes the amount, type and way information is presented to individuals, the order in which it is presented and the question format. There is a wide body of evidence to suggest that survey design can affect responses. Survey design requires framing a realistic decision concerning the environment where the monetary question to be asked is accepted as a possible state of the world in which individual respondents might find themselves. Important decisions for the analyst include a reason for the payment and how, including how often, funds will be raised (the bid vehicle). For example Rowe *et al.* (1980) found that WTP to preserve landscape quality was higher when an income tax increase was suggested than when entry fees were used. The technique for bid elicitation may be an open-ended question, a dichotomous choice, or a bidding game. Also, at this stage information on physical changes will be summarized and the method of their description chosen (for example text, graphics, maps).

Due to the sensitivity of responses to the information supplied, the pre-testing of the survey has become of increasing importance. This can be conducted via a small sample test run of the survey or a focus group. The pre-test will enable the identification of problems with regard to the framing of the decision problem as well as divergence between encoding and decoding of information.

The conduct of the main survey can use several variations. The in-house interview is now most favoured, although the expense of this approach often means surveys are completed in the street, by telephone interviewing or mail. The sample is often weighted in terms of the local or regional population which is seen as politically more important to the decision and likely to have strong direct economic connections to the outcome.

Typically, median bids are less than mean bids so both are reported. At this stage the treatment of 'protest bids' becomes problematic and these are often omitted from the mean calculation. Protest bids are zero bids given for reasons other than a zero value being placed on the resource in question. For example, a respondent may refuse any amount of compensation for loss of an environmental asset which they regard as unique or a species which they feel should be protected at all costs. Respondents may refuse to state a WTP/WTA amount because they reject the survey as an institutional approach to the problem, or because they have an ethical objection to the trade-off being requested, for example a lexicographic preference.

Analysis of the bid curve is used to test construct validity, that is that the socio-economic variables have the expected signs, and the regression is statistically significant. Other relationships can also be investigated at this stage. In general bid curve analysis has tended to be of academic, as opposed to policy, interest despite the relevance for judging whether the exercise has produced the expected results in accordance with economic theory.

The method of aggregating data, both across time and space, requires deciding on the relevant population, the method of aggregating from the sample bid, and the time period or discounting procedure for aggregation. These are major concerns in CBA and have serious impacts on any resulting monetary values. The sensitivity of the results to variations in such factors should be tested and presented as a central aspect of the findings, however this is rarely the case. Sensitivity analysis in CBA is generally ignored or extremely limited.

Final reflection upon the CVM study can include convergent validity and success of repeatability where there exist other similar studies. The overall success of the exercise will also become apparent as the results are being analysed, for example a high number of protest bids. There are several specific problems which are recognized as possible causes of bias, some of which have been mentioned: strategic bias, design bias (choice of bid vehicle, prompting a bid). More problematic are the impact of information, as this is by necessity restricted but can have serious influence upon the resulting bids, and the problem of embedding as raised by Kahneman and Knetsch (1992). These two issues are discussed next.

Information provision   In a hypothetical market, respondents combine information provided to them regarding the good to be valued, and how the market will work, with information they already hold on that good. Their responses may be influenced by either hypothetical market or commodity-specific information given to them in the survey. This phenomenon implies that WTP/WTA values are endogenous to the valuation process. Samples *et al.* (1986) found that bids to preserve different animal species varied significantly according to the information provided by researchers. Ajzen *et al.* (1996) concluded from experimental research that the nature of the information provided in CVM surveys can profoundly affect WTP estimates, and that subtle contextual cues can seriously bias these estimates under conditions where the good is of low personal relevance. Whitehead and Blomquist (1991) show both theoretically and empirically how information on environmental substitutes changes the value of related goods. In their research, telling respondents about alternative wetland sites significantly altered WTP to protect the Clear Creek wetland in Kentucky. However, Randall (1986) has argued that CVM answers should vary under different information sets, otherwise the technique would be insensitive to significant changes in commodity framing. The divergence of opinion here relates to information provided which economists regard as important to the decision and should therefore have an impact but fails to do so, and information which would be regarded as peripheral or irrelevant by economists but which does have an impact on stated behaviour.

Indeed, the effects of information may be inappropriately labelled as bias, depending on the way in which WTP/WTA is changed. Information which improves the knowledge of an individual concerning the characteristics of a good can be regarded as informing a consumption decision. Information which alters the preferences is more problematic in the neo-classical framework and could be regarded as creating a bias. For example, Baron and

Maxwell (1996) show that individuals' WTP can be biased by information on the cost of provision of public goods and suggest eliminating information from which costs could be inferred, so that respondents can focus more easily on benefits alone. While such redesign may avoid some types of bias, a more general issue that remains, is how far individual preferences can be regarded as exogenous to the valuation process and especially when goods are unfamiliar and/or never traded in a market.

Part–whole bias and embedding   This problem arises when the component parts of an individual's valuation are evaluated separately and when summed are found to exceed the valuation placed upon the whole. Evidence that such behaviour exists was provided by Seip and Strand (1990). CVM studies have found part–whole bias, also termed embedding, and this has been attributed by some to valuation of the moral satisfaction from contributing to a worthy cause ('warm glow') rather than the good itself (Kahneman and Knetsch, 1992). The counter reaction has been that CVM surveys finding embedding are flawed in some way which creates the part–whole bias, and that this can be corrected by careful survey design (Carson and Mitchell, 1993, 1995; Hanemann, 1994). However Bateman *et al.* (1997) have provided experimental evidence for the existence of part–whole bias for private goods outside of the CVM context. They therefore suggest the problem lies with economic preference theory rather than the CVM approach.

Choice of welfare measure   WTP and WTA are the two welfare measures available for a CVM survey. Willig (1976) showed that the two measures would be close if the ratio of consumer's surplus to income (expenditure) was sufficiently small, and if the income elasticity of demand for the good in question was sufficiently low. Where these conditions failed to hold, precise limits on the difference between the two measures could be calculated. Whilst Bockstael and McConnell (1980) criticized the applicability of Willig's findings to environmental benefits, Randall and Stoll (1980) extended Willig's theorem which was derived for price changes to the quantity changes more commonly encountered in environmental valuation. Despite this, stated WTP has still been found to be significantly lower than stated WTA (for example Rowe *et al.*, 1980; Hammack and Brown, 1974), and lower than the Willig approximation would suggest. In addition, experimental work by Knetsch and Sinden (1984) and Gregory (1986) has also found that WTA exceeds WTP.

On practical grounds, the status quo reference position is preferable in terms of the property rights structure. If an alternative is imposed by the blanket imposition of WTP formats in all CVM surveys, the result can be to create an unrealistic trade-off, hypothetical market bias and protest bids.

Thus, rather than follow a generic prescription always to use WTP formats as a conservative estimate of values (for example guidelines suggested by NOAA, 1994), the property rights prevalent in a given situation should be used as guidance. This reinforces the theoretical argument for using WTA to measure a loss and WTP for a gain (Knetsch, 1994).

Conjoint analysis

Conjoint analysis (CA) is closely related to CVM with respondents to a survey being required to trade-off money for an environmental commodity whose attributes are hypothesized to alter marginally. CA has been used extensively in the marketing literature to infer implicit weights for each attribute of a multi-attribute commodity (Louviere, 1996). Some interest has been shown in using the technique for the assessment of non-market environmental goods (Roe *et al.*, 1996; MLURI, 1996; Adamowicz *et al.*, 1994; Mackenzie, 1992).

Under CA the respondent is asked to rank commodities/options which have varying characteristics/attributes. This involves choosing both relative rankings of commodities and ratings for each commodity. Responses can be obtained by either multiple ranking or binary choice. Binary choice CA is nearly identical to dichotomous choice CVM, and they share the same problems: choice of bid price, selection of functional form (linear versus non-linear), and utility consistent specification. The advantage of CA is the potential to vary commodity characteristics and, by including price as an attribute, derive implicit prices for each. The potential to disaggregate costs and benefits in this way is one of the principal attractions of CA.

However, CA also has disadvantages. It assumes cardinal preferences which is in contrast to modern welfare economics. Although ordinal preferences should be obtainable from CA, Roe *et al.* (1996) found that mixed statistical results across ratings differences, rankings and binary choice models prevented transition to ordinal preferences. CA also fails to request an explicit entry into the market trade-off scenario, unlike CVM which requests acceptance of a bid. This problem might be rectified for use values by the inclusion of a contingent-behaviour question. However, Roe *et al.* (1996) conclude that, because of this, CA is of particularly limited application for the assessment of non-use values.

Choice experiments

Choice experiments (CEs) arose from CA. Instead of rating or ranking alternatives as in CA, in CEs individuals are asked to choose from several bundles of goods or services. Hence CEs are consistent with random utility theory. According to Adamowicz *et al.* (1998), CEs have considerable merit over CVM in measuring passive use values, being able to examine values for attributes and their levels, as well as a precise scenario. Obtaining values for characteristics of scenarios rather than one specific scenario is also useful when designing substitution possibilities. However, as with CVM, CE studies require much effort in the design stage (several methodological issues remaining unresolved) and administration, especially the development of the relevant scenarios and their attributes, and the statistical design. Statistical analysis of the results from CA and CE can often appear as a black box from which results appear.

CVM and rural resource management

CVM can in theory, although to varying degrees, address most of the non-market value categories related to rural land use changes, with the exception of biodiversity and ecosystems functions. Biodiversity itself has rarely been valued in CVM, instead individual species (rather than their diversity) have been a focus of research. Aesthetics have been subject to benefit estimation by HP and CVM, with Graves (1991, p. 225) regarding CVM as having several advantages, that is distinguishing the aesthetic dimension of a policy change; generating data rather than relying on remote proxies; imposing fewer behavioural assumptions; and yielding plausible results, particularly in applications to visibility. However, defining aesthetic qualities and conveying them to individuals so they become familiar with the concepts in a commodity framework can be difficult or impossible. Also, the description of an aesthetic quality may itself introduce distortions.

One practical issue in terms of applying CVM concerns the disaggregation of benefit categories. Whilst the CVM survey can, in theory and as mentioned, be applied to a range of value categories, any one survey will be limited in scope and is normally restricted to an aggregate assessment of total benefits, as with the other methods. The most common disaggregation is by direct use and passive use (that is two categories) and in some cases by use, option, existence and bequest values (that is four categories). This kind of disaggregation could be carried out for classes of an externality by one of three main methods. First, obtain a total bid and then ask respondents to split the total, for example state the percentage attributable to each category. Second, ask for an evaluation of each externality either by the same individual or, if a large enough sample is available, by different individuals (that is sub-samples for each externality). Both these approaches may be difficult for individuals to comprehend. Third, develop alternative scenarios so that aspects of the externality are removed (for example noise/no noise) for different sub-samples. The problem here is to develop realistic scenarios responsible for creating the change in the externality.

The issue of disaggregating benefits by externality and the preceding discussion highlights the continuing experimental nature of the CVM approach.

In areas where an environmental change can easily be described and under-stood in terms of a choice based upon individual preferences, and the market trade-off implied is accepted as appropriate to the decision then CVM seems applicable. However, where aesthetics, cultural and historical values and ecosystems functions and biodiversity are concerned these conditions often seem unlikely to hold. Where only certain aspects of such environmental concepts are easily explained and/or captured in commodity terms the result-ing monetary valuation will be a poor reflection of the environmental values they encapsulate.

CONCLUSIONS

Table 5.1 provides a summary of the methods discussed so that the economic valuation techniques suitable for use in the context of rural land use changes can be easily identified. There is some danger in presenting such a simplified table, and the qualifications and limitations of methods, as summarized in this chapter, must be kept in mind. In addition, there are general qualifica-tions to the use of CBA. For example, income distribution is taken as given so that prices and monetary estimates will reflect relative purchasing power in society. Adjustments could be made to the results to test for the impact of changing income distribution, but, as with other sensitivity analysis, this is rarely done in practice.

Table 5.1   Current suitability of CBA methods for assessing the economic externalities of rural land use changes

Non-market value category	Method			
	TCM	PFA	HP	CVM
Aesthetics	?	✗	?	?
Cultural and historical values	?	✗	✗	?
Health and safety	✗	✓	?	✓
Ecosystems functions and biodiversity	✗	?	✗	?
Peace and quiet	?	✗	✓	✓
Recreation and tourism	✓	✗	?	✓
Water and air quality	?	✓	✓	✓

Key:
✗   Of little or no use
?   Sometimes useful
✓   Potential for application strongest

HP can assess certain aspects of externalities after they have occurred and have been capitalized. The PFA is generally inapplicable due to a lack of scientific data. TCM is primarily concerned with recreation and tourism values at a site prior to any development. As can be seen CVM provides the most potential for comprehensive coverage of externalities and could be conducted before or after a change in land use. In terms of including option, existence and bequest values only CVM can attempt to do so. CVM also provides considerable flexibility in the types of non-market value which can be addressed in the survey. However, there are several aspects of implementing CVM which restrict the extent to which it will be able to assess environmental values. In practical terms, the cost of and time needed for conducting a CVM survey can be relatively high and have increased due to the extent to which various design features are now regarded as required practice. However, CVM remains an experimental technique which has been accelerated into public policy use by legal action in the USA over natural resource damages. Perhaps the greatest contribution the technique is now making is in terms of forcing economists to reconsider the content and meaning of both observed and intended human behaviour with regard to a plurality of environmental values.

REFERENCES

Adamowicz, W., J. Louviere and M. Williams (1994), 'Combining revealed and stated preference methods for valuing environmental amenities', *Journal of Environmental Economics and Management,* **26**, 271–92.

Adamowicz, W., P. Boxall, M. Williams and J. Louviere (1998), 'Stated preference approaches for measuring passive use values: choice experiments and contingent valuation', *American Journal of Agricultural Economics,* **80**, 64–75.

Adams, R.M. (1983), 'Issues in assessing the economic benefits of ambient ozone control: Some examples from agriculture', *Environment International,* **9**, 539–48.

Ajzen, I., T.C. Brown and L.H. Rosenthal (1996), 'Information bias in contingent valuation: effects of personal relevance, quality of information and motivational orientation', *Journal of Environmental Economics and Management,* **30**(1), 43–57.

Atkinson, S. and T. Crocker (1992), 'Econometric health production functions: Relative bias from omitted variables and measurement error', *Journal of Environmental Economics and Management,* **22**(1), 12–24.

Baron, J. and N.P. Maxwell (1996), 'Cost of public-goods affects willingness-to-pay for them', *Journal of Behavioural Decision Making,* **9**(3), 173–83.

Bateman, I., A. Munro, B. Rhodes, C. Starmer and R. Sugden (1997), 'Does part–whole bias exist? An experimental investigation', *Economic Journal,* **107**(441), 322–32.

Beaufoy, G. (1994), 'Impact of the CAP Reform on land use and rural amenities', in A. Dubgaard, I. Bateman and M. Merlo (eds), *Economic Valuation of Benefits from Countryside Stewardship,* Kiel: Wissenschaftsverlag Vauk, pp. 27–46.

Bockstael, N.E. and K. McConnell (1980), 'Calculating equivalent and compensating variation for natural resource facilities', *Land Economics*, **56**, 56–62.

Bonnieux, F. and P. Le Goffe (1997), 'Valuing the benefits of landscape restoration: a case study of the Contentin in Lower-Normandy, France', *Journal of Environmental Management*, **50**, 321–33.

Bromley, D. and I. Hodge (1990), 'Private property and presumptive policy entitlements: reconsidering the premises of rural policy', *European Review of Agricultural Economics*, **17**(2), 197–214.

Cameron, T.A. (1992), 'Combining contingent valuation and travel cost data for the valuation of nonmarket goods', *Land Economics*, **68**(3), 302–17.

Carson, R.T. and R.C. Mitchell (1993), 'The issue of scoping in contingent valuation studies', *Journal of Agricultural Economics*, December, 1265–7.

Carson, R.T. and R.C. Mitchell (1995), 'Sequencing and nesting in contingent valuation surveys', *Journal of Environmental Economics and Management*, **28**, 155–73.

Clark, C.W. (1976), *Mathematical Bioeconomics*, New York: Wiley.

Fishbein, M. and I. Ajzen (1975), *Belief, Attitude, Intention and Behavior: An Introduction to Theory and Research*, Reading, Massachusetts: Addison-Wesley.

Freeman, A.M. (1986), 'The ethical basis of the economic view of the environment', in D. van der Veer and C. Pierce (eds), *People, Penguin and Plastic Trees: Basic Issues in Environmental Ethics*, Belmont, CA: Wadsworth Publishing Co., pp. 218–27.

Freeman, A.M. (1993), *The Measurement of Environmental and Resource Values: Theory and Methods*, Washington, DC: Resources for the Future.

Garrod, G. and P. Allinson (1991), *The Choice of Functional Form for Hedonic House Price Functions*, Discussion paper 23, Countryside Change Initiative, University of Newcastle-upon-Tyne.

Graves, P.E. (1991), 'Aesthetics', in J.B. Braden and C.D. Kolstad (eds), *Measuring the Demand for Environmental Quality*, Amsterdam: North-Holland, pp. 213–26.

Gregory, R. (1986), 'Interpreting measures of economic loss', *Journal of Environmental Economics and Management*, **13**, 325–37.

Hammack, J. and G. Brown (1974), *Waterfowl and Wetlands: Towards Bioeconomic Analysis*, Baltimore: Johns Hopkins Press.

Hanemann, W.M. (1994), 'Valuing the environment through contingent valuation', *Journal of Economic Perspectives*, **8**(4), 19–43.

Hanley, N. and C.L. Spash (1993), *Cost–Benefit Analysis and the Environment*, Aldershot: Edward Elgar.

Hartwick, J.M. and N.D. Olewiler (1986), *The Economics of Natural Resource Use*, New York: Harper and Row.

Hughes, W.T. and C.F. Sirmans (1992), 'Traffic externalities and single-family house prices', *Journal of Regional Science*, **32**(4), 487–500.

Kahn, J. (1991), 'Atrazine pollution and Chesapeake fisheries', in N. Hanley (ed.), *Farming and the Countryside: An Economic Analysis of External Costs and Benefits*, Oxford: CAB International, pp. 137–58.

Kahneman, D. and J. Knetsch (1992), 'The purchase of moral satisfaction', *Journal of Environmental Economics and Management*, **22**(1), 57–70.

Kling, C.L. (1997), 'The gains from combining travel cost and contingent valuation data to value non-market goods', *Land Economics*, **73**(3), 428–39.

Knetsch, J. (1994), 'Environmental valuation: some problems of wrong questions and misleading answers', *Environmental Values*, **3**, 351–68.

Knetsch, J. and J. Sinden (1984), 'Willingness to pay and compensation demanded:

Experimental evidence of an unexpected disparity', *Quarterly Journal of Economics*, **94**(3), 507–21.

Loomis, J.B. (1995), 'Models for determining environmental quality effects on recreational demand and regional economics', *Ecological Economics*, **12**(1), 55–65.

Louviere, J. (1996), 'Relating stated preference measures and models to choices in real markets: calibration of CV responses', in D.J. Bjornstad and J.R. Kahn (eds), *The Contingent Valuation of Environmental Resources: Methodological Issues and Research Needs*, Cheltenham: Edward Elgar, pp. 167–88.

Mackenzie, J. (1992), 'Evaluating recreation trip attributes and travel time via conjoint-analysis', *Journal of Leisure Research*, **24**(2), 171–84.

Mendelsohn, R., J. Hof, G. Peterson and R. Johnson (1992), 'Measuring recreation values with multiple destination trips', *American Journal of Agricultural Economics*, **74**(4), 926–33.

Michaels, R. and V. Smith (1990), 'Market segmentation and valuing amenities with hedonic models: the case of hazardous waste sites', *Journal of Urban Economics*, **28**, 232–42.

MLURI (1996), *Valuation of the Conservation Benefits of Environmentally Sensitive Areas*, Aberdeen: Macaulay Land Use Research Institute.

NOAA (1994), 'Natural resource damage assessment: proposed rules', *Federal Register*, **59**(5), 1062–191.

Pruckner, G. (1995), 'Agricultural landscape cultivation in Austria: an application of the CVM', *European Review of Agricultural Economics*, **22**(2), 173–90.

Randall, A. (1986), 'The possibility of satisfactory benefit estimation with contingent markets', in R. Cummings, D. Brookshire and W. Schulze (eds), *Valuing Public Goods: An Assessment of the Contingent Valuation Method*, Totowa, NJ: Rowan and Allanheld, pp. 114–22.

Randall, A. (1994), 'A difficulty with the Travel Cost Method', *Land Economics*, **70**(1), 88–96.

Randall, A. and J. Stoll (1980), 'Consumers surplus in commodity space', *American Economic Review*, **70**(3), 449–55.

Roe, B., K.J. Boyle and M.F. Teisl (1996), 'Using conjoint analysis to derive estimates of compensating variation', *Journal of Environmental Economics and Management*, **31**(2), 145–59.

Rowe, R., R. d'Arge and D. Brookshire (1980), 'An experiment on the economic value of visibility', *Journal of Environmental Economics and Management*, **7**, 1–19.

Samples, K., J. Dixon and M. Gowen (1986), 'Information disclosure and endangered species valuation', *Land Economics,* **62**(3), 306–12.

Seip, K. and J. Strand (1990), *Willingness to Pay for Environmental Goods in Norway: a Contingent Valuation Study with Real Payment*, Memorandum 12, Dept. of Economics, University of Oslo.

Silvander, U. and L. Drake (1991), 'Nitrate pollution and fisheries protection in Sweden', in N. Hanley (ed.), *Farming and the Countryside: An economic analysis of external costs and benefits*, Oxford: CAB International, pp. 159–76.

Spash, C.L. (1997), 'Assessing the economic benefits to agriculture from air pollution control', *Journal of Economic Surveys*, **11**(1), 47–70.

Spash, C.L. (1998a), *Environmental Values and Wetland Ecosystems: CVM, Ethics and Attitudes,* Cambridge: Cambridge Research for the Environment, Department of Land Economy, University of Cambridge.

Spash, C.L. (1998b), 'Investigating individual motives for environmental action:

Lexicographic preferences, beliefs and attitudes', in J. Lemons, L. Westra and R. Goodland (eds), *Ecological Sustainability and Integrity: Concepts and Approaches* 13, Dordrecht: Kluwer Academic Publishers, pp. 46–62.

Spash, C.L. (2000), 'Multiple value expression in contingent valuation: economics and ethics', *Environmental Science & Technology*, **34**(8), 1433–8.

Spash, C.L. and N. Hanley (1995), 'Preferences, information and biodiversity preservation', *Ecological Economics*, **12**, 191–208.

Stevens, T.H., J. Echeverria, R.J. Glass, T. Hager and T.A. More (1991), 'Measuring the existence value of wildlife: what do CVM estimates really show?', *Land Economics*, **67**(4), 390–400.

Twigger-Ross, C.L. and D.L. Uzzell (1996), 'Place and Identity Processes', *Journal of Environmental Psychology*, **16**(3), 205–20.

Tyrvainen, L. (1997), 'The amenity value of the urban forest: An application of the hedonic pricing method', *Landscape and Urban Planning*, **37**(3–4), 211–22.

Whitehead, J. and G. Blomquist (1991), 'Measuring contingent values for wetlands: Effects of information about related environmental goods', *Water Resources Research*, **27**, 2523–31.

Willig, R. (1976), 'Consumers surplus without apology', *American Economic Review*, **66**, 589–97.

PART II

Cases on the Interaction between Agriculture and Nature

6. Water availability in the Mediterranean region

Consuelo Varela-Ortega, José Sumpsi and María Blanco

INTRODUCTION

In this chapter we will investigate the interactions between agriculture and nature, focusing on the major role that water resources play for preserving Mediterranean ecosystems and ensuring socio-economic stability. The Mediterranean region is characterized by an uneven distribution of rainfall both in time and space. Agricultural production shows marked regional differences, and also interacts with the availability of water for natural habitats. Degradation of the natural resource base is calling for a sustainable use of water resources. Our analysis focuses on the degradation of wetlands in Spain and seeks to integrate environmental and economic objectives for a cost-effective adoption of policy measures. Agri-environmental programmes (AEP) have been introduced in this region to reduce water abstraction and to recover wetland ecosystems. These measures have improved viability of the rural countryside, but the cost-effectiveness of these programmes requires a careful analysis. Other policy options, such as cross-compliance, also need to be considered.

The first section presents a framework for the analysis of water resources in the Mediterranean region. In addition, trends on water demand are presented. The second section focuses on the impacts of irrigation on wetland ecosystems. This is followed by the identification of CAP measures (including Agenda 2000) that are suitable to achieve a sustainable management of water resources and preserve a valuable wetland in Spain. The chapter is completed with some concluding remarks on policy choice for environmental and socio-economic integration.

General Overview

Global water resources are becoming increasingly scarce, and access to water resources is a major problem in many countries. Water consumption rate has more than doubled the population growth during the last decades and growing demands of water have resulted in a number of regions with water scarcity problems (UNO, 1997). Projections for the year 2025 show that around two thirds of the world population will be living under water stress. Renewable water resources are falling in a growing number of countries around the southern Mediterranean region. In this region, they get below the critical level of 1000 m³ per person, which represents a severe constraint for economic development (FAO, 1995; Seckler *et al.*, 2000).

Irrigation is a key factor for food production and has become the world's largest user of water. Irrigation agriculture consumes 70 per cent of all fresh water resources in the world, but this proportion can mount up to 90 per cent in dry regions (Seckler *et al.*, 1998). Irrigation strategies have long considered water as an inexhaustible resource and therefore consisted in the progressive development of new water captions by constructing new dams and reservoirs. Water was subsidized, and the natural resource base became increasingly exhausted. At present, further investments in new water supplies are questioned because of mounting costs, decreasing farm income and environmental damage (Rosegrant, 1997).

Increasingly, society demands a sustainable use of water, and the Second World Water Forum (The Hague, March 2000) has expressed the need to consider ecological values and socio-economic benefits of integrated water management to conserve wetland ecosystems. The International Water Management Institute (IWMI) evaluated the Annual Water Resources (AWR) at country level, which is defined as the average annual amount of water provided in a sustainable manner. Depletion of aquifers is not counted as part of the AWR because it is considered a non-sustainable activity (Seckler *et al.*, 1998).

Such a vision to integrate environmental objectives with the management of water resources in the Mediterranean region demands for appropriate policies. The region has a fragile environment and a high seasonal variation of rainfall, with droughts and an increasing dependence upon irrigation agriculture. These factors have resulted in severe water depletion problems, salinity from marine intrusion and water contamination. In addition, frequent torrential rains produce soil erosion, uncontrolled runoff and irregular water flows. However, water resources are not distributed evenly across the 25 countries bordering the Mediterranean Sea. Water-abundant countries coexist with intensely water-scarce countries and regions. The northern water-abundant Mediterranean region is characterized by low population growth, stable water demand and moderate pressure on water resources. Environmental protection has been developed in EU Mediterranean countries as a response to augmenting degradation of water resources. In contrast, the southern Mediterranean region has high demographic pressure, increasing demand for water and a strong strain on water resources. Structural shortages of water are foreseen in this area where resources are already saturated and expected to aggravate, calling for more sustainable policies (Margat and Vallée, 1999).

Water Conservation in the Mediterranean Region

The Blue Plan for the Mediterranean has defined specific projections for water use in the region, taking into account its special characteristics (Margat and Vallée, 1999). The projections build on scenarios proposed by the IWMI (Seckler *et al.*, 2000), and enable the identification of instruments for water conservation. One scenario represents a conventional trend and the other represents a sustainable development trend. The conventional trend scenario stabilizes pressures on water resources in the northern Mediterranean countries by a selective localized control of water depletion and pollution. However, the overall development process is considered not to be sustainable. Conversely, the sustainable development scenario integrates social, economic and environmental aspects, stabilizes pressure on the natural environment and offers a long-lasting balance of supply and demand for water renewable resources. The main lines of the two scenarios are summarized in Figure 6.1.

Table 6.1 shows current water demand in the EU countries bordering the Mediterranean Sea, and Table 6.2 shows projected demands for the two scenarios considered. Except in France, irrigation agriculture is the largest consumer of water in all countries. Its share is highest in Spain and Greece. These countries grow water-demanding crops such as fruits and vegetables. Spain has 3.5 million ha of irrigated land, the largest area of all EU Member States, and is also the major user of irrigation water (24 km^3 per year) to supply water intensive crops in the Mediterranean littoral.

Water demand needs to be reduced by 20 per cent if a sustainable development trend is to be attained in the EU countries bordering the Mediterranean Sea. The agricultural sector needs to reduce water demand by 25 per cent, and countries like Spain and Greece even need a 30 per cent reduction to achieve sustainable use of water resources. The projected irrigation area will not need to be substantially reduced for attaining a sustainable use of the resource (Figure 6.2). In fact, in Spain, irrigation will concentrate further in water intensive market-oriented crops, such as vegetables and fruit. Increasing efficiency of irrigation networks and of on-farm water use will achieve the projected reduction in water demand. Countries like France and Italy that grow crops with lower water demands, such as cereals and oilseeds, will face larger reductions in irrigation area.

The scenarios determine policies that will best attain the objectives. The sustainable development scenario includes instruments to attain socio-economic goals, a sustainable management of water resources and the protection

Conventional trend
- Continuation of current trends (economic, demographic and technological).
- Growing pressure on water resources and water ecosystems.
- Maintenance of current policies and low participation of local entities and stakeholders.
- Increase in export crops and decrease in traditional Mediterranean production systems.
- Increase in total water demands (almost 40 per cent). Stabilization of the increase in irrigation area and the increase in irrigation efficiency.
- Water conservation and water quality policies only in the northern Mediterranean countries.

Sustainable development
- Water management includes social and environmental elements to ensure a sustainable development of water resources.
- Increasing participation of local agencies and stakeholders in water management and development of integrated basin management of water resources.
- Increasing profitability of low water-intensive crops.
- Development of water conservation policies that will include cost-share instruments among competing users (agriculture, environment) and income compensation mechanisms for agricultural production.
- Increasing use of recycled and desalinated water and eco-technologies.
- Decrease in total water demands (–12 per cent in the region), reduction in irrigation area in the north Mediterranean and large increase in irrigation efficiency.
- Priority to water conservation and water quality policies.

Source: Margat and Vallée (1999) and own elaboration

Figure 6.1   Scenarios for the water sector in the Mediterranean until 2025

of ecosystems and water quality. The improvements in water management will prevent the development of new water catchments. Policies will be designed to reduce water demand in irrigation agriculture (especially in the over-exploited aquifers). They will promote investments in augmenting water conveyance efficiency and a better adjustment of water volumes in the crops.

In Table 6.3 we have summarized impacts of the scenarios on nature, as well as on the private and public sectors. No doubt a sustainable development

Table 6.1   Water demand in the Mediterranean countries of the EU (1995)

Country	Water demand (km^3/year)				Agriculture (% of total)	Per capita (m^3/year)
	Total	Agriculture	Urban	Industry[c]		
Portugal[a]	10.85	6.41	0.65	3.79	59	1,105
Spain[b]	35.32	24.09	4.67	6.56	70	908
France	40.67	4.97	5.93	29.77	12	720
Italy	44.60	20.30	7.90	16.40	45	775
Greece	7.03	5.66	1.15	0.22	80	700

Notes:
a.   Caldas (1999).
b.   includes desalinated and recycled water.
c.   includes hydroelectric (cooling)

Source: Own calculations based on Margat and Vallée (1999).

Table 6.2   Projected water demand for 2025 by scenario

		Water demand (km^3 per year)				
		Total		Agriculture		
Country	Scenario	Volume	Change (%)[a]	Volume	Change (%)[a]	Average (m^3 /ha/year)
Portugal	T	11.2	+3	5.3	−17	4 000
	S	7.1	−34	4.0	−37	3 600
Spain	T	40.7	+15	25.7	+7	4 000
	S	26.9	−24	17.2	−29	3 500
France	T	50.0	+23	5.8	+17	2 300
	S	32.3	−20	4.0	−19	2 000
Italy	T	44.4	0	31.7	+56	3,800
	S	27.0	−29	17.2	−15	3 500
Greece	T	11.2	+59	9.0	+58	2 300
	S	5.2	−26	4.0	−30	2 000

Notes:
T: trend scenario
S: Sustainable development scenario
a. Relative change from baseline scenario (1995) (%)

Source: Margat and Vallée (1999) and own calculations

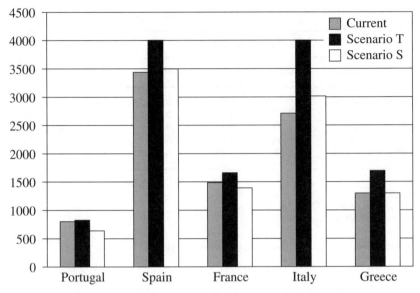

Scenario T: Conventional trend   Scenario S: sustainable development

Source: Own calculations based on OECD (1998) for current scenario and Margat and Vallée (1999) for the year 2025

Figure 6.2   Irrigation area (1995) and projected water demand for 2025 by type of scenario (× 1000 ha)

policy will be beneficial for the environment but will require large public expenditures. The protection of natural resources for future generations will require substantial financial resources and farmers will seek for compensation of any income losses they might face with the application of the Polluter Pays Principle (PPP). The farmers' property rights to use their entitled water allotments will be affected. Public authorities will play a major role in the attempt to manage water resources at basin level, because participatory policy decisions need the involvement of a large number of stakeholders.

EFFECTS OF IRRIGATION ON WETLAND ECOSYSTEMS

We will build on Table 6.3, and focus on a particular case study on water conservation policies for recovering a wetland ecosystem in Spain. We will first present an analytical overview of the EU policy context that presides over the interactions of agricultural production, the use of water resources

Table 6.3   Policy impacts by type of scenario for 2025

Policy impact	Scenario	
	Conventional trend	Sustainable development
Nature	• Preservation of ecosystems only in selected sites. • Limited progress in the protection of wetlands. • Preservation of resources already in use.	• Preservation of ecosystems. • Preservation of natural wetlands. • Pollution control of surface and groundwaters. • Protection of aquatic flora and fauna.
Private sector	• Moderate application of the PPP. • Limited participation of stakeholders in decision making. • Limited environmental constraints.	• Wide adoption of the PPP. • High participation of stakeholders in decision making. • Large private–public partnership in integrated basin management of irrigation systems. • Compliance to tight environmental constraints. • Income-loss compensated.
Public sector	• Water supply approach is dominant. • Infrastructure and water diversion costs increase. • Expenditure increases but moderately. • Low social equity.	• Water demand management approach is dominant. • Public sector will regulate and control water management. • High increase in expenditure. • Increase in social equity.

Source: Own elaboration, after Margat and Vallée (1999)

and their effects on the environment in the particular case of groundwater courses. Second, we will focus on a case study for recovering a valuable wetland ecosystem in Spain. Here, agricultural policies have encouraged intensification of water demand for irrigation purposes, and thus have been responsible for the aquifer's depletion and the subsequent wetland degradation. Also, regional agri-environmental programmes have been implemented to recover the lost wetlands. This combination of instruments calls for the integration of socio-economic and environmental issues and lays the ground for an assessment on the role of agricultural measures introduced under Agenda 2000.

Intensification of Production and Groundwater Depletion

Groundwater is a strategic source of water in regions with an uneven distribution of rainfall, such as the Mediterranean region. The extraction of groundwater for irrigation has expanded as an easily accessible source of water to a large number of irrigators who use private wells at low costs. As a result valuable water ecosystems in the European Mediterranean countries have been progressively degraded. Being rare and unique ecosystems of great ecological value, their preservation requires the adequate policy framework for achieving an integrated approach of land use and water management. In the EU context we can distinguish two broad regions in which the impacts on groundwater is determined largely by the different agricultural systems that characterize, in general terms, the northern and southern areas of the EU (Table 6.4).

Table 6.4   Environmental effects of intensification of production on aquifers in the EU by region

Region	Production pattern	Primary effects	Secondary effects	Appropriate Directive
North	Intensive production systems	• Accumulation of nitrates and pesticides	• Water pollution	• Nitrate Directive • Drinking Water Directive
South	Intensive irrigation systems	• Over-exploitation of aquifers • Salinization • Water scarcity	• Loss of wetlands • Loss of aquatic flora and fauna	• Habitats Directive • Natura 2000

Intensive agriculture in the northern Member States causes water pollution problems due to the accumulation of fertilizers and pesticides in the aquifers. In the southern areas of the EU, intensive irrigation has produced excessive water mining from groundwater, which has led to progressively declining water tables and salinity from marine intrusion in the sea littorals. This has created severe water shortage problems and the subsequent drying of wetlands and loss of aquatic species.

Depletion of aquifers from intensive irrigation has occurred in several regions in Spain of great environmental value. Past policies have encouraged the development of irrigation, and have been furthermore reinforced by the production-related payments, as in other countries of south Europe (Baldock and Long, 1988; Varela-Ortega and Sumpsi, 1998; Rainelli and Vermersch, 1998). Overdrafting takes place when water-mining rates exceed the rate of natural recharge, causing aquifers to become exhausted and wetlands degraded. Recovering these wetlands requires effective environmental protection policies, which promote environmental sustainability through elimination of groundwater overdraft (that is appropriate regulatory policy, incentives policy and an adequate institutional framework).

The reform of the CAP under Agenda 2000 searched for policy instruments that are compatible with nature protection and farmers' income, without inflicting a major burden on public expenses. In this context, in the southern EU countries, the protection of water resources of highly valued aquifers provides a good example of policy options for attaining the compatibility of agricultural production and the protection of natural ecosystems.

Spain needs policy instruments that integrate water conservation, economic efficiency and environmental sustainability. However, it should be taken into account that in Spain public ownership of water determines that irrigators are usufructuaries of water allotment rights through administrative concessions. For this reason, policy options have to take into consideration that significant social unrest will arise if public authorities resort, for environmental reasons, to developing water conservation policies intended to restrict the use of water. These policies will face high transaction costs if they impose compulsory limitations on the water used by the farmers below their consolidated water allotment rights. This has been the case of groundwater management problems in several areas in the world (Provencher and Burt, 1994; Ledoux, 1997; Shah *et al.*, 2000) as well as in the valuable wetlands of the national park 'Tablas de Daimiel' in the region of La Mancha in Spain's southern central plateau. This fragile aquatic ecosystem had been progressively degraded as a result of the over-exploitation of the aquifer by the intensively irrigated nearby farms (Llamas, 1995; Sancho Comins *et al.*, 1993). We will discuss this particular case in the next section.

A Case Study on the Preservation of Wetlands in Spain

The 'Tablas de Daimiel' in the region of Castilla-La Mancha is one of the most peculiar geographical formations in the landscape of the Spanish south central plain. The geomorphologic and hydrological conditions that come together in the High Basin of the River Guadiana give rise to a network of small lakes and areas flooded by the fluvial overflowing of the surrounding rivers. The resulting wetland area is included in Category A – exceptional interest – in the Catalogue of the Wet Areas of Europe, as a habitat for the conservation of European and North African aquatic birds. The high ecological productivity and biodiversity of these wetlands in La Mancha give them not only a high environmental value but also a geochemical and limnological singularity in Europe. These environmental conditions enable the existence of a large number of species and large populations of nest-building and hibernating waterfowl. All these environmental merits have attracted special national and international recognition for the area's conservation value. It is catalogued as a UNESCO Biosphere Reserve, RAMSAR agreement site, a Special Bird Protection Area under the Birds Directive 79/409, a Natura 2000 site under the Habitats Directive 92/43 and under a number of other international and national designations (Baldock *et al.*, 2000).

In the decade before Spain's entry into the EC, irrigation agriculture expanded progressively in the region of La Mancha in the Spanish central plateau as a response to national structural policy programmes. This trend was further reinforced by the application of the CAP programmes upon Spain's integration into the EC in 1986. The increase of irrigated land on the plains of La Mancha was possible thanks to the recourse of subterranean water and the construction of wells and infrastructure by the farmers. The use of water from the Western La Mancha aquifer number 23, with an area of 5000 km^2 in its geographical centre, was particularly significant. Until the middle of the 1970s, the hydric balance of the aquifer could be regarded as surplus. But between 1980 and 1987, the rhythm of drillings and extractions accelerated due to good returns from irrigated land and public subsidies for irrigation transformations. In the early 1990s, water extractions from the aquifers in the region exceeded the natural recharge rate. The irrigated area in the zone has increased from 30 000 ha in the early 1970s to 120 000 ha in the early 1990s. In addition to this, groundwater mining from the aquifers had mounted to reach an annual extraction rate of more than 500 million m^3 largely surpassing the estimated natural recharge rate of 230 million m^3 per year (MOPTMA-CGH, 1995). Consequently the water table was progressively lowered, the natural water return flows diminished and the aquifers became gradually depleted. As a result, this produced salinization of the subterranean water, contamination and eutrophication of the surface water. Also, it produced a substantial reduction in nesting areas, changes of vegetation, peat fires, a generalized subsidence of land with the concomitant impact on the landscape and the loss of traditional exploitations (for example crayfish sellers). Moreover, the drying up of the aquifer, by up to 40 metres, together with long periods of drought, induced the breaking up of riverbeds and their contamination by nutrients and pesticides. Since the end of the 1970s, all this has not only had a devastating effect on the flora and fauna but it has also jeopardized irrigation farming as a result of the drop in profitability due to the decreasing availability of water (Sumpsi and Varela-Ortega, 2000).

Policy responses to eliminate groundwater depletion
Overexploitation of groundwater resources in the Guadiana river basin motivated the Water Authority to adopt a specific regulation in 1991 to impose a strict Water Management Regime. This regulation restricted water extractions from the individual wells and redefined the previously established water allotment rights of the private irrigators by substantially reducing their entitled water assignments. A range of upper limits on water consumption were established depending on farm size, with largest farms facing tightest limitations. On average, the maximum permitted amount was fixed at 2000 m³/ha. No compensation payments are granted to the farmers for their derived income loss in achieving these compulsory measures. Water extraction restrictions from the aquifer are measured indirectly by means of the crops grown by each individual farmer, making the policy control a costly and difficult procedure. As in many other similar cases, this environmental policy faces large implementation difficulties due to arduous control and monitoring of the individual farmers (Eggertsson, 1990; Whitby *et al.*, 1998). Furthermore, this difficulty is reinforced by the large incentives that farmers have to avoid the cropping restrictions imposed by the water-limitation policy in response to lucrative price incentives. As a result, extremely high enforcement costs have resulted in a very limited uptake of this national policy.

Regulation 2078/92 was designed to promote agricultural production systems compatible with the requirements of the protection of the environment and the maintenance of the countryside. By 1993, only the region of Castilla-La Mancha had implemented this policy where one of the most successful zonal programmes focused on the recovery of wetland areas in Castilla-La Mancha and Campo de Montiel in the southern central plateau of Spain. This is the most expensive of all environmental programmes in Spain and one of the most expensive in all the EU with a total budget of 104 million ECU for a five year period (1993–97). The programme's environmental objective was to recover the natural wetlands of the National Park 'Tablas de Daimiel' by reducing water extractions from the aquifers. The programme aimed to maintain the agricultural activity in the nearby area by compensating the farmers irrigating their land for measures they needed to take. The region includes about 120 000 ha and 8400 farms. Income compensation payments are reported to be beneficial for attaining social, economic and environmental objectives (Viladomiu and Rosell, 1997).

By mid-1997, almost 3000 farms had joined the programme covering close to 90 per cent of the total area affected. Annual water extractions had been reduced by almost 300 million m³, exceeding the programme's target (255–270 million m³ per annum) and equivalent to an average reduction of 60 per cent (Consejería de Agricultura y Medio Ambiente, 1997). Meeting largely its environmental and socio-economic objectives, the programme has produced a much larger impact than was foreseen. It has contributed to the reduction of social distress in the area caused by the long lasting years of severe drought and has brought about agricultural extensification. It has encouraged farmers to limit crops with high water demand, change to dry farming and reduce input use (machinery and agrochemicals). These measures need to promote production techniques, with limited pressure on the environment.

The adoption of the agri-environmental measures was voluntary, and the obligation for all farmers to comply with the Water Management Regime created synergy in policy. Trends on the use of water in the region of Daimiel are presented in Table 6.5.

Table 6.5   Evolution of water consumption in the region of Daimiel

Applied measures	Year	Volume abstracted (million m³)	Irrigated area (ha)
	1985	478	107,767
Pre MacSharry	1986	525	117,200
	1987	553	123,739
	1988	568	121,276
	1989	561	121,626
National policy to limit water extractions rules	1990	522	117,212
	1991	427	93,255
	1992	410	89,280
Agri-environmental programmes under Regulation 2078/92	1993	310	89,494
	1994	236	73,505
	1995	217	73,582
	1996	215	73,300
	1997	203	73,015

Source: Consejería de Agricultura y Medio Ambiente (1997)

A FRAMEWORK TO EVALUATE POLICIES FOR WATER CONSERVATION AND WETLAND PROTECTION

Policy Options in the EU Context

One of the most widespread criticisms of the Common Agricultural Policy (CAP) is that it absorbs large public resources. In addition, the CAP has also been criticized for its insufficient specification of environmental objectives and its harmful effects on the environment, natural resources and landscape. For this reason, the Fifth Environmental Action Programme 'Towards Sustainability' has propounded the necessity to integrate environmental objectives within the common structural policies and market support policies. This is particularly relevant to the CAP that absorbs about one half of the total EU budget.

Environmental objectives have been integrated into the CAP through the agri-environmental programmes under Regulation 2078/92. These programmes currently cover less than 5 per cent of the total CAP budget. Along the same lines, the EU has enacted several directives, such as the Nitrate Directive. The application of this directive has been delayed, especially in the southern Member States.

The 1999 reform of the CAP under Agenda 2000 provides new possibilities for the consideration of environmental conditions in the market regimes. These policy instruments include cross-compliance, in which direct payments are subject to meeting specific conditions for environmental and resource conservation. The potential strength to apply cross-compliance is being considered. Solid investigations, based on quantitative analysis, need to be done. Good prospects for cross-compliance have been reported in some countries such as the Netherlands (Brouwer, 1999), but its widespread applicability remains questionable. Indeed, a great majority of farmers in the EU receive direct payments that are crucial to the viability of these holdings. Thus, imposing a restricted access to these income support payments might seriously impair the viability of many farms. Therefore, cross-compliance has been regarded as a regulatory mechanism rather than as a pure economic instrument (Baldock and Mitchell, 1995; Spash and Falconer, 1997). Thus, its effectiveness will be determined largely by the definition of environmental requisites and by the penalties established if these requisites are not respected (for example a reduction or even withdrawal of direct payments).

The 1999 CAP reform established that

> where agricultural activity within the scope of common rules Regulation is concerned, Member States shall take the environmental measures they consider to be appropriate in view of the situation of the agricultural land used or the production

concerned and which reflect the potential environmental effects. These measures may include: 1) support in return for agri-environmental commitments; 2) general mandatory environmental requirements and 3) specific environmental requirements constituting a condition for direct payments (Article 3 of Common Rules Regulation 1259/1999, in Dwyer *et al.*, 2000, p. 8).

The third option is known as cross-compliance.

Generally speaking, farmers prefer to receive agri-environmental payments for meeting certain environmental objectives (such as reducing water extractions) independently of the direct payments they receive from CAP regimes. Strong opposition might be expected from the farmers' organizations if direct payments are conditioned to meeting certain environmental requisites (cross-compliance). For all these reasons, flexibility and variability in the application of cross-compliance options is to be expected in most EU countries (Brouwer and Lowe, 2000).

Farmers have joined agri-environmental programmes in the case study area, where payments were subject to reducing water extractions. In addition, they forcefully opposed the non-compensating national water policy based on mandatory limitations of water extractions from the aquifer (mandatory environmental requirements).

It has been argued that the agri-environmental programme applied in this area might not be a cost-effective tool for reducing water extractions and ultimately recovering the valuable wetlands of the adjacent National Park 'Tablas de Daimiel' (Varela-Ortega and Sumpsi, 1999). Other policy instruments might reach similar objectives at lower public costs. Consequently, policies other than the existing agri-environmental programmes have been proposed that incorporate more cost-effective instruments for reducing public costs. Policies identified in Table 6.6 could all contribute to reduce groundwater extractions. They include price-responsive water management instruments and are defined by the establishment of a varied system of water levies that will encourage the reduction of water used by the irrigators (Varela-Ortega and Sumpsi, 1999).

However, Agenda 2000 provides a new set of policy options, including cross-compliance. Cross-compliance might contribute to attaining the combined goal of economic development and ecological sustainability. In fact, there is a need to examine the prospects of this policy tool to link agriculture with nature conservation.

Table 6.6 shows the expected economic and environmental effects of these policies. Direct payments without any agri-environmental measures are only beneficial for farmers' income but do not reduce depletion of water resources and have brought about an increase in budget expenses. In contrast, the introduction of agri-environmental programmes had a beneficial effect on nature by encouraging water conservation practices and the replenishment of

Table 6.6   Policy choice matrix

		Effects of measures		
Type of policy		Nature	Farm income	Public sector budget
CAP measures	CAP (92)	–	+	–
	CAP (92) and AEP 2078/92	+	+	– –
	Agenda 2000 and cross-compliance[a]	+	–	+
Environmental policies	Water use limitation (water quotas)	+	–	+
	Water pricing policies (water tariffs)	+	–	+

Note: a.   Agri-environmental programmes (AEP) not included in this policy option

the aquifer. Cross-compliance options (without agri-environmental pro-grammes) are envisaged to meet economic and environmental goals at lower public expenses. To what extent these options may inflict income losses to the farmers, remains questionable and needs further assessment.

The Role of Cross-compliance

Up to the present, two different policies have been applied to limit water extractions in the irrigated area of La Mancha and to ensure the sustainable management of the aquifer of Daimiel. One is compliance with the compul-sory Spanish royal decree enacted in 1991, under which water volumes are restricted and farmers are not compensated for their income loss. The other is the agri-environmental programme under Regulation 2078/92, which com-pensates farmers who voluntarily reduce the amount of water extracted. However, other policy alternatives as proposed in Agenda 2000 for attaining a sustainable management of the aquifer have not yet been examined.

In this policy choice context, the objective of this case study is the comparative assessment of several policy options whose common objective is to achieve economic and environmental sustainability. For this purpose, we have analysed the effects of different scenarios of CAP on water use, farmers' income and the public budget in the region of Castilla-La Mancha

(Sumpsi *et al.*, 2000). Therefore, the main objective of this case study is to investigate whether the implementation of Agenda 2000 may contribute to the reduction of groundwater abstractions from the region's valuable aquifers without inflicting severe penalties on the farmers' income and the public expenses.

Methodology

A dynamic mathematical programming model has been used to assess the farmers' responses to different policy measures (Sumpsi *et al.*, 1998, Varela-Ortega *et al.*, 1998). The model evaluates an increase of irrigation in the zone by comparing the relative profitability of irrigated crops and dry crops. It allocates arable land into different types of irrigated crops, and quantifies the relative profitability of high and low water demanding crops. Consequently, the simulation results will assess the influence of different policy options on water consumption, that is, on the amount of water extracted from the aquifer. These results will provide an empirical base for policy analysis and policy recommendations to conserve the available water resources.

The zone of study has been represented by a set of statistically based representative farms (F-1, F-2, F-3, F-4) (Table 6.7) that characterize the variety of production systems found in the irrigation district of Daimiel. It covers an area of 20 000 ha in the Guadiana river basin, located in the region of Castilla-La Mancha in central Spain. The technical and economic parameters of the farms have been obtained from a survey conducted in the study area in 1995 (Sumpsi *et al.*, 1998) and further revised in 1999 (Sumpsi *et al.*, 2000). The farms have been classified according to size, soil type, cropping pattern and irrigation techniques.

Table 6.7   Farm typology

	F-1	F-2	F-3	F-4
Area (ha)	8	24	30	70
Soil quality	low	high	medium	medium and low
Cropping pattern	vine	horticulture and arable crops	melon/sugarbeet, arable crops and vine	arable crops
Coverage (% of area)	22	19	28	31

For each farm type we have designed a farm model in which a profit function has been maximized subject to technical constraints (availability of land, water, labour, equipment, production possibilities), financial constraints (liquidity and loans), economic constraints (prices of inputs and products, rates of interest) and policy constraints (CAP measures, crop limitations and investment subsidies).

Policy options
Four policy options have been defined within the framework of the CAP. Scenarios included focus on the price reductions of cereals, oilseeds and protein crops (COP) products, as part of the CAP reform in 1992, agri-environmental programmes under Regulation 2078/92, and the adoption of Agenda 2000 measures. We assess the implications of cross-compliance for water conservation and hence for attaining a sustainable management of water resources. Policy options selected include direct payments (a hectare premium, which differentiates between irrigated and dry lands). Therefore, progressive rates of reduction of payments have been considered, including 25, 50, 75 and 100 per cent.

The policy options are:

● *Scenario E1* corresponds to the 1992 CAP reform without the agri-environmental payments. It will be taken as the reference scenario or baseline.
● *Scenario E2* corresponds to the 1992 CAP reform, complemented by the agri-environmental measures. Farmers receive direct payments for their arable crops and income compensation payments, subject to measures they take to reduce the amount of water extracted.
● *Scenario E3* corresponds to the application of Agenda 2000 with cross-compliance. We first consider that prices for the arable crops are equal to the reference scenario (E1) (initial prices). In addition, prices are 10 or 20 per cent below initial prices.
● *Scenario E4* corresponds to the application of Agenda 2000 without the adoption of cross-compliance. Three price reduction levels have been considered as in scenario E3.
● *Scenario E5* is composed of the total elimination of direct payments, and replaced by agri-environmental measures.

Cross-compliance considers that direct payments are subject to meeting the required reduction in water extractions. This follows up on Article 3 of Regulation 1259/1999. Average water consumption in the area was 4000 m³/ha before the Water Management Regime was enacted and the maximum permitted volume for the aquifer's recovery was set at 2000 m³/ha. Therefore, farmers will face no deduction of direct payments if water use does not exceed 2000 m³/ha. Income support is reduced by 30 per cent if water use is between 2000 and 3000 m³/ha, and by 60 per cent if water use is between

3000 and 4000 m³/ha. Support is fully withdrawn if they consume more than 4000 m³/ha.

Results

Table 6.8 shows the aggregated effects of the policy options considered on farm income, water consumption and public expenses. The reference scenario (1992 CAP reform without environmental payments) and the policy from the mid-1990s (1992 CAP reform and environmental payments) are based on 1998 prices of COP crops (initial prices). However, the other policy options (cross-compliance scenario and the 'no-direct payments' or radical reform scenario) are based on the consideration of three different alternative price levels that are intended to reflect the range of price fluctuations on the

Table 6.8   Results of policy options

Policy option		Farm income (€/ha)		Water consumption (m³/ha)		Public expenditure (€/ha)	
		Total	%	Total	%	Total	%
Reference policy (E1)		618	100	3,985	100	174	100
Current policy (E2)		698	113	1,500	38	386	222
Agenda 2000	Initial prices[a]	581	94	2,080	52	189	109
with cross-	10% lower[b]	544	88	2,046	51	172	99
compliance (E3)	20% lower[c]	519	84	2,046	51	168	97
Agenda 2000	Initial prices[a]	655	106	3,776	95	212	122
without cross-	10% lower[b]	575	93	2,359	59	182	105
compliance							
(E4)	20% lower[c]	538	87	2,180	55	181	104
Radical reform	Initial prices	593	96	1,035	26	267	154
(E5)	10% lower	581	94	1,035	26	267	154
	20% lower	562	91	1,035	26	267	154

Notes:
(E1)   1992 CAP reform direct payments (1998) without agri-environmental programmes.
(E2)   Same as (E1) plus agri-environmental payments (1998).
(E3)   Agenda 2000 direct payments with cross-compliance option.
(E4)   Agenda 2000 without cross-compliance.
(E5)   No direct payments and only agri-environmental payments (1998).
a.   Current 2000 market prices and Agenda 2000 direct payments.
b.   Price reduction of 10 per cent and Agenda 2000 direct payments maintained.
c.   Price reduction of 20 per cent and Agenda 2000 direct payments maintained.

world market. The first alternative considers that current (initial) prices are maintained, whereas the second and third alternatives consider a 10 or a 20 per cent reduction of initial prices.

The reference policy option (E1, 1992 price reduction)   The reference scenario (E1) does not promote any water conservation practices among farmers. Water use is high, mounting to almost 4000 m³/ha. This is well above the maximum limit of 2000 m³/ha as established by Spanish regulation to recover the aquifer. Farmers grow irrigated crops with a clear predominance of water demanding crops, such as maize and horticulture products. Dry farming appears to be profitable only when the difference in payments between irrigated and dry lands is reduced. If farmers received similar payments irrespective of whether or not land is irrigated, they would reduce irrigation by 50 per cent.

The present policy option (E2) (1992 CAP reform, also including agri-environmental payments)   Scenario E2 reflects conditions from the late 1990s, and incorporates agri-environmental payments. This scenario meets water conservation objectives. Water consumption is reduced by more than 60 per cent, and farmers' income increases by 13 per cent. However, this policy option requires considerable public resources, double those required in the case without agri-environmental payments. Even in the case where these payments are offered without price support (scenario E5), public funding will increase by more than 50 per cent relative to the reference policy.

Agenda 2000 with cross-compliance option (E3)   Agenda 2000 with the adoption of cross-compliance would also reduce water consumption to a level below that required by law. Water demand is expected to be reduced by almost 50 per cent, and will reach a level of around 2000 m³/ha. This amount is around the maximum water extraction volumes permitted for the aquifer's recovery. However, in contrast to the agri-environmental measures, this policy does not increase public expenses. In addition, farm income is hardly reduced relative to the reference policy. In fact, if prices of the COP crops were to be maintained, water use would be sharply reduced to 52 per cent, farm income would be slightly (6 per cent) lower than in the reference policy and public funds would increase only by 9 per cent. If prices declined by 10 or 20 per cent, cross-compliance would be less costly than 1992 CAP programmes and public expenses reduced by 3 per cent. Water demand would be fairly stable in all three cases.

Agenda 2000 without cross-compliance (E4)   Compared to the reference level, Agenda 2000 (without cross-compliance and prices remaining unchanged) would reduce water consumption by 5 per cent only. Therefore, this scenario would not sufficiently reduce water consumption, and water demand would still exceed the limit of 2000 m³/ha. If crop prices decrease by 10 or 20 per cent, water consumption will decrease substantially, because crops with high water demand become less viable. This scenario clearly indicates the effects of crop prices on water consumption, on the condition that the farmers do not have to comply with any additional environmental requirements. Farm income will increase by 6 per cent when prices are maintained. When crop prices are reduced, and irrigation farming becomes less profitable, incomes decline substantially and reach levels similar to the Agenda 2000 cross-compliance scenario (90 to 85 per cent of baseline scenario).

Comparing the cost of the different policy options, the currently applied policy (E2) (direct payments and agri-environmental aids) requires an average payment per ha of € 386. In the case where no direct payments are applied and only agri-environmental payments are considered (E5), the costs per ha continue to be high and reach a level of almost € 270 per ha. However, if agri-environmental payments are eliminated, such as in the reference policy (E1), the costs per ha decrease to around € 175. This is only slightly below the case of the cross-compliance option (E2) which amounts to € 190/ha. This difference vanishes, however, when prices for COP crops are expected to decrease by 10 or 20 per cent in the cross-compliance option, which diminishes to € 168/ha.

A cross-compliance option in Agenda 2000 clearly encourages water saving strategies among farmers who will grow fewer water-demanding crops, such as barley. In the present situation where irrigated lands receive higher direct payments than dry lands, rain-fed farming is scarce. But when these differentials are reduced, rain-fed farming increases progressively and occupies close to 60 per cent of the average farm surface when direct payments are the same for all types of lands. Only crops such as melon and vine with low water requirements will be cultivated in the irrigated lands.

CONCLUSION

The analysis offers evidence that all policy options are more cost-effective than the measures with the 1992 CAP reform direct payments, complemented with agri-environmental support measures. This policy was implemented in the Spanish region of Castilla-La Mancha for reducing excessive water extraction from the aquifer and hence for recovering the nearby wetlands.

Unquestionably, the incorporation of water-saving measures into agri-environmental programmes has met the policy's environmental goal of water conservation and has also been beneficial for assuring a social and economic balance in the area. However, from a public perspective, this policy is expensive. It requires high acreage payments to compensate the farmers for not using up their total entitled water volumes and consequently for their derived income loss. If less water is available for agriculture, irrigation will be reduced, crop profitability will diminish and farm income will decline. Therefore, farmers will voluntarily join this programme only if direct compensation payments are offered to them. In consequence, with respect to environmental effectiveness, the currently applied programmes will reduce water consumption at a comparatively high cost.

Conversely, cross-compliance would attain the desired reductions in water extractions for the aquifer's replenishment and would only need half of the public funds compared to the case with agri-environmental programmes.

Looking at the private sector, all policy options will inflict some income losses on the farmers if compared to the currently applied policy. In fact, in this policy, as farmers are eligible to a dual direct-payment source of income (CAP reform of 1992 and agri-environmental support measures), they actually obtain higher income gains than with the baseline policy. Being an expensive policy, it remains socially questionable whether farmers need to be compensated for meeting environmental standards that are beneficial for nature's protection and long-term social well-being.

From an integrated social and environmental perspective, Agenda 2000 with cross-compliance allows for a more balanced cost-effective combination of ecological and socio-economic objectives. This policy option will largely attain the projected water conservation objectives with lower costs for the public sector and will inflict minor income losses on the private farmer. This will be reinforced if the payment differential between irrigated and dry lands is mitigated. In addition to that, the effects of this policy on water use, farm income and public expenditure are very inelastic to crop price reductions. That is, this policy option has the advantage of being considerably stable across price variations and hence it will reduce the effects of the uncertainty related to future international price fluctuations.

Conversely, the combination of economic and environmental objectives is not efficiently met under Agenda 2000, when cross-compliance is not adopted. In fact, water use will not be reduced unless crop prices diminish. In that case, a derived decrease in irrigation agriculture will lower farm income at higher public expenditure requirements than in the Agenda 2000 cross-compliance option.

Deciding on whether the farmer or government will pay for the cost of reducing water use in agriculture is a major question of policy choice, where economic efficiency, nature's preservation for future generations and social equity will have to be considered.

To estimate the value of water and full cost of supply, economic and environmental externalities have to be included, so that integrated water management includes ecological values, as wetland ecosystems are both economic users and economic suppliers of water. In this context, the questions for debate will be the following: When a given environmental regulation (the preservation of aquatic ecosystems) imposes a restriction (a limitation on water extractions) on the farmers, do these farmers have to be compensated for complying with the existing regulation? If irrigators have consolidated water rights, can the irrigators' property rights to use water resources be expropriated? The answer is a matter of policy choice and a necessary consistency between policy options and policy instruments. If the PPP is applied the irrigators will not be compensated, public costs will be small, but high social unrest will make the policy difficult to enforce. If incentive schemes are applied, farmers will be compensated but the cost to the public sector will be high and monitoring costs will be substantial. Cross-compliance options as a regulatory mechanism will have lower cost requirements but will inflict some income loss on the private sector.

Ultimately an efficient management of water resources will require the development of technical, economic, social and institutional approaches and the need to involve all stakeholders in the decision-making process, that is, the public sector (the taxpayers), the private farmers and the environment (that is the future generations).

REFERENCES

Baldock, D. and A. Long (1988), *The Mediterranean environment under pressure: the influence of the CAP on Spain and Portugal and the IMPs in France, Greece and Italy*, Report to World Wildlife Fund, London: Institute for European Environmental Policy.

Baldock, D. and K. Mitchell (1995), *Cross-Compliance within the Common Agricultural Policy: a Review of Options for Landscape and Nature Conservation*, London: Institute for European Environmental Policy (IEEP).

Baldock, D., J. Dwyer, J. Sumpsi, C. Varela-Ortega, H. Caraveli, S. Einschütz and J-E. Petersen (2000), *The Environmental Impacts of Irrigation in the European Union*, Report to the European Commission, Brussels: European Commission.

Brouwer, F. (1999), 'Options for cross-compliance in the Netherlands', Working paper, The Hague: Agricultural Economics Research Institute (LEI-DLO).

Brouwer, F. and P. Lowe (eds) (2000), *CAP Regimes and the European Countryside: Prospects for Integration between Agricultural, Regional and Environmental Policies*, Wallingford: CAB International.

Caldas, J.C. (1999), *A Irrigaçao em Portugal*, Lisbon: Lisbon Technical University, Department of Agrarian Economy and Rural Sociology.

Consejería de Agricultura y Medio Ambiente (1997), *Solicitud de prórroga para el periodo 1998–2002 del programa de compensación de las rentas agrarias en las*

Unidades Hidrogeológicas de Mancha Occidental y Campo de Montiel, Toledo: Comunidad de Castilla-La Mancha.

Dwyer, J., D. Baldock and S. Einschütz (2000), *Cross-compliance under the Common Agricultural Policy – A report to the Department of the Environment, Transport and the Regions*, London: Institute for European Environmental Policy (IEEP).

Eggertsson, T. (1990), *Economic Behavior and Institutions,* Cambridge: Cambridge University Press.

FAO (1995), 'Reforming Water Resources Policy', FAO irrigation and drainage paper no. 52, Rome: United Nations Food and Agriculture Organisation.

Ledoux, L. (1997), 'Irrigation management in a coastal wetland: The Camargue', paper presented at the Eighth annual Conference of the European Association of Environmental Economists, Tilburg, The Netherlands (26–28 June).

Llamas, R. (1995), *Explotación y gestión de las aguas subterráneas y la conservación de los humedales españoles: Estado actual, perspectivas y aplicaciones territoriales*, Proceedings of the seminar: Las Aguas Subterráneas en la Ley de Aguas Española: Un decenio de experiencia, Murcia, Spain.

MAPA (1997) (Ministerio de Agricultura, Pesca y Alimentación) Dirección General de Planificación y desarrollo rural. Analisis de resultados ejercicio 1996.

Margat, J. and D. Vallée (1999), *Mediterranean vision on water, population and the environment for the XXIst century*, Report, Mediterranean Technical Advisory Committee (MEDTAC) – Global Water partnership (GWP). Blue Plan for the Mediterranean, Valbonne, France.

MOPTMA-CGH (1995), *El problema hidraúlico de la Cuenca alta del Guadiana*, Madrid: Ministerio de Obras Públicas Transportes y Medio Ambiente.

OECD (1998), *Sustainable Management of Water in Agriculture: Issues and Policies; The Athens Workshop*, Paris: Organization for Economic Co-operation and Development (OECD).

Provencher, B. and O. Burt (1994), 'A private property rights regime for the commons: The case for groundwater', *American Journal of Agricultural Economics*, **76**, November, 875–88.

Rainelli, P. and D. Vermersch (1998), 'Irrigation in France: Current situation and reasons for its developments', Paper presented at the workshop: CAP and the Environment in the EU (FAIR 3–CT96–1793), Wageningen: LEI.

Rosegrant, M.W. (1997), *Water Resources in the Twenty-first Century: Challenges and Implications for Action. Food, Agriculture and the Environment*, Discussion paper 20, Washington DC: International Food Policy Research Institute (IFPRI).

Sancho Comins, J., J. Bosque and F. Moreno (1993), 'Crisis and permanence of the traditional agromediterranean lands in the central region of Spain', *Landscape and Urban Planning*, **23**, 155–66.

Seckler, D., D. Molden, U. Amarasinghe and C. de Fraiture (2000), 'Overview of the data and analysis' in: International Water Management Institute (IWMI), *World Water Supply and Demand: 1995–2025*, Colombo: Monograph. IWMI, pp. 3–32.

Seckler, D., U. Amarasinghe, D. Molden, R. Da Silva and R. Barker (1998), *World Water Demand and Supply, 1995 to 2025: Scenarios and Issues*, Research Report 19, Colombo: International Water Management Institute (IWMI).

Shah, T., D. Molden, R. Sakthivadivel and D. Seckler (2000), *The global groundwater situation: Overview of opportunities and challenges*, Research report, Colombo: International Water Management Institute (IWMI).

Spash, C.L. and K. Falconer (1997), 'Agri-environmental policies: cross-achievement and the role for cross-compliance', in F. Brouwer and W. Kleinhanss (eds), *The*

Implementation of Nitrate Policies in Europe: Processes of Change in Environmental Policy and Agriculture, Kiel: Vauk Publisher, pp. 23–42.

Sumpsi, J. and C. Varela-Ortega (2000), *Environmental Impacts of Irrigation in Spain*, Madrid: Department of Agricultural Economics, Polytechnical University of Madrid.

Sumpsi, J., M. Blanco and C. Varela-Ortega (2000), 'Políticas agrarias alternativas para reducir el uso del agua en los regadíos de Daimiel', Working paper, Research report for ADENA-WWF, Madrid: Department of Agricultural Economics, Polytechnical University of Madrid.

Sumpsi, J.M., A. Garrido, M. Blanco, C. Varela-Ortega and E. Iglesias (1998), *Economía y política de gestión del agua en la agricultura*, Mundi-Prensa, Madrid: MAPA.

UNO (United Nations Organization) (1997), *Comprehensive Assessment of the Freshwater Resources of the World*, Commission on Sustainable Development, Department for Policy Coordination and Sustainable Development (DPCSD), UNO.

Varela-Ortega, C. and J. Sumpsi (1998), 'Spain', in F. Brouwer and P. Lowe (eds), *CAP and the Rural Environment in Transition. A Panorama of National Perspectives*, Wageningen: Wageningen Pers, pp. 201–40.

Varela-Ortega, C. and J. Sumpsi (1999), 'Assessment of cost-effectiveness of policy instruments for sustainable development in environmentally sensitive irrigation areas', paper presented at the IXth Congress of the European Association of Agricultural Economists (EAAE), Warsaw, Poland.

Varela-Ortega, C., J.M. Sumpsi, A. Garrido, M. Blanco and E. Iglesias (1998), 'Water pricing policies, public decision making and farmers response: implications for water policy', *Agricultural Economics*, **19**(1–2), 193–202.

Viladomiu, L. and J. Rosell (1997), 'Gestión del agua y política agroambiental: el Programa de Compensación de Rentas por reducción de regadíos en Mancha Occidental y Campo de Montiel', *Revista Española de Economía Agraria,* **179**, 331–50.

Whitby, M., C. Saunders and C. Ray (1998), 'The full cost of stewardship policies', in S. Dabbert, A. Dubgaard, L. Slangen and M. Whitby (eds), *The Economics of Landscape and Wildlife Conservation*, Wallingford: CAB International, pp. 97–112.

World Water Forum (2000), *From Vision to Action. Water and Economics*, Forum reports, The Hague.

7. Agricultural policy and nature conservation in the UK

Bob Crabtree

INTRODUCTION

Habitat protection in Britain took a major step forward in the 1980s with two major pieces of legislation. The first, the 1981 Wildlife and Countryside Act, strengthened instruments for the protection of Sites of Special Scientific Interest (SSSIs) from potentially damaging operations, especially on farmland. The act was not designed to provide for the more general protection of valued countryside from changes in land use. Since agriculture was outside the planning system, farmers were free to do much as they wished with their land. Progressive destruction of habitat through conversion of grassland to arable cropping, drainage, and reclamation, all facilitated by mechanization, price support and grant aid, had resulted in major changes in land cover (Bowers and Cheshire, 1983; Whitby and Lowe, 1994).

The loss of traditional landscape and farmland habitats provoked an increasingly strong reaction from the public and certain interest groups. This crystallized in a variety of protests but one in particular was important through its impact on agricultural policy. This was the demonstration against continued drainage and conversion to arable land of the Halvergate Marshes in the Norfolk Broads. In 1985, faced with growing public concern, the Agriculture ministry (MAFF) together with the Countryside Commission established a scheme of incentive payments to induce farmers in the Halvergate Marshes not to engage in environmentally damaging land use change. This second piece of legislation established a system of fixed rate payments that was to become the benchmark for future agri-environmental intervention in the UK (Colman and Lee, 1988). As an outcome of these experiences and continuing pressure from environmental groups, the UK government was instrumental in promoting agri-environmental measures as an element of the CAP under Regulation 797/85. This was a response driven by the politics of countryside change in Britain where MAFF looked for mechanisms that would both be acceptable to farmers, and control the loss of public good output as agriculture modernized. Only at a later stage

(MAFF, 1991) was the economic argument for agri-environmental payments to farmers more fully specified.

ENVIRONMENTALLY SENSITIVE AREAS

The perception in the 1980s was that the general thrust of agricultural development only needed to be moderated in specific areas of high environmental value. Hence, the focus was on targeting areas (geographically delimited zones) of high wildlife or landscape value that were under threat from agricultural change. In the UK, agri-environmental measures were introduced in the form of Environmentally Sensitive Areas (ESAs) and these have been the flagship of UK agri-environmental policy ever since. The scheme is a zonal one in which farmers in selected areas are offered payments for activities that contribute to nature conservation. Areas are targeted after consultation with environmental agencies and environmental interests. There are currently over 19 000 farmers in the UK with ESA management agreements covering an area of 1.5 million ha. The scheme is voluntary and uses incentive payments as the mechanism for encouraging farmers to enter an environmental contract. Typically there are two tiers. Farmers participating must enter a Tier 1 contract in which they are paid to comply with measures to protect the environment, including wildlife habitats and landscape. They may additionally contract into Tier 2 which consists of specific management and investment activities aimed at enhancing habitats and biodiversity. In this tier they agree on a selection of activities from a menu of possibilities, each with an associated payment, developed for each ESA. There is thus some flexibility for the scheme to adapt to the characteristics of different farms and the interests of the farmers.

The details of the scheme are described in greater detail in Whitby (1994) and Coates (1999). In essence, an ESA can be designated where the conservation interest is dependent on the adoption, maintenance or extension of particular farming practices. The scheme aims to protect and enhance wildlife by applying measures to secure and extend habitats by modifying farming practices. It also protects and extends landscape features such as stone walls, hedges and historic and archaeological features. An agreed five-year management plan defines the contract between government and farmer; it defines a set of activities that the farmer will (and will not) engage in, including appropriate capital investment and changes to stocking or cropping practices.

The argument for concentrating public expenditure on selected zones is that these are those areas where the expected loss in environmental value is greatest due to changes in farm practices. However, such objective assessment is difficult since data on environmental change is highly fragmented. In practice, area selection has become a political decision that takes into account the pressures both from interest groups and farmers.

Conceptually the benefits from the ESA scheme can be depicted as a response to declining natural capital value at time t due to agricultural change (Figure 7.1). Without policy intervention the environmental value is expected to fall during the period to t^1. However, the environmental value of the area can be maintained by protecting habitats and landscape. With a higher level of incentives some enhancement of the capital would take place leading to a recovery in value. At time t^1 the public benefit from ESA policy under Tier 1 is measured by the distance a between the 'no policy' value and the value associated with a 'protection' policy (Tier 1). The benefit from an 'enhancement' policy (Tier 2) is given by the distance b. In England and Wales there has been an emphasis on the use of the scheme to protect areas against change (using Tier 1 payments). In Scotland, the emphasis has shifted over time to concentrate almost entirely on enhancement through Tier 2 measures; farmers must now enter both Tier 1 and Tier 2 of the scheme. This reflects the more limited threat from agriculture in Scotland where livestock farming predominates and technical progress is limited. Typically, enhancement measures include reductions in stocking rate, bird-friendly grass cutting dates, measures to improve woodland (for example by stock exclusion), fencing of water margins and measures to protect archaeological sites.

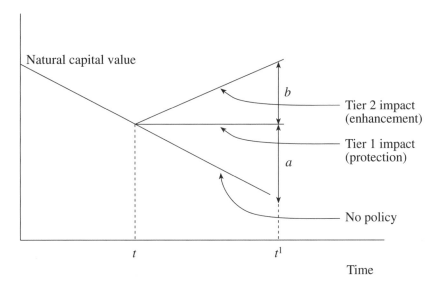

Figure 7.1   Benefits from ESA policy

OTHER AGRI-ENVIRONMENTAL SCHEMES

A number of other schemes were introduced in the 1980s and 1990s to address environmental issues not covered by the ESA scheme. The principal ones which either have primary or secondary impacts on biodiversity and landscape, or may facilitate the public use of such benefits, are:

- Countryside Stewardship (CSS);
- Nitrate Sensitive Areas (NSA);
- Organic Aid Scheme;
- Habitat Scheme; and
- Countryside Access Scheme.

Table 7.1 indicates the areas under agreement in England under each of the schemes, with the expenditure in payments to farmers in 1998/99 (from Coates, 1999). Other countries in the UK tend to have similar schemes adapted to regional conditions. Compared with the public expenditure on agricultural support the spending on the agri-environment is quite limited and this has been a source of constant criticism from interest groups.

Table 7.1   Major agri-environmental schemes in England

Scheme	Area under agreement (ha)	Public expenditure 1998/99 (£m)
Environmentally Sensitive Areas	516 000	38.0
Countryside Stewardship	162 000	20.0
Nitrate Sensitive Areas	28 000	4.8
Organic Aid Scheme	15 000	1.5
Habitat Scheme	6 900	1.8
Countryside Access Scheme	1 600	0.08
TOTAL	729 500	66.18

Countryside Stewardship[1]

The Countryside Commission in England developed this scheme as a means of protecting and enhancing habitats and landscape, and providing public access to farmland (Countryside Commission, 1992). The targeting in this scheme is by habitat/landscape type, concentrating on valued types outside ESAs such as limestone grasslands and lowland heath. The scheme uses a similar management agreement approach to ESAs but is discretionary in that farmers who apply pass through a selection procedure designed to concentrate the expenditure on those farms and environmental goods that will provide the greatest value for money for the public. MAFF took the scheme over in 1996 and it is now part-financed under the EU agri-environmental measures (Regulation 2078/92).

Nitrate Sensitive Areas (NSA)

This scheme was established under national financing in 1990 in response to the anticipated EU Nitrates Directive (MAFF, 1994). It targeted 32 zones where the nitrate level in surface water was at, or was greater than, the EU limit of 50 mg per litre. Farmers were offered a set of voluntary options to change agricultural practices and reduce nitrate leaching, each option having an associated standard payment. The options were based on reductions in fertilizer usage, conversion of arable land to grassland, use of cover crops and control of organic manure spreading. Incentive payments were offered, based on calculated opportunity costs in order to encourage voluntary participation. Manteuffel Szoege *et al.* (1996) assessed the cost effectiveness of the different options offered. The scheme was effective in changing land use and reducing nitrate leaching, although the aim of achieving the European standard was not always achieved through the voluntary approach. Options that required relatively minor changes to farming practices (for example limited reductions in fertilizer use) were not effective in achieving the required changes in nitrate leaching.

The scheme was primarily driven by human health considerations and impending legislation. Whilst the changes to land use and water quality might be expected to benefit biodiversity, no detailed investigation into these secondary benefits has been made. The scheme is now being wound up and the regulatory measures defined in the Nitrates Directive are being implemented to address excess nitrate problems. Hence, an incentive approach to environmental protection is being replaced by a regulatory and uncompensated one. It reflects a shift in property rights given that the directive defines an upper limit on collective rights to emit nitrates. More pragmatically, however, the incentive-based NSA scheme was a mechanism for obtaining rapid reductions in emissions without major income effects on producers in sensitive catchments.

Organic Aid Scheme

Under this scheme, farmers were offered payments to assist in the conversion to organic farming (MAFF, 1997). It has now been superseded with similar schemes offering higher payment levels. The main aim of the Organic Aid Scheme was to facilitate a supply of 'healthier' food in a situation where the disruption of output and income during the prolonged conversion process might prevent adoption of organic techniques. By reducing the use of fertilizers and pesticides the scheme should indirectly confer conservation benefits through improvements to some wildlife habitats and to water quality. However, such potential benefits depend critically on the intensity and management of farms prior to entering the scheme. On arable or intensive livestock farms some conservation benefits would be expected but much would depend on the scale of organic farming in an area. However, the fixed payment system is most attractive to farms where the costs of conversion are lowest, and gains to the environment will be correspondingly small. The majority of organically farmed land is grassland with very limited uptake on arable and horticultural holdings. In Scotland, the great majority of entrant farms have been in upland areas where use of inorganic fertilizer is minimal. Here, no clear evidence has emerged of benefits to biodiversity at least in the short-term.

Habitat Scheme

This scheme embodies a much more radical approach to habitat creation than anything contained in the ESA or CSS schemes. It aimed to create new habitat with high perceived environmental value from land previously in farming. The types of priority habitat differ between countries and include upland scrub, lowland heath, saltmarsh, water margins and former set-aside land. This is a scheme with the clear aim of enhancing the area of priority habitat. The additionality of the payments is thus more obvious as compared with the ESA and CSS schemes, where much of the expenditure is on environmental protection. Even so, the costs of creating new habitat are high, particularly on arable land, because of the loss of agricultural output and associated support. The payment levels offered have not been sufficient to attract a high uptake (Table 7.1) and this possibly reflects some caution on the part of policymakers about the value to the public of additional farmland habitat. The long (20-year) contract period between farmer and government may also have limited entry (HM Government, 1997). This scheme has now been closed to new entrants.

Countryside Access

Under this scheme, payments are made to farmers who permit public access to set-aside land for informal recreation. Uptake has been low (1600 ha) and there is little available information on the benefits obtained. It follows a pilot scheme run by the Countryside Commission on set-aside land, later extended to form an option under the Countryside Stewardship Scheme (see above). An appraisal of the value for money of such incentive payments for public access by the author (Crabtree, 1997) suggested that they produce variable but generally quite limited benefits in relation to the exchequer costs involved. Low value for money reflects deficiencies in the quality of access and in the information about new access available to the public. Together, these factors resulted in low rates of use by the public of the access procured under the schemes.

MECHANISMS FOR PROVIDING NATURE CONSERVATION

The UK government has used a variety of methods for protecting and enhancing natural assets and the range is described in Colman *et al.* (1992). The type of instrument can be related to the underlying presumed property rights and the associated legislation. For example, under European environmental legislation the emphasis is on environmental protection and the removal of rights to damage the environment. Regulation is the normal route to environmental protection with economic instruments less commonly applied. Despite the limitations of regulatory instruments they are preferred in policy because of their simplicity and reliability. Under the Nitrates Directive, to give one example, water quality and river ecology are protected through restrictions on farming activities defined in local action plans. Previous presumed 'rights' to emit nitrates are thus removed without compensation.

A rather different principle has been applied for the protection of special biodiversity sites (SSSIs and sites designated under the Birds Directive and Habitats Directive). Here, farmers receive compensation for the imposition of restrictions on damaging activities. However, only those farmers wishing to engage in such operations are compensated. This is an example of what Hanley *et al.* (1998) call a Beneficiary Pays Principle, with taxpayers providing the compensation and a subset of the public being the beneficiaries. Whitby and Saunders (1996) have explored the efficiency of such payment systems and conclude that they are more cost-effective than fixed incentives. Nevertheless, negotiated payments systems have become discredited on several counts. It was widely perceived that the compensation process was characterized by hidden information (Williamson, 1985) where the public agency is not well informed about the decision making and opportunity costs of the landowners. It has encouraged some farmers to propose damage artificially, with the intention of obtaining excessive levels of compensation for not proceeding with damaging actions. Negotiations have often been protracted and associated with high legal fees; this has created an aura of conflict between farmers and environmental agencies. This made environmental protection an increasingly contentious and litigious issue and has driven policy towards a more incentive-based approach (Leonard, 1982). In the economics literature, the alternative contract designs form part of a wider literature dealing with principal–agent issues and public procurement (Arrow, 1991).

Operating under the CAP agri-environment Regulations 797/85 and 2078/92, the UK government has used incentive payments as the principal mechanism to deliver agri-environmental output. The state thus creates a quasi-market in environmental goods in which output is procured from those farmers wishing to supply at the price set by government or its agencies. The mechanism is a contract in the form of a management agreement in which a farmer agrees to a set of actions in exchange for a payment. MAFF (1991) provide an economic justification for this procurement by indicating that taxpayers will fund general protection and enhancement of the countryside through funded schemes where direct market mechanisms do not exist. Payments would also be made for contracts that restrict farming activities where these go beyond 'good agricultural practice'. Hence property rights over the environment were seen to rest firmly with farmers leaving the state to intervene, where it was considered appropriate, through voluntary schemes. In this situation, farmers aiming to maximize income cannot lose since they will only participate if this enhances income.

Fixed payment incentive schemes are not entirely cost-efficient in procuring conservation output. This is illustrated in Figure 7.2. The curve S is the supply curve for 'conservation' on farms eligible for a conservation scheme. It reflects the fact that different farms will have different opportunity costs for adhering to a management agreement. If all farms are paid a price p^1, A is supplied and the hatched area is the rent payment over and above the minimum procurement cost for each farm. It represents the policy dead-weight. The problem for policy is that the costs of participation of individual farms are unknown and, where this is the case, the only feasible incentive system is to offer a fixed payment. The contract problem is exacerbated when farms have different qualities of biodiversity and this information is not available to the policymakers when fixing payment. Payments then cannot be differentiated according to the value of the environmental goods on offer and the problem of 'adverse selection' becomes even greater. However, fixed payments do have the merit of simplicity and this reduces transaction costs. They also remove the conflict that often occurs when prices are negotiated separately with each producer.

The inefficiencies in fixed payments have stimulated the search for more effective contract design to reduce policy costs. Some efficiency gains can be achieved through price segmentation. In Figure 7.2, if higher cost producers can be identified and offered a price p^2 to deliver an extra area $(B–A)$ there is a

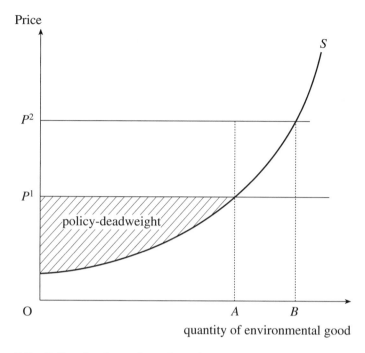

Figure 7.2   Policy dead-weight under a fixed payment incentive system

substantial saving as compared with the total cost of offering all farmers p^2. Crabtree *et al.* (2000) explore the benefits from discretionary schemes where farms are selected according to the value of the environmental output procured. In their example quite large investments could be justified to obtain information on which discretionary entry could be exercised. The Countryside Stewardship Scheme in England uses such a discretionary system to increase its value for money. Scoring of farms for biodiversity potential is increasingly being adopted to improve the effectiveness of agri-environmental schemes by selecting those where the highest value of output can be procured per pound spent. A number of recent studies have explored the extent to which other instruments such as auctions, that elicit information from farmers, might also be used to increase the efficiency of procuring environmental goods (for example Latacz-Lohmann and Van der Hamsvoort, 1997; Moxey *et al.*, 1999).

Policy Effectiveness

The predominant method used in the EU to procure environmental output from farming has been to establish incentive payment systems. These have resulted in substantial sums being paid to farmers, although it is important to bear in mind that they represent only a fraction of the cost of agricultural support. Even so, schemes are regularly monitored and reviewed in order to determine their effectiveness.

Voluntary schemes can only be effective if sufficient numbers of farmers participate to allow objectives to be achieved. It is self-evident that if payments are pitched too low or scheme conditions are perceived as too onerous, then the scheme will fail through low uptake. A number of agri-environmental schemes in the UK have suffered this fate due to excessive caution or miscalculation on the part of the schemes' designers. In some cases the EU Commission's rules on maximum payment levels have restricted payment levels and contributed to policy failure. Some variation in the level of policy success seems inevitable given that policymakers are attempting to design measures with little information either on the economic value of the environment or on farmers' reactions to specific measures.

Participation Rates

Uptake levels in the ESA scheme have been quite variable. In England, in the 22 ESAs, it averages just under 50 per cent of the eligible area. The range is from 5 to 92 per cent. For the 10 Scottish ESAs uptake was 44 per cent of the eligible area in 1997, varying by area from 26–75 per cent (Crabtree *et al.*, 1999). It is not easy to interpret these figures. Policymakers appear to consider a 50–60 per cent uptake as satisfactory but this has no clear basis apart from the fact that with such an uptake level the majority of the ESA area is protected.

If the policy aim is to maintain and enhance the stock of biodiversity and landscape assets then the required participation rate depends on the expected rate of loss under a policy-off scenario. Figure 7.3 describes two possible situations in which an incentive policy designed to both protect and enhance natural capital is in operation. In Case *A*, there is no benefit from protection measures since no depreciation in natural capital is anticipated even if participation in the scheme is zero. Any benefits are those from enhancement. In this case, the higher the uptake rate the greater the enhancement but payments to farmers for protection are wasted – these payments simply pay farmers for doing what they would have done anyway. In this situation policy effectiveness is greatest if all the measures are targeted at enhancement. This approximates to the Scottish ESAs where threats of major environmental loss are not easy to identify and policy is directed at Tier 2 (enhancement) measures. The key issue here is the value of the enhanced biodiversity and landscape in relation to policy costs.

By contrast, under situation *B* there is an expected deterioration in biodiversity and landscape under the policy-off scenario, characterized by a

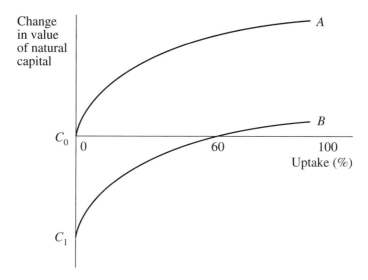

Figure 7.3   Effect of participation rate on protection and enhancement of natural capital

reduction in natural capital from C_0 to C_1 at zero uptake in the figure. A 60 per cent participation rate is needed simply to stabilize the situation, with additional investment by entrants compensating for losses in natural capital on non-entrant farms. Where the threat is from radical destruction of assets, such as occurred in the original Halvergate Marshes context, a 100 per cent uptake might need to be the target in order to protect existing habitats. With the diminishing threat from such land use change the emphasis of the ESA scheme has rightly shifted towards enhancement measures (HM Government, 1997).

Biodiversity and Landscape Benefits from Agri-environmental Schemes

Quantifying the benefits from agri-environmental policies has proved a contentious issue in the UK. In the political context it is the areas under agreement (that is participation) and the perceived 'value' of the associated biodiversity that is presented as the prime measure of success (Coates, 1999). There is an implication that biodiversity would have been lost without the policy, but evidence for this is not easy to find. That said, there are major difficulties in evaluation because the counterfactual (policy-off) situation cannot be observed, hence removing the baseline for comparison. And the ecological response in habitats and species generally takes place over a long time period making measurement of policy benefits difficult. Even so, ecological monitoring has been extensive. In England, in the 1996–97 round, a number of positive effects were noted (Hanley *et al.*, 1999). These were:

- In the South Downs ESA, landscape quality had been enhanced due to reversion from arable land to grassland;
- Declines in meadow diversity had been halted, and in some cases reversed, in the Pennine Dales;
- Bird numbers increased in the Somerset Levels and Moors ESA, compared with a situation of rapid decline prior to the policy being introduced;
- However, land outside the ESA boundary and on non-agreement land had experienced intensification in the Somerset levels and Pennine Dales.

In Scotland, ecological monitoring over periods of 5 and 10 years has tended to find little change in target habitats on participant farms. Biodiversity in ESAs is being maintained but there is little evidence for enhancement. For example, where farmers are paid to fence woodland to prevent grazing by livestock and encourage natural regeneration, tree regeneration from seed has not generally succeeded due to grazing by deer or growth of rank vegetation. It has become apparent that many such ecological processes are either too complex or not well enough understood to allow a simple set of contractual conditions to be written that will ensure success. Nevertheless valuable experience on the ecology of habitat creation is being obtained and this should lead to more successful management in the future.

Asking farmers about the ways the scheme has affected their farming activities is another route for discovering the likely environmental impact of the scheme. Crabtree *et al.* (1999) interviewed farmers participating in the Scottish ESA scheme. Impacts on farming varied between ESAs but were small overall. Only 12–13 per cent of farmers had changed fertilizer or spray levels but 12 per cent of farmers had not undertaken potentially damaging drainage or reclamation that they would otherwise have undertaken. The scheme was thus performing an environmental protection role by preventing some changes to land use. Changes in variable costs and output as a consequence of entry were generally very small. Some reductions in sheep output were recorded, particularly in the Southern Uplands, where most of the stock reduction was concentrated. Elsewhere, impacts on stock numbers and enterprise gross margins were generally quite small. To some extent this reflects the low total expenditure under the scheme on stock disposal (5.4 per cent of total ESA payments). Where the prescription required stock control, fencing off wetland or woodland and so on it appeared that farmers were able to accommodate this without any great impact on their businesses, for example by renting additional land or entering habitat areas in the scheme that had little agricultural value. Overall, it is difficult to find evidence of pervasive extensification as an outcome of the scheme; farmers were in most cases able to propose a prescription that resulted in minimal changes to their farming activities.

A limited impact of the scheme on farming might be interpreted as indicating low additionality for the conservation objectives of the scheme; that is farmers were being paid for what they were doing anyway. There was clearly no shift to more extensified, low input systems typically associated with high nature value farming. Much higher payments and tighter prescriptions would be needed to produce this effect. Any benefits were therefore localized to specific habitats or features that were often peripheral in a business sense. Quite substantial payments (25 per cent of the total costs of the scheme) were made for archaeology and non-habitats (mainly dyking), where impacts on farming would be minimal. Twenty-four per cent of expenditure was on woodland and wetland which again was likely to play a very limited agricultural role. Other measures such as water margins and herb-rich pasture were generally peripheral to the business or could be accommodated with minimal cost. Only longer-term monitoring will indicate the extent of the benefits produced by these measures.

An encouraging sign for conservation in the long-term was the fact that the majority of entrants indicated a greater interest in conservation since joining the scheme, although almost half indicated that they would revert to some pre-ESA practices if the payments stopped. The conclusion is that quite a lot of the less durable ESA benefits could be lost if the scheme were terminated, especially if farmers were under financial pressure at that time.

Benefits to the Public

Various researchers have tried to estimate the welfare benefits to the public from agri-environmental measures. They have typically used contingent valuation as the method, eliciting the public's willingness to pay (WTP) for the anticipated benefits. In the Scottish ESA context, respondents are given a description of the expected changes in biodiversity following imposition of the policy, together with photomontages to illustrate the likely landscape effects (Hanley *et al.*, 1996). Table 7.2 summarizes the household WTP estimates from the main studies where the public were segmented into local residents, visitors and the remainder. As might be expected, valuations by local residents and visitors tend to be higher since these groups benefit directly from access to the area. The general public valuation primarily reflects the existence value benefits. Nevertheless, it is the general public's WTP that dominates the total benefit procured under a scheme, and this has

Table 7.2   Mean household WTP estimates for ESAs (£/year)

ESA	Residents (£)	Visitors (£)	General public (£)
Hanley *et al.* (1996)			
Breadalbane	31.4[1]	98.0[2]	22.0[1] (42–57)[2]
Machair	13.7[1]	378.0[2]	13.4[1] (48–78)[2]
Willis *et al.* (1993)			
South Downs	27.52[1]	19.47[1]	1.98[1]
Somerset Levels	17.53[2]	11.84[1]	2.45[1]
Gourlay (1995)			
Loch Lomond	20.6[1]	1.98[1] (individual, per visit)	not estimated
Stewartry	13.0[1]	2.53[1] (individual, per visit)	not estimated
Bullock and Kay (1997)			
Southern Uplands	not estimated	69.0[3]	83.0[3]

Notes:
1   open-ended
2   discrete choice, adjusted
3   discrete choice

in most cases been considerably greater than the cost of the scheme to the exchequer. Thus in cost–benefit terms the schemes appear to pay off very substantially with ratios of net value to exchequer costs varying from 3:1 to more than 260:1. The same conclusion can be drawn from Hanley (1990) and Foster and Mourato (1997) who evaluated benefits from the Nitrate Sensitive Area and Organic Aid schemes respectively.

However, whilst the CVM evaluations have been avidly used by politicians to justify agri-environmental expenditure they have been subject to considerable criticism. The methodological problems associated with contingent valuation are well documented, particularly those of part–whole bias and yea saying. More specifically, there are difficulties both in specifying the counterfactual and the impacts of policy. Mis-representation of either would affect the net benefit. Typical scenarios presented to the public suggest clear deterioration of habitats without an ESA policy (the counterfactual) and significant enhancement under the ESA policy. Such expectations as have been used about the size and scale of benefits look increasingly unrealistic as evidence is gathered about the impact of ESAs on farming practices (Crabtree *et al.*, 1999). The net effect of the policy is then unduly optimistic because 'there is a failure to establish a clear and realistic description of the likely outcome of the policy' (Hodge and McNally, 1998).

Benefits to Farmers and Local Economies

Most farmers look to their businesses to provide an adequate income. In deciding whether to participate in incentive policies there is no shortage of evidence that the potential for income gains dominates farmers' decisions. Farmers with a strong interest in nature conservation may require less in the way of income benefit or even be prepared to part-finance investment (Crabtree and Appleton, 1992). The income support offered by an ESA-type policy can be important in producing conservation benefits if it keeps farmers in business and prevents structural change that may be environmentally damaging. In the Scottish study (Crabtree *et al.*, 1999) this effect varied markedly between regions depending on how much pressure there was on farm incomes. In some ESAs no farmers were intending to leave farming, whereas in the Western Isles and Cairngorms 30 per cent indicated that without the ESA payments they would have given up farming because of low incomes. There are also benefits to local economies as farmers spend on ESA-related supplies and may increase other farm investment or household consumption. All these effects are important to a political assessment of agri-environmental policies, because the agri-environmental measures are assessed for what they contribute to overall agricultural policy objectives.

Crabtree *et al.* (1999) undertook the most detailed UK investigation into the income benefits from ESA policy. Not only were the net income gains to farmers calculated but also the employment creation from the net injection of spending by farmers into the local economy. Table 7.3 summarizes the impacts. In Scotland, the ESA scheme was expected to pay £23.4m to 1 349 entrants, an average of £17 361 per household. In 1997 the mean increase in household income across the 10 ESAs was £3 359 and, after taking into account the knock-on effects of farmer spending associated with the scheme the total expected job creation was 514 full-time equivalent jobs. These spin-off effects of agri-environmental policy are substantial and enhance its appeal to policymakers because of the support they can give to remoter rural areas.

CONCLUSIONS

There can be no doubt that the major agri-environmental schemes in the UK have produced nature conservation benefits. They have proved politically acceptable to government and farmers as clear evidence of a commitment to protect landscapes and biodiversity, and to engage in a positive partnership

Table 7.3 *Summary of economic impacts in Scottish ESAs*

ESA Scheme	Number of Entrants at 1st Nov 1997	Payments committed at 1st Nov 1997 (£000)	Mean payment per entrant (£)	Principal prescription elements[1]	Mean increase in household income, 1997 (£)	Net injection of income into local economy (£000)	Employment creation (FTEs)[3]
Cairngorm Straths	82	1 841	22 450	Woodland, wetland	+5 524	405	39
Loch Lomond	36	669	18 582	Woodland, stock control	+3 129	214	19
Breadalbane	104	2 120	20 383	Woodland, herb rich pasture, non-habitat payment[2]	+4 360	483	43
Shetland Islands	197	1 782	9 048	Grassland bird measures, stock control	+1 747	329	32
Western Isles Machair	187	919	4 915	Grassland bird measures, cropping with seaweed	+1 205	677	64

Argyll Islands	215	3 227	15 011	Grassland bird measures, wetland, herb rich pasture	+4 955	686	65
Western Southern Uplands	104	2 655	25 531	Non-habitat payment, stock control	+5 480	573	51
Central Southern Uplands	187	4 538	24 266	Stock control, non-habitat payment	+1 782	619	69
Stewartry	163	4 236	25 985	Non-habitat payment, archaeology	+3 901	1 081	110
Central Borders	74	1 434	19 375	Non-habitat payment, woodland	+788	N/a	23
Total	1 349	23 421	17 361		+3 359	N/a	514

Note:
1 elements ordered by expenditure up to 50% of the total expenditure
2 mainly dyking (building stone walls)
3 full-time equivalent jobs

for stewardship of the countryside. The National Audit Office's (1997) study of ESAs concluded that the five initial ESAs had been 'generally successful in maintaining the traditional character of the landscape and arresting environment decline'. However, the cost of the schemes in relation to the possibly limited extent of the benefits has left a degree of scepticism amongst some economists. Whitby (2000) states that 'key questions remain to be answered'. Whilst the risk of major loss from land use change has been averted, evidence for other benefits in some ESAs has proved difficult to find. Colman (1994) concludes that ESA policy in some areas has 'achieved comparatively little' since 'farmers are rewarded for doing what they would in any case do'. The environmental lobby has been more muted in its criticism, preferring instead to focus on adjusting policy in directions that they regard as most beneficial. Even so, the ESA type of scheme has become increasingly divorced from mainstream environmental policy where the driving force has been biodiversity targets for habitats and species following the Rio summit and Agenda 21. Clear threats to specific areas from agricultural change have also receded. The pressures for the future are thus focused on obtaining greater policy cohesion and effectiveness in procuring environmental enhancement.

Effectiveness means obtaining greater additionality and value for money from expenditure. This involves a move to instruments that involve discretion on the part of policymakers to select farms and proposals by farmers. Scoring systems are being used in more recent schemes as a crude system of valuing the environmental assets procured from spending. Even so, these are subject to their own limitations since they tend to select large diverse farms and omit those with fewer habitats regardless of habitat quality. There may yet be a greater shift to so-called challenge funding where farmers are asked to bid for available funds in order to drive down the rents to farmers. Falconer and Whitby (1999) have raised the issue of high transaction costs associated with some agri-environmental measures. These are borne both by government and by farmers and need to be taken into account in assessing the performance of different instruments.

Greater policy cohesion is being achieved through stronger linkages between agri-environmental and other agricultural and environmental policies. In particular some effort is being made to link agri-environmental policy more firmly both to environmental policy and other agricultural objectives including Less-Favoured Area policy. The new Rural Development Regulation (1257/1999) provides the framework in which this is occurring (CEC, 1999). There is also a more transparent underlying rationale to agri-environment expenditure – that it should be used to purchase specific public goods and services for which priorities have been defined.

A major concern with existing policies, which typically have 5-year contracts, is what happens if government or participants choose not to renew contracts. In the Scottish ESA study it was encouraging that the majority of entrants said that the scheme had increased their interest in wildlife conservation. However, half of the entrants indicated that they would revert to some or all of the pre-ESA practices if payments were to stop. The extent of reversion was dependent on the income pressures faced by farmers; those under pressure to maintain incomes would revert to previous practices most readily. This suggests that cessation of a scheme could lead to a loss of much of the investment in biodiversity that had taken place under the scheme.

Governments are likely to face difficulty with payment schemes that continue into the very long term. Such commitments limit the flexibility to engage in new conservation initiatives as priorities change over time. In addition, payment levels may need to increase over time where farm systems that enhance biodiversity diverge progressively over time from those that maximize farm incomes. In this situation, the cost of maintaining biodiversity will inevitably increase and greater prioritization will be needed. Evidence for this trend is not difficult to obtain. Further ESAs will not be designated in the UK, and in the future existing ESA entrants will have to compete under discretionary arrangements. The effect will be that some farms currently participating in the ESA scheme will no longer be eligible. There is also a shift towards greater regulation and cross-compliance as a means of protecting the environment. This places the burden on farmers rather than the taxpayer. The UK government, for example, has stopped the NSA scheme leaving the weaker regulatory measures of the Nitrates Directive to operate, and widespread cross-compliance measures are being introduced as part of Regulation 1257/1999 (CEC, 1999).

In the UK we are seeing policy moving away from targeted areas towards payments to procure protection and enhancement of specified habitats and landscapes. Increasing the area under organic agriculture is also a priority. There appears to be considerable public support for these policies, as indicated in the contingent valuation and other studies. However, even in special landscapes, such as those targeted under the CSS scheme, one might question whether taxpayers will be willing to pay the increasing cost of large-scale intervention to maintain historic practices and their associated landscapes for an indefinite period.

NOTE

1. A similar scheme, Tir Cymen, has been operated in Wales.

REFERENCES

Arrow, K.J. (1991), 'The economics of agency', in J.W. Pratt and R.J. Zeckhauser (eds), *Principals and Agents: the Structure of Business*, Boston: Harvard Business School Press, pp. 37–54.

Bowers, J.K. and P.C. Cheshire (1983), *Agriculture, the Countryside and Land Use: An Economic Critique*, London: Methuen.

Bullock, C.H. and J. Kay, (1997), 'Preservation and change in the upland landscape: the public benefits of grazing management', *Journal of Environmental Planning and Management*, **40**, 315–34.

CEC (1999), *Council Regulation (EC) 1257/1999*, Official Journal of the European Communities, L160/80, 26.6.99, Brussels: Commission of the European Communities.

Coates, D. (1999), 'The implementation of agri-environmental policies', in S.T.D. Turner and D. Alford (eds), *Agriculture and the Environment: Challenges and Conflicts for the New Millennium*, Wolverhampton: ADAS, pp. 26–35.

Colman, D. (1994), 'Comparative evaluation of environmental policies', in M. Whitby (ed.), *Incentives for Countryside Management, The Case of Environmentally Sensitive Areas*, Wallingford: CAB International, pp. 219–52.

Colman, D. and N. Lee (1988), *Evaluation of the Broads Grazing Marshes Conservation Scheme 1985–1988*, Manchester: Department of Agricultural Economics, University of Manchester.

Colman, D., J.R. Crabtree, J. Froud and L. O'Carroll (1992), *Comparative Effectiveness of Conservation Mechanisms*, Manchester: Department of Agricultural Economics, University of Manchester.

Countryside Commission (1992), *Countryside Stewardship, an Outline*, CCP346, Cheltenham: Countryside Commission.

Crabtree, J.R. (1997), 'The supply of public access to the countryside – a value for money and institutional analysis of incentive policies', *Environment and Planning* (A29), 1465–1476.

Crabtree, J.R. and Z. Appleton (1992), 'Economic evaluation of the farm woodland premium scheme', *Journal of Agricultural Economics*, **43**, 355–67.

Crabtree, J.R., J. Potts and T. Smart (2000), 'Statistical modelling of incentive design under limited information – The case of public access to farmland', *Journal of Agricultural Economics*, **51**, 239–51.

Crabtree, J.R., A. Thorburn, N. Chalmers, D. Roberts, G. Wynn, N. Barron, F. Barraclough and D. Macmillan (1999), *Socio-economic and Agricultural Impacts of the Environmentally Sensitive Areas Scheme in Scotland,* Economics and Policy Series 6, Aberdeen: Macaulay Land Use Research Institute.

Falconer, K. and M. Whitby (1999), 'The invisible costs of scheme implementation and administration' in G. Van Huylenbroeck and M. Whitby (eds), *Countryside Stewardship: Farmers, Policies and Markets*, Oxford: Elsevier Science, pp. 67–88.

Foster, V. and S. Mourato (1997), 'Behavioural consistency, statistical specification and validity of the contingent ranking method: evidence from a survey of the impacts of pesticide use in the UK', *CSERGE Working Paper 97–09*, Norwich: University of East Anglia.

Gourlay, D. (1995), *Loch Lomond and Stewartry ESAs: a Study of Public Perceptions of Policy Benefits*, Unpublished PhD Thesis, University of Aberdeen.

Hanley, N.D. (1990), 'The economics of nitrate pollution', *European Review of Agricultural Economics*, **17**, 129–51.

Hanley, N., H. Kirkpatrick, I. Simpson and D. Oglethorpe (1998), 'Principles for the provision of public goods from agriculture: Modelling moorland conservation in Scotland', *Land Economics*, **74**, 102–13.

Hanley, N., I. Simpson, D. Parsisson, D. Macmillan, C. Bullock, and R. Crabtree (1996), *Valuation of the Conservation Benefits of Environmentally Sensitive Areas*, Economics and Policy Series 2, Aberdeen: Macaulay Land Use Research Institute.

Hanley, N., M. Whitby and I. Simpson (1999), 'Assessing the success of agri-environmental policy in the UK', *Land Use Policy*, **16**, 67–80.

HM Government (1997), 'Environmentally sensitive areas and other schemes under the agri-environmental regulation', *Response of the Government to the Second Report (1996–1997) from the Agriculture Committee, Cm 3707*, London: HMSO.

Hodge, I. and S. McNally (1998), 'Evaluating the environmentally sensitive areas: the value of rural environments and policy relevance', *Journal of Rural Studies*, **14**, 357–67.

Latacz-Lohmann, U. and C.P.C.M. van der Hamsvoort (1997), 'Auctioning conservation contracts; a theoretical analysis and an application', *American Journal of Agricultural Economics*, **79**(2), 407–18.

Leonard, P. (1982), 'Management agreements: a tool for conservation', *Journal of Agricultural Economics*, **33**, 351.

MAFF (1991), *Our Farming Future*, London: Ministry of Agriculture, Fisheries and Food.

MAFF (1994), *The New Nitrate Sensitive Areas Scheme*, London: Ministry of Agriculture, Fisheries and Food.

MAFF (1997), *Review of the Organic Aid Scheme*, London: Ministry of Agriculture, Fisheries and Food.

Manteuffel Szoege, H., J.R. Crabtree and A. Edwards (1996), 'Policy cost-effectiveness for reducing non-point agricultural groundwater pollution in the UK', *Journal of Environmental Planning and Management*, **39**, 205–22.

Moxey, A., B. White and A. Ozanne (1999), 'Efficient contract design for agri-environmental policy', *Journal of Agricultural Economics*, **50**, 187–202.

National Audit Office (1997), *Protecting Environmentally Sensitive Areas*, London: The Stationery Office.

Whitby, M. (ed.) (1994), *Incentives for Countryside Management, The Case of Environmentally Sensitive Areas*, Wallingford: CAB International.

Whitby, M. (2000), *Challenges and options for the agri-environment*, Presidential address to the Agricultural Economics Society, Manchester.

Whitby, M. and P. Lowe (1994), 'The political and economic roots of environmental policy in agriculture', in M. Whitby (ed.), *Incentives for Countryside Management, The Case of Environmentally Sensitive Areas*, Wallingford: CAB International, pp. 1–24.

Whitby, M. and C. Saunders (1996), 'Estimating the supply of conservation goods in Britain: A comparison of the financial efficiency of two financial instruments', *Land Economics*, **72**, 313–25.

Williamson, O. (1985), *The Economic Institutions of Capitalism*, New York: The Free Press.

Willis, K.G., G.D. Garrod and C.M. Saunders (1993), *Valuation of the South Downs and Somerset Levels and Moors Environmentally Sensitive Area Landscapes by the General Public*, A Report to the Ministry of Agriculture, Fisheries and Food, Newcastle upon Tyne: University of Newcastle upon Tyne, Centre for Rural Economy, Department of Agricultural Economics and Food Marketing.

8. The pivotal role of the agricultural land market in the Netherlands

Jan Luijt and Carel P.C.M. van der Hamsvoort

INTRODUCTION

One of the most significant problems confronting the Netherlands at the start of the 21st century is the use and organization of the limited land available. The high level of economic growth in recent years and the increasing prosperity have resulted in a greatly heightened demand for land for home construction, infrastructure, business premises, and nature and landscape. On the other hand, the amount of land is limited and most of it (69 per cent) is reserved for agriculture. The growth in demand and the limited availability of land is being translated into developments in the real estate market.

In the Netherlands, however, the real estate market is not a free market. The government regulates the use of space by means of the *Wet op de Ruimtelijke Ordening* (WRO; 'Town and Country Planning Act') and thus restricts the allocation options for the available space. Moreover, the development potential of various agricultural and non-agricultural sectors is influenced to a greater or lesser extent by sector-specific policy, such as agricultural policy, nature and landscape policy, and environmental policy. All these developments affect the supply of and demand for land in the Netherlands, which has important consequences for the developmental possibilities of different economic sectors.

The central theme in this chapter is an analysis of the effect both of government policies in respect of agriculture, nature and landscape, and the environment and developments in agricultural and non-agricultural sectors on the price of agricultural land. The empirical relevance of this analysis is to be found in the crucial role played by the agricultural land market in the achievement of policy objectives for the environment, nature and landscape, and the developmental possibilities of agricultural enterprises. Moreover, a number of recent developments suggest the existence of conflicting policy in this area. A couple of examples will illustrate this point.

Since the mid-nineties, the necessary expansion of acreage of continuable agricultural enterprises has been stagnating due to numerous non-agricultural claims and the ensuing resettlement of farmers who have been bought out. And even if land is on offer in the vicinity of the farms, it is often too expensive for farmers due to high land prices. In addition, the process of handing over the land to the next generation is becoming increasingly costly, because succession is taxed on the basis of the increased price of land on lease. Finally, higher land prices are causing the amount of regularly leased acreage to decrease more rapidly. Although the price of leased land also continues to rise, the difference with the free land price is becoming greater, so that the capital gain for the lessor on purchase of the freehold is greater.

Higher land prices stimulate the use of fertilizers, since they form a substitute for land in the case of a considerable number of agricultural crops.[1] As a result, environmental pollution caused by agriculture increases, seriously threatening a number of policy objectives in respect of the environment. Moreover, high agricultural land prices, combined with limited land mobility, hinder land acquisition by the *Dienst Landelijk Gebied* (DLG; 'Countryside Department') and thus the realization of the expansion of the *Ecologische Hoofdstructuur* (EHS; 'Ecological Main Structure').[2] More and more money is required for the purchase of nature reserves and nature development areas and agricultural nature conservation demands increasingly higher payments.

The structure of this chapter is as follows. The next section begins with a description of the real estate market segments, after which we focus on the agricultural real estate market segment. Developments in agriculture and agricultural policy that influence the price of agricultural land will be examined. This is to be followed by an examination of the extent to which 'non-agricultural' developments are responsible for the development of the price of land in the agricultural segment of the real estate market. The following section examines the relative importance of a number of different agricultural and 'non-agricultural' factors affecting the level of the 'agricultural' land price. Finally, this chapter offers a conclusion and a look at the future.

SEGMENTATION OF THE REAL ESTATE MARKET VIA THE *WET RUIMTELIJKE ORDENING*

The government via the 'Town and Country Planning Act' regulates land use in the Netherlands. By means of dos and don'ts, it lays down what use is or is not permitted to the private sector at a given location. The justification for this is derived from the conviction that government intervention in town and country planning is of benefit to society since the free market is found wanting on two counts. In the first place, because the utilization of land by one user may in some cases have negative consequences (negative external effects) for the welfare of the user of the neighbouring land. For example, the welfare of the inhabitants of a residential area may be negatively affected when adjacent plots are used for an industrial estate or rubbish dump. And secondly, because of the public nature of some uses of land, such as dams, roads, nature reserves, and so on.

For various reasons, the result is that the Dutch territory, consisting of 3.4 million hectares of land (and 0.8 million hectares of water), was allocated as follows in 1996: 69 per cent for agriculture, 14 per cent for 'green' activities such as woodlands and nature reserves areas and 16 per cent for 'red' activities such as housing and other buildings, traffic, and recreation, and so on (see Table 8.1).

Table 8.1   Land use in the Netherlands (1996)

Use	Size (× 1000 ha)	Share of total (%)
Agricultural	2 351	69.4
Woodlands	323	9.5
Nature	138	4.1
Recreation	83	2.4
Housing	224	6.6
Other buildings	96	2.8
Traffic	134	4.0
Other land use	39	1.1
Total (excl. water)	3 387	100

Source: Centraal Bureau voor de Statistiek (1997)

In particular, land use for housing, other buildings, traffic and recreation (the so-called 'red' activities), as well as for woodlands and nature reserves (the 'green' activities) has been expanding over recent decades at the expense of land allotted for agriculture. Table 8.2 illustrates this development for the 'red' activities. In the 1950–1995 period, land use for housing and work and infrastructure increased by 88 per cent and 50 per cent respectively, while the area in use for recreation was 22 times greater in 1995 than in 1950.

The distribution of land use would have been completely different if 'town and country planning' had been left entirely to the free market. Under such circumstances, the 'red' area would have been considerably larger than is now the case. This area has been restricted or kept artificially scarce by means of the 'Town and Country Planning Act'. This results in segmented real estate markets. Five segments are distinguished (Centraal Planbureau, 1999): (i) business premises; (ii) housing; (iii) infrastructure; (iv) agriculture

Table 8.2   Development of urban land use 1950–1995 (× 1000 ha)

Year	Housing and work	Recreation	Infrastructure	Total
1950	178.6	3.7	95.1	277.3
1967	220.5	15.4	64.6	300.4
1978	296.1	64.6	126.9	487.6
1989	323.5	78.4	137.4	539.4
1995	336.1	85.0	142.2	563.4

Source: Farjon *et al.* (1997)

and horticulture; and (v) woodlands and nature areas. Within the separate real estate market segments there are sub-segments, each with its own land price. These differences do not result only from the 'Town and Country Planning Act', but also from other laws and regulations. Within the agricultural segment, for example, not all forms of agriculture and horticulture are permitted at every location. Combined with the immobility of agricultural entrepreneurs, this leads to regional sub-markets with permanent regional differences in agricultural land prices. Another example is the *Boswet* ('Woodlands Act'), which designates the locations in the 'woodlands and nature areas' segment that must in any case remain forested, thus creating sub-segments with this segment.

All sub-markets and their components have their own land prices, usually related to the profitability of the permitted land use. Under the pressure of social and economic developments, the 'Town and Country Planning Act', taking the democratic rights of all parties into account, permits continuous modifications of land use. Expansion of real estate market segments at the cost of the agricultural/horticultural segment thus has spin-off effects on the agricultural market segment and affects the 'agricultural' land price. After all, most land is used for agriculture. Thus, segmentation does not mean that the sub-markets cannot affect each other. In consequence of the constant process of reallocating agricultural land, the price of agricultural land is determined not only by its expected profitability in agriculture, but also by its expected value following possible reallocation. The more probable a possible future reallocation of a plot or area becomes, the greater the influence of the new use on the price level. An additional influence on the price of agricultural land in other areas is the resettlement of 'bought-out' agricultural enterprises triggered by the reallocation.

Figure 8.1 illustrates the effect of the 'Town and Country Planning Act' on prices and acreage in three real estate market segments: business, housing and agriculture/horticulture. D_B, D_H, and D_A are the demand curves for land

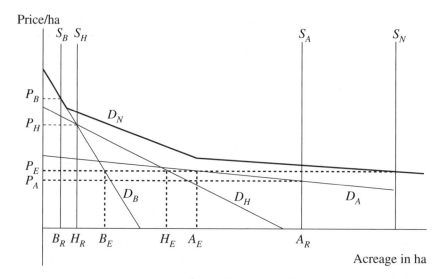

Figure 8.1   The effect of the 'Town and Country Planning Act' on price and acreage in the business, housing and agriculture/horticulture real estate market segments

for business premises, housing and agriculture/horticulture respectively. The bold line shows the cumulative demand curve, D_N. The vertical supply curves S_B, S_H, and S_A indicate the number of hectares on which the 'Town and Country Planning Act' permits business premises, housing and agriculture/horticulture respectively. S_N, finally, shows the amount of land available in the Netherlands (3.4 million hectares). Note that we show only three segments, so that the horizontal sum of the available land in the sub-markets is not equal to the total area of land in the Netherlands. Each real estate market segment has its own land price, which is the result of the interaction between the segmented demand for land and the artificially limited supply. The highest hectare price is found in the business segment (P_B), followed by housing (P_H) and agriculture/horticulture (P_A). The accompanying acreages are B_R, H_R, and A_R. Now imagine that the 'Town and Country Planning Act' disappears and that the allocation of land is left to free market processes. Real estate market segments will disappear and there will be a single hectare price throughout the Netherlands. This equilibrium price (P_E) is shown in the figure at the intersection of the cumulative demand curve (D_N) and the national available acreage (S_N). The accompanying acreages for business, housing and agriculture/horticulture respectively are B_E, H_E and A_E. Under free market processes, the 'red' surface area will increase considerably at the expense of the agricultural and horticultural acreage and the price of land will be higher than the price of agricultural land, but quite a bit lower than the prices in the business and housing segments under the 'Town and Country Planning Act'.

PRICE FORMATION IN THE AGRICULTURAL SEGMENT OF THE REAL ESTATE MARKET

Calculation of the Price of Agricultural Land

With a very strict application of the 'Town and Country Planning Act', the free agricultural land price would primarily be the result of the expected future land yields in agriculture. Under such circumstances, the price of agricultural land is equal to the capitalized future net yield from an extra hectare of land in agriculture (value of marginal product of agricultural land). It is a matter of a simple fraction:

Land price = Net Cash Value land income = land income/(discount rate – growth rate land income)

The discount rate is influenced by expectations with regard to the amount of the future interest, while the annual land income is influenced by the expected growth of land productivity on the one hand and the expected development of the 'agricultural terms of trade' on the other (the quotient of 'prices received by farmers and prices paid by farmers'). Land productivity in agriculture has been improving constantly for decades (Dijksterhuis, 2000). Changes in the expectations of agricultural entrepreneurs with regard to the constant improvement of land productivity and the agricultural terms of trade have great influence on the price of land. An example may clarify this. Income from land amounting to € 1350 per hectare per year and a discount rate of 5 per cent results in a land price of € 27 000 per hectare (€ 1350 / 0.05). Suppose that the expected growth rate of income from the land, through improved land productivity and/or agricultural terms of trade, is 1 per cent per year. The price of the agricultural land will thereby rise by 25 per cent to € 33 750 per hectare (€ 1350 / [0.05–0.01]).

The agricultural terms of trade are greatly influenced by agricultural support, the EU market and price policy (support to trade: intervention and export support), and, via the agricultural terms of trade, the price of agricultural land as well. Gylfason (1995: p. 11) expresses this as follows:

> (....) but in the long run, the benefits of farm support accrue primarily to landowners, and then mostly to those who own the largest estates (Winters, 1987; Martin *et al.*, 1989). This is not surprising. Price support raises rents because land is

essentially fixed in supply, but it cannot raise the return to farm labour, because the potential entry of workers into agriculture from other sectors is unrestricted, and price support cannot be used to prevent the inevitable exit of labour from agriculture. According to Johnson (1991), a sixth or at most a fifth of all farmers in the industrial countries are responsible for two-thirds to three-fourths of all farm sales and receive support commensurately.

A number of factors within agriculture which are of importance for the development of the price of land, such as milk quotas, manure legislation, compulsory extensive land use and alternative applications will now be examined in detail.

Milk Quotas 1984

With regard to the EU market and price policy, it is primarily the milk price supports combined with milk quotas that are of great importance for the price level of agricultural land in the Netherlands. After all, dairy farms make use of two-thirds of the total agricultural acreage in the Netherlands and are thus by far the largest land users. In the first half of the 1980s, the EU decided to employ price supports but to limit the rising production of milk by means of production restrictions. Although the price of land was maintained by the implementation and even expansion of this support, there also arose an indispensable means of production for dairy farmers, which like all other means of production required compensation. In the beginning, the government still attempted to buy up the milk quotas for € 0.30 per kilogram, but soon thereafter (1985) it was calculated that a large group of dairy farmers were able to offer about € 1.15 for a kilogram of levy-free milk (Luijt, 1985). When the government then tried to buy up the milk quota at € 1.15 per kilogram, the quota price had again risen due to the value of the dollar, which by that time had been halved. With the weaker dollar, imported concentrates became very inexpensive, so that the margin on a litre of milk rose even further, ultimately to the present level of nearly € 1.80 per kilogram. Due to the higher quota price, the leeway to pay for the other means of production decreased. Since variable means of production, such as energy, continued to require the same payments as before the superlevy, payment declined in particular for the fixed means of production land and labour. The milk quotas thus had and have a negative effect on the price of land. After all, the cake must now be divided among more means of production.

Manure Legislation 1987

Price supports and their influence on the price of agricultural land have also had other consequences. We are concerned here with the damage to the environment and the landscape. Winters (1990, pp. 254–5) provides an extensive survey:

> It is sometimes argued that farm support enhances visual amenity because it encourages rural population stability and the careful and tidy management of farmland. On the other hand, high output prices encourage intensive cultivation and the use of marginal land, while capital grants and tax expenditures encourage building and land improvement. The result is a tendency towards monoculture, extensive building, the closure of footpaths, the destruction of hedgerows and woodlands, the draining of pastures and the use of chemicals. … Overall, therefore, it is probable that current farm policies do more harm than good to visual amenity.

Although Winters describes the specific situation in the UK, the essence of his ideas equally applies to the Dutch case. In reaction to the damage to the environment, nature and landscape caused by agriculture, the soil protection legislation (*Wet Bodembescherming*) and the manure legislation (*Meststoffenwet*) came into force in 1987 (Baarda, 1999), followed by the *Natuurbeleidsplan* in 1990 ('Nature Policy Plan'; Ministerie van Landbouw, Natuurbeheer en Visserij, 1990). Broadly speaking, the manure legislation restricts the spreading of manure on agricultural land and sets requirements for its storage and the manner in which it is spread. On the one hand, it thus leads to higher storage costs, which are covered at the expense of payments for other means of production, such as land. On the other hand, land acquires an extra value because a certain amount of manure can be spread on it. Since this manure does not need to be disposed of in another manner, no costs will be incurred in this respect. The extra value of the land is equal to the costs saved. On balance, the manure legislation resulted in an increase in the price of land. In addition it created a property right for manure disposal, which received economic value in the market.

Compulsory Extensive Land Use: 2.5 Livestock Units per Hectare

Environmental policy can also trigger even more land price effects. A recent report (Goedgeluk *et al.*, 1999) gave evidence that the price of land resulting from environmental policy can rise considerably higher when the environmental requirements are stricter than the restrictions resulting from limitations on milk production. After all, limiting the intensity of land use, the number of animals per hectare, to for instance 2.5 livestock units per hectare will lead to a situation in which dairy farms with intensive land use (more than 2.5 livestock units per hectare) are suddenly facing either an excessive milk quota or too little available land. Table 8.3 shows that this concerns nearly 27 per cent of the dairy farms. Such farms will either have to sell milk quotas or purchase land. As a result, the milk quota price will fall and the price of land

Table 8.3 Livestock units (only milk cows and calves) per hectare of cultivated land (1999)

Livestock units per ha	Dairy farms (number)	Land area (ha)	Milk cows (number)
<2	12 109	404 359	509 378
2–<2.5	9 401	304 697	528 335
2.5–<4	6 985	177 303	402 624
4–<8	835	13 856	51 284
≥8	93	324	3 509
Total	29 423	900 539	1 495 130

Source: Landbouw-Economisch Instituut/Centraal Bureau voor de Statistiek (1999)

will rise. In fact, the quota price then overflows into the land price. At an average litre price of € 1.75 and an average milk quota of 12 000 litres per hectare, the quota value and thus the maximum overflow amounts to € 21 000. Given an average agricultural land price exclusive of milk quota of € 29 500 per hectare and of € 50 500 including the milk quota (29 500 + 21 000), this amounts to about 42 per cent of the land price (21 000/50 500).

Alternative Applications in Agriculture

Thus, besides the expected income from land and the expected interest rate, the price level of agricultural land is also influenced by production restrictions in agriculture and environmental policy applicable to agriculture, as well as by the future expectations of agricultural entrepreneurs in this regard. In addition, there is also the effect of alternative land uses, both within and outside the field of agriculture.

Within agriculture, competition for land between agricultural and horticultural sectors affects the price level of agricultural land in a given area. If the land is suitable for other, more intensive forms of cultivation with higher added value per hectare, and if this more intensive cultivation is prominent in the area, then the price of land will partly be influenced by the expected chance of future expansion of these more intensive forms of cultivation, such as glasshouse horticulture, bulb cultivation, arboriculture and intensive dairy farming. Through this competition, the outlook for, in particular, extensive grain farming and extensive stockbreeding becomes in time less favourable.

ALTERNATIVE APPLICATIONS OUTSIDE AGRICULTURE

Particularly when the economy is booming, the expected growth of non-agricultural use of agricultural land has great influence on the agricultural land price. We are concerned here with the influence of the other real estate market segments on the agricultural segment. The major claims on agricultural land in connection with a booming economy are made by the expansion of nature reserves and recreation areas and by ongoing urbanization.

Expansion of the Ecological Main Structure

Implementation of the expansion of the Ecological Main Structure (*Ecologische Hoofdstructuur* or EHS) planned in 1990 demands a great deal of agricultural land. The survey in Table 8.4 shows that 190 000 ha of the planned total of 700 000 ha must still be acquired. This acreage is composed of 71 000 ha of managed areas, 69 000 ha of reserve areas and 50 000 ha of nature development areas. In managed areas, management agreements are concluded with the owners of the land, usually farmers. In reserve areas and nature development areas, on the other hand, policy is concentrated on acquiring agricultural land with high natural value that requires management specifically focused on nature. The area concerned amounts to 119 000 ha, which places a considerable claim on the land offered on the free market.

Table 8.4   Overall composition of Ecological Main Structure

Overall composition EHS	Area in ha
Existing	510 000
• Nature areas	185 000
• Rural estates	25 000
• Woodlands (in EHS)	270 000
• Managed areas	13 000
• Reserve areas	17 000
New	190 000
• Managed areas	71 000
• Reserve areas	69 000
• Nature development areas	50 000
Total EHS (land)	700 000

Source: Rijksinstituut voor Volksgezondheid en Milieu (1997)

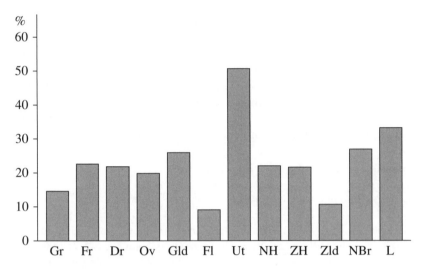

Source: Rijksinstituut voor Volksgezondheid en Milieu (1998)

Figure 8.2   *Percentage-wise demand for nature development on the total*
              voluntary supply of land in the provinces of Groningen (Gr),
              Friesland (Fr), Drenthe (Dr), Overijssel (Ov), Gelderland
              (Gld), Flevoland (Fl), Utrecht (Ut), Noord-Holland (NH), Zuid-
              Holland (ZH), Zeeland (Zld), Noord-Brabant (NBr), and
              Limburg (L)

The government's demand for voluntarily supplied land can be extremely
high in some areas, varying from 8 per cent to 50 per cent of the total supply.
In the provinces of Utrecht and Limburg in particular, little land for expansion remains in the land-based agricultural sectors (Figure 8.2).

It should be clear that a major market party such as the Countryside
Department can drive up the price of agricultural land. On the one hand, this
is because the government, in attempting to achieve its acquisition objectives
via the Countryside Department, is making more demands on the market for
agricultural land. On the other hand, it is because farmers must offer more for
neighbouring land than the government in order to achieve their own often
essential expansion objectives.

Figure 8.3 shows that an increase of 150 000 ha in the demand for nature
areas causes agricultural acreage to decline by the same amount. When the
demand for land for agriculture remains the same and the demand for land for
nature areas rises, the result is an increase in the total 'green' demand for
land. The consequence is a higher price level, with the area under agriculture
declining by 150 000 ha and the area devoted to nature expanding by the

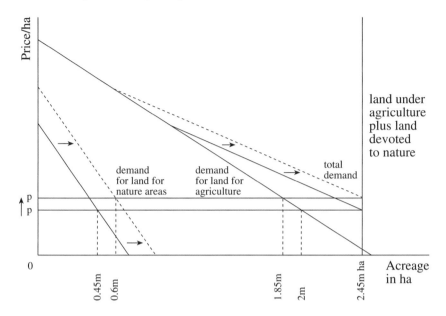

Figure 8.3   Long-term effect on the price of agricultural land of the planned expansion of the EHS by 150 000 ha: from 0.45m ha in 1995 to 0.6m ha in 2018

same amount. The price of this land will also remain higher because more limited agricultural acreage in the future will ultimately mean that only the more profitable crops are retained.

Ongoing Urbanization

The artificial limitation of the 'red' area via the 'Town and Country Planning Act' has created a substantial price difference between 'red' and 'green' zoned land. Table 8.5 illustrates this by comparing hectare prices 'inside and outside VINEX districts'. VINEX stands for *Vierde Nota Ruimtelijke Ordening Extra* ('Fourth Memorandum on Town and Country Planning Extra'). On the map of the Netherlands it points out the new areas for urbanization. 'Outside VINEX districts' means that 'green' activities are concerned. 'Inside VINEX districts' indicates that the area is zoned for 'red' uses. The difference between 'green' and 'red' prices is substantial and increasing year by year. In 1993, for example, the 'red' price was nine times higher than the 'green' price, while the difference in 1997 amounted to a factor of twelve.

The rising demand for residential areas, business premises, infrastructure and nature areas are expressions of an economic upturn. After all, the price

Table 8.5   Development of prices of agricultural land (in €/ha) outside and inside VINEX districts in the 1993–97 period

Year	Outside VINEX districts Price/ha	Inside VINEX districts Price/ha
1993	17 200	156 000
1994	17 100	174 000
1995	18 100	207 000
1996	20 000	250 000
1997	21 900	253 000

Source: Luijt *et al.* (1999)

level of real estate and the consequent price of building land are supported by the expected growth in income, that is by economic activity (Draper, 1983). The recent boom years and the related price development of real estate are putting a high pressure on the agricultural real estate market segment and the 'Town and Country Planning Act'. This finds expression in the price development of agricultural land, which, as can be seen from Figure 8.4, has been following the general price level of real estate fairly closely over the years.

According to the Central Bureau of Statistics, the price of agricultural land rose from an average of € 24 000 in 1998 to € 29 500 in 1999. The growth begins increasingly to resemble the explosive growth in land prices of the second half of the seventies. The current rise began in 1995 and there are as yet few signs of stabilization, let alone decline. Corrected for inflation, the high level of the late seventies has now been more or less reached.

Despite the fact that there are a number of significant differences between the present situation and the situation at the end of the seventies, such as the interest rate, inflation, agricultural land price policy, environmental policy, and so on, there is one important similarity: the general increase in real estate prices supported by the booming economy.

Figure 8.4 shows the average price development of agricultural land in the Netherlands. However, the price development differs considerably from region to region, despite the levelling effect of fiscally attractive resettlement within agriculture. While the seventies were primarily characterized by purchases by farms to expand their acreage, now farmers who have been bought out, mainly for 'red' but also for 'green' purposes, are purchasing more and more whole large farms. The fiscally favourable resettlement of agricultural enterprises has not, however, been able to eliminate the regional differences. Figure 8.5 illustrates this and also shows that the prices of agricultural land

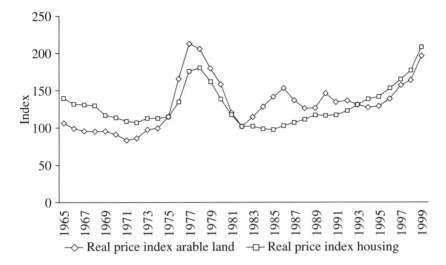

Figure 8.4 Development of the prices of arable land and homes (1982=100) in the 1965–99 period

are highest in areas where urbanization is taking place (VINEX areas). Finally, Figure 8.6 provides an overall survey of the different factors affecting the price of agricultural land.

RELATIVE IMPORTANCE OF FACTORS DETERMINING LAND PRICE

Polman *et al.* (1999) attempted to estimate the relative importance of the factors determining the price of agricultural land. In the study, a connection was assumed between, on the one hand, the paid market price for land and, on the other, the income from land in agriculture, the share of horticultural land in an area, and the claims on agricultural land under the *Vierde Nota Ruimtelijke Ordening Extra* (VINEX to 2005) and the *Ecologische Hoofd Structuur* (EHS to 2018):

$$P_{paid} = a_1{}^*P_{shadow} + a_2{}^*VINEX + a_3{}^*EHS + a_4{}^*Horticulture$$

Where: P_{paid} = the land price paid by a farmer
P_{shadow} = shadow price of agricultural land
VINEX = area VINEX/agricultural acreage
EHS = area EHS/agricultural acreage

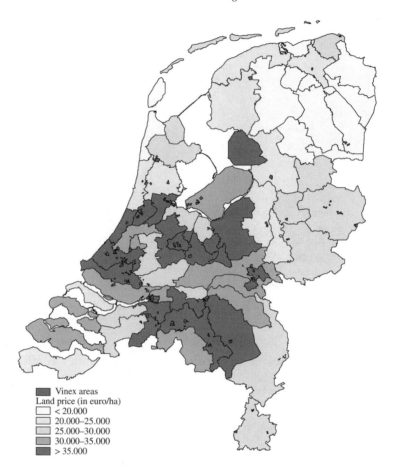

*Figure 8.5   VINEX areas and prices of agricultural land zoned for
           agricultural purposes in 66 agricultural areas in 1998 (€/ha)*

Horticulture = area horticultural land/agricultural acreage
a_1, a_2, a_3, a_4 = parameters

The shadow price of dairy farms indicates what farmers, with respect to
the contribution of extra land to the operating result, can pay for this on an
annual basis. The shadow price is calculated by means of a balance function.
The share of expensive horticultural land in an area reflects the pressure on
the price of agricultural land from the horticultural sector. The share of
VINEX and EHS claims in an area reflects the non-agricultural pressure on
the price of agricultural land for housing, work and nature development. All

	Effect on the price of agricultural land
Within agriculture	
Annual income from land	
● Productivity improvements	+
● Deterioration of agricultural terms of trade	–
Policy interventions	
● Production restrictions	–
● Manure legislation	+
● 2.5 livestock units per hectare	+
Competition between agricultural sectors	+
Outside agriculture	
Demand for preservation of nature	+
Demands of ongoing urbanization (incl. resettlement)	+
Low interest	+

Figure 8.6   Survey of factors affecting the price of agricultural land

variables are expected to exert a positive influence on the price of land. The results of the estimate confirm this expectation (Table 8.6).

The figure shows that the price of land can largely be explained by means of the four variables, judging by the high declared variance of 0.82 ($R^2=0.82$). Moreover, each of the variables provides a reliable contribution to the explanation of the price of land. This is apparent from the t-values of the variables, which are all higher than two. In statistical terms, the variables deviate significantly from zero at a 5 per cent significance level.

Table 8.6   Estimated coefficients for the paid land prices on dairy farms in the 1992–95 period ($R^2=0.82$)

	P_{shadow}	*VINEX*	*EHS*	*Horticulture*
Mean	933.50	0.011653	0.06868	0.063722
Coefficient	18.13	190,444	217,190	31,349
T-ratio	(11.1)	(2.9)	(9.1)	(2.5)

The shadow price of land has a positive influence on the paid land price. Based on an infinite time scale, the result is an estimated discount rate of 0.055 (=1/18.13). This is a very plausible result. On average, purchasers demand a return of nearly 5.5 per cent on capital invested in land. To a significant extent, the price of land is determined by the contribution of the maximum bid price for agricultural land. By multiplying the coefficient by the average value (Table 8.6), we find this contribution amounting to some € 7700. The effect of the VINEX and EHS also seems very plausible. The average VINEX pressure in the Netherlands is 0.011653 (VINEX hectares in an agricultural area divided by the agricultural acreage in that area). And the average EHS pressure is 0.06868 (EHS hectares in an agricultural area divided by the agricultural acreage in that area). We observed a VINEX share in the land price of € 1000 and an EHS share of € 6750. Together, this is more than the estimated bid price for agricultural land (€ 7700) and thus comparable with the agricultural share. Furthermore, the fact that the EHS share is larger than the VINEX share is plausible. After all, in the case of the EHS the acreage to be transferred is much greater. On the other hand, the purchase prices in the case of VINEX are usually much higher.

In the medium term, the effect of the joint non-agricultural claims on the price of agricultural land is thus roughly as great as the profitability of land on the dairy farm (the shadow price), approximately 47 per cent. The remainder, some 6 per cent, was accounted for by land-intensive horticulture. The total of these contributions amounts to more than € 16 000. The difference with the observed paid land price in the 1992–1995 period should be ascribed to the unexplained portion of the variance.

FUTURE: A LAND PRICE SPIRAL?

The use and organization of the limited land available in the Netherlands is one of the most challenging issues for the coming decades. As yet, the issue is far from being resolved. Viewed separately, the environmental, nature, and agricultural policies might be consistent with the goals they are supposed to achieve, but in interaction they are conflicting and preclude the simultaneous achievement of these very same objectives. The agricultural land market was shown to play a pivotal role in this network of interactions. Among the chapter's major conclusions are the following:

High (higher than on the world market) guaranteed prices (EU market and price policy) in combination with technological development lead to expansion of production and increase of scale. Since increase of scale via expansion of acreage is only possible in dribs and drabs, due to the mainly demographically determined rationed supply of agricultural land and the massive non-agricultural claims on it, land use is becoming more and more intensive, although it is sometimes curbed by production restrictions such as quotas that give rise to costly production rights.

The expansion of production, primarily through intensification, has had effects both on the price of land and on the environment. After all, the whole situation gave rise to high land prices, an increasingly strict environmental policy and a demand for nature policy. Initially, environmental policy took shape through restrictions on manure deposits on the land. On balance, that led to an increase in the price of land. And when environmental policy also starts setting requirements with regard to the intensity of cattle holding (2.5 livestock units per hectare in 2008), land prices will rise even more since the quota price will then overflow into the land price. Finally, nature conservation policy is taking shape via the acquisition of agricultural land in the agricultural segment of the real estate market, until now on a voluntary basis. In consequence, an extra demand for land will be made, with the result that the price of land will rise once again. In addition, a high price may nourish proprietors' beliefs that the price increase is not yet at an end. As a result, landowners dampen the supply of agricultural land and inflate the price again.

When the economy is booming, the demand for agricultural land for urbanization heightens greatly, which in combination with an unsteady 'Town and Country Planning Act', drives up land prices. High prices severely complicate the achievement of environmental and nature policy objectives in at least two ways. First, it raises the cost of acquisition of agricultural land for the Ecological Main Structure. Second, it increases the pace of development of the agricultural structure, resulting in a continuing decline in the number, but an increase in the scale of agricultural enterprises. Economies of scale contribute to the efficiency of the remaining agricultural enterprises, but at the risk of an increased uniformity in terms of outward appearance, causing rural areas to lose their natural identity.

To sum up, the EU market and price policy, with the exception of the milk quotas, caused the price of land to rise, and subsequently the land price rose again due to the environmental and nature policy needed to compensate for the negative effects of that agricultural policy. Finally, the present economic boom is creating a great many 'red' claims on agricultural land, causing the price of agricultural land to rise along with the general increase in real estate prices. For farmers, the resulting extremely high land price is reason to make even more intensive use of land. The interaction between agricultural policy, environmental policy, nature policy and town and country planning policy via the real estate market is plain to see.

NOTES

1. Winters (1990: p. 256) 'Fertiliser is a substitute for land in many agricultural processes so the strong positive relationship between price support and land prices stimulates fertiliser use. Kawagoe *et al.* (1986) estimate that a 1 per cent increase in the price of land relative to fertiliser increases the relative use of the latter by 1.4 per cent in the United States and 0.4 per cent in Japan. It is also likely that the tendency towards crop specialisation stimulates pollution. Whereas mixed farming makes relatively balanced demands of the eco-system and is able to counter certain diseases by alternating crops and livestock in particular fields, specialised farms often require additional chemicals to maintain fertility and additional drugs to control disease (Bowers and Cheshire, 1983).'
2. The *Dienst Landelijk Gebied* ('Countryside Department') is a delegated government department whose tasks include the acquisition of land for the implementation of the *Ecologische Hoofdstructuur* (EHS; 'Ecological Main Structure'). The EHS is an interrelated network of ecosystems of (inter)national importance which are to be permanently maintained, as indicated in the Nature Policy Plan (Ministerie van Landbouw, Natuurbeheer en Visserij, 1990).

REFERENCES

Baarda, C. (1999), *Politieke Besluiten en Boerenbeslissingen. Het draagvlak van het Mestbeleid tot 2000* (Political and farmer decisions. The public support for the Manure policy until 2000), ICS dissertatiereeks 58, Groningen: Rijksuniversiteit Groningen.

Bowers, J.K. and P.C. Cheshire (1983), *Agriculture, the Countryside and Land Use: An Economic Critique*, London: Methuen.

Centraal Bureau voor de Statistiek (CBS) (1997), *Bodemstatistiek* (Soil statistics), Voorburg: CBS.

Centraal Planbureau (CPB) (1999*), De grondmarkt. Een gebrekkige markt en een onvolmaakte overheid* (The land market. An imperfect market and a defective government), Den Haag: Sdu.

Dijksterhuis, G.B. (2000*), De agrarische grondmarkt. Ontwikkelingen en Verwachtingen* (The agricultural land market. Developments and Expectations), Utrecht: Stafgroep Economisch Onderzoek, Rabobank Nederland.

Draper, D.A.G. (1983), *De investeringen in woningen: een econometrische studie* (Investments in housing: an econometric study), Amsterdam: Economisch Instituut voor de Bouwnijverheid (EIB).

Farjon, J.M.J., N.F.C. Hazeldonk and W.J.C. Hoefnagel (1997), *Verkenning natuur en verstedelijking 1995–2020* (Enquiry nature and urbanization 1995–2020), Achtergronddocument Natuurverkenning '97 (Background document Nature enquiry 1997), Wageningen: Informatie- en Kenniscentrum Natuurbeheer.

Goedgeluk, R., J. Helming, J. Luijt and K. Schotten (1999*), Groene grond in ruimtelijke perspectieven* (Green land in spatial perspectives), Den Haag: Landbouw-Economisch Instituut (LEI), rapport 4.99.18.

Gylfason, Th. (1995), *The Macroeconomics of European Agriculture,* Princeton, New Jersey: Princeton University, Department of Economics, Princeton Studies in International Finance, No.78.

Johnson, D.G. (1991), *World Agriculture in Disarray*, 2nd edition, London: MacMillan.

Kawagoe, T., K. Otsuka and Y. Hayami (1986), 'Induced bias of technical change in agriculture: the US and Japan, 1880–1980', *Journal of Political Economy*, **94**(3), 523–44.

Landbouw-Economisch Instituut (LEI) / Centraal Bureau voor de Statistiek (CBS) (1999), *Land- en tuinbouwcijfers 1999* (Agriculture and horticulture statistics), Den Haag: Landbouw-Economisch Instituut (LEI).

Luijt, J. (1985), 'De maximale biedprijs van landbouwgrond in combinatie met het leveringsrecht van heffingsvrije melk' ('The maximum bid price of agricultural land in conjunction with the licence to deliver duty-free milk'), in L.B. van der Giessen (ed.), *Economische en structurele gevolgen van de superheffing* (Economic and structural effects of the superlevy), Den Haag: Landbouw-Economisch Instituut (LEI), Mededeling 336.

Luijt J., J.H. van Rijswijk and M. van Heusden (1999), *Prijzen van landbouwgrond in en om VINEX-locaties* (Prices of agricultural land in and around VINEX areas), Den Haag: Landbouw-Economisch Instituut (LEI), rapport 4.99.02.

Martin, J.P., J.M. Burniaux, F. Delorme, I. Lienert and D. van der Mansbrugghe (1989), 'Economy-wide effects of agricultural policies in OECD countries: simulation results with WALRAS ', *OECD Economic Studies*, **13**, 131–72.

Ministerie van Landbouw, Natuurbeheer en Visserij (1990*), Natuurbeleidsplan; regeringsbeslissing* (Nature policy plan; government decision), Den Haag: Ministerie van Landbouw, Natuurbeheer en Visserij.

Polman N., J. Luijt, M. Mulder and G. Thijssen (1999), *'Going concern'-waarde en marktprijs van landbouwgronden. Berekening en analyse van het verschil* ('Going-concern' value and the market price of agricultural land. Computation and analysis of the difference), Den Haag: Landbouw-Economisch Instituut (LEI), rapport 6.99.02.

Rijksinstituut voor Volksgezondheid en Milieu (RIVM) (1997), *Natuurverkenning 97* (Nature enquiry 97), Alphen aan den Rijn: Samson H.D. Tjeenk Willink.

Rijksinstituut voor Volksgezondheid en Milieu (RIVM) (1998), *Natuurbalans 98* (Nature audit 98), Alphen aan den Rijn: Samson H.D. Tjeenk Willink.

Winters, L.A. (1987), 'The economic consequences of agricultural support: a survey', *OECD Economic Studies*, **9**, 7–54.

Winters, L. Alan (1990), 'The So-Called "Non-Economic" Objectives of Agricultural Support', *OECD Economic Studies*, **13**, 237–66.

9. Broadening the sectoral perspective on agricultural policy in Greece

Leonidas Louloudis and Nikos Beopoulos

INTRODUCTION

A major article in a well-known Greek newspaper recently noted that all the latest public opinion polls show a 'discrepancy between the expectations of urban and rural citizens'. According to this article, the discrepancy

> underlines regional inequalities and can be directly correlated with the level of development, the speed with which changes are absorbed in society, the time lag in the utilisation of technological advancements, and most importantly the persistence exhibited in the regions furthest from the centre on traditional structures of social organisation and production.

The article completed by stating that 'the government has every reason to support new activities in the countryside which would offer opportunities for income outside the agricultural sector'.[1] As is often the case in the daily press, this article, while it does reflect the reality of rural citizens' low expectations, does not take into account the noteworthy state initiatives in the agricultural sector. Such initiatives respond to the greater cohesion process of the Greek and European economies (Greece's entry into the European Monetary Union), and, more specifically, to the adaptation of national agricultural and regional policies to the corresponding European ones after the adoption of the Maastricht Treaty. The real question concerns the speed, quality, and the efficiency of trial rural development policies at the national level.

Previous studies have indicated that the government only recently became aware of the harmful effects of agriculture on the environment (Louloudis *et al.*, 2000) and Greek farmers were not adequately prepared for the new significance ascribed in European agriculture to environmental protection (Beopoulos and Louloudis, 1997). Despite these factors hampering the implementation of measures to integrate environmental requirements in farming, major changes have taken place in the pattern of rural development. Rural development has changed in response to the application of new EU policies in the 1990s, whether they be specific measures in the context of the agri-environmental regulation, or in the context of the Habitats Directive. An adequate assessment of these changes would require considerations regarding their effects in the areas of employment as well as overall rural development in the application of, for instance, LEADER I and II initiatives.

The main objective of this chapter is to examine changes that have taken place during the past few decades in the rural countryside of Greece. Geopolitical conditions, for example the immigration since the end of the 1980s, have largely changed the demographic conditions of rural areas, as well as the structure of their economies and labour markets. In addition, social changes have taken place as well. The question posed concerning these changes is whether, and to what extent, they can be effectively articulated into a new plan emphasizing an integrated development of the countryside. In addition, we will also examine the above question by means of evaluating the up-to-present implementation experience in Greece of those particular EU policies. The implementation of these measures is associated with the integration of the environmental dimension into agricultural practices, and with the development of opportunities for employment outside agriculture, as a supplement of income generated by agriculture. This multi-sectorial type of policy approach to rural space is gaining increasing importance, as Greece is a typical example of a country in which, at least from the post-war period on, single-sector policies were applied almost exclusively, and focused on the development of the primary sector.

HOW AGRICULTURAL HAS THE RURAL COUNTRYSIDE REMAINED?

The changes in agricultural society have been dramatic, especially after the entry of the country into what was then (1981) the European Community. National demographic and employment trends (Kasimis and Zakopoulou, 2000) reflect them. In the second half of the 20th century, Greece was transformed from an agricultural country (almost half of the population was employed in agriculture during the early 1950s) towards a society focusing on the service sector. However, although the share of agriculture to the GNP has declined, it has remained significant through to the end of the 1990s (7.9 per cent in 1998). About 1.5 million inhabitants are part of the agricultural society and the rural areas in which they live cover about 100 000 km². This means that 76 per cent of the Greek territory has a population density of 15 inhabitants per km². The dramatic rates of population decrease in agricultural regions, which were recorded in the 1960s and 1970s slowed down in the 1980s and stabilized in the 1990s. In 1991 the agricultural population composed 28.2 per cent of the total population of the country, which again turned down to around 19 per cent at the end of the 1990s. This decrease is not surprising and is largely due to the mechanization process in agriculture. But within this development, three social phenomena can be a cause for concern. The first is the ageing of the population, the second is the absence of women of the 'reproductive' age group (25–29 years), and the third is low literacy. The current age distribution of the rural population and the ongoing trend for young women to leave agricultural areas reflects the entrenchment of cultural norms of disdain for agricultural professions, and an attraction for the urban way of living.[2] Equally serious is the deficiency at the level of education. Even in 1981, 10.1 per cent of the farmers had never gone to school while 84.7 per cent had completed only some or all of their primary education.

The agricultural labour force constitutes 20 per cent of the nation's total, as opposed to 30 per cent some twenty years ago. Measured in Annual Work Units (AWU), the amount fell from 956 000 AWU in 1980 to 644 000 AWU in 1996. The rate of employment in the primary sector among residents of agricultural areas has fallen below 50 per cent for those between the age of 20 and 44. This means that in agricultural areas, more than one half of those of working age, between 20 and 44, are employed predominantly outside agriculture.[3] Employment in the agricultural sector has increased in semi-urban and urban areas, from 16.7 per cent in 1981 to 23 per cent in 1996. This reflects that the agricultural sector is currently less identified with rural areas, at least in the way those areas continue to be defined based on conventional statistical categories (that is settlements with less than 2000 inhabitants). The rate of unemployment in the rural areas (around 5 per cent) is well below the national average of 10 per cent. This gap, however, has diminished since the early 1980s. In both cases, unemployment affects mainly the younger populations. In recent years empirical studies have focused on the significance of part-time employment and pluri-activity. The average farm size is only 4.5 ha, while only 0.1 per cent of agricultural holdings are larger than 100 ha. Due to the large number (estimated at 773 800 for 1995) of small-scale agricultural holdings, as well as their structures of production, Greek agricultural holdings do not ensure, on average, full employment for even one person (average 0.9 AWU per farm in 1993). Consequently, it should not be surprising to find high rates of part-time employment among members of households involved in such holdings. According to Eurostat data from 1993, 65.4 per cent of the holders and 78 per cent of the household members that are involved in the holdings contribute less than half-time to this occupation, a rate which increased from 1985 to 1993.

A recent study (Zakopoulou, 1999) has brought a new dimension of this issue to light. This study showed there are many 'pluri-active' people who have agriculture as their first or second occupation, both in the agricultural sector and in the country as a whole, which is due to the relatively large number of agricultural holdings. When those that are farmers for their main occupation engage in other employment, this occurs largely within agriculture, while agriculture remains the most 'popular' second occupation for almost all of the professional categories. Because of this situation, we can more accurately speak of 'multi-employed holders of agricultural enterprises' rather than 'multi-employed farmers'. Empirical field research has repeatedly confirmed these findings. Field work in Polykastro-Peonia gave evidence that 'forms of employment revolving around the *nikokyrio* (household), namely self- and family employment, involved 52 per cent of the economically active population, whilst the category of salaried/wage workers accounted for some 44 per cent'. This region includes 17 communities and three municipalities that embrace 27 villages and three small towns, During the early 1990s these figures are rather well representative for rural areas and small towns in Greece as a whole. Moreover, the figures for Peonia and especially Polykastro conceal a large number of employees who receive supplementary incomes through their involvement in agriculture. They obtain their incomes either from leasing-out of their holding or from micro-cultivation. Fieldwork investigation conducted during the same year with the latest population census indicated that approximately two out of every five employees received some income from agriculture (Kalantaridis and Lambrianidis, 1999).

All of the above indicates that the so-called agricultural space of Greece is in transition, at least from a sociological point of view. The share of agriculture in the rural countryside has changed significantly, thus calling into question some of the sector's traditional features for having a significant share of rural populations. The first feature to be called into question is that primarily residents of the rural countryside practise agriculture, and the second is that professional farmers practise it. The main question remains whether farmers have farming as their single activity, even in a traditionally agricultural country such as Greece. This again questions how efficient policies for agricultural development can be, which are aimed only at those employed exclusively in agriculture. Of course this 'pluri-activity' is a long-term feature of agricultural societies, and we cannot agree with the hasty adoption of the term 'non-farmer' to describe those engaged in such activities. Yet the issue remains, as articulated by Djurfeldt (1999), that 'the peasantry needs to be reconceptualised.'

This is not simply a theoretical discussion. The 1992 reform of the CAP was intended to achieve more sustainable production methods, which was bolstered after the adoption of the Structural Funds for the period 2000–2006. In addition, society did prepare to implement certain EU directives such as the Habitats Directive and the Nitrates Directive. At the same time, programmes such as agro-tourism and eco-tourism are being promoted with the aim of providing recreational services and utilizing special local skills and practices to make products of distinguished quality and origin. All these developments, already in the planning stages and beyond, are realized in an eco-geographical and socio-economic arena which identifies them primarily with agriculture and, conventionally, because of the practice of single-sectoral policies such as agricultural policy. Today, given the medium- and long-range span of the above multi-sectoral policies and, after two decades of the application of CAP and the coming socio-economic changes, a reorientation of this sphere is necessary. The practical goal of such a reorientation is the better adaptation of agriculture to the new conditions of 'rural development', or, more precisely, 'development of the countryside'. Meanwhile, the Ministry of Agriculture had incorporated this goal by changing its name to Ministry of Agriculture and Development of the Countryside. The following part of this chapter is intended to offer evidence to the concerted action which would be needed to achieve this goal following the period of applying single-sector policies.

The Dual Pattern of Rural Development

The land area of Greece covers a total of 131 957 km^2. Out of this total, 105 834 km^2 is on the mainland and 26 123 km^2 is on the islands. The length of the coastline is over 15 000 km and out of this, 11 000 km are island coasts. This coastline, in offering opportunities for summer holidays, has lent Greece the image of a predominantly maritime country, an image reinforced by the number of foreign tourists as well as the large populations of seaside urban centres. But Greece is primarily a mountainous country. Of the total land, 39 per cent is under 200 metres, 28 per cent is between 200 and 500 metres, and 30 per cent is between 500 and 1500 metres. About 3900 km^2 (2.9 per cent) is higher than 1500 metres, and of this, 500 km^2 are over 2000 metres above sea-level. The area used agriculturally in Greece is about 3.9 million ha, and 29 per cent of the land is irrigated. The irrigated areas are to a large extent in the lower, flat areas or fertile plains, where modern intensive agriculture is practised. In these areas, subsidized arable cultivation predominates, exemplified by the highly subsidized cotton which takes up about one-third of the irrigated land, contributing 80 per cent of total cotton production in the EU. If market and price support measures constitute half of the total family income of small enterprises, their significance is obvious for the economy in the periphery. In the Thessalian plains, a traditionally agricultural region and chiefly an eco-geographic zone of development in cotton cultivation, the average family income is almost double the national average, while in the more northern areas of Macedonia and Thrace, it is half the average. However, there has been pressure from the European Commission to control Greek agriculture, which until now has been favoured by the CAP. There are two reasons for this; first, the expansion of cotton produced is not in line with the intended decrease in protection offered by the CAP, and second, the expected impacts on the environment are serious. Recent investigations on the consequences of Agenda 2000 for agriculture in the lowland areas, showed that a 10 per cent decrease in prices of cereals would in the medium-run further increase the area of cotton production, at the expense of corn. A similar phenomenon occurred in the country in 1993–1995 due to the application of the CAP reform, when the cultivation of manufactured tomatoes and sugarbeet, which could have been used as an alternative, could not be expanded because of existing quotas (Spathes *et al.*, 1998). But the Ministry of Agriculture no longer permits a further increase in land use for cotton cultivation.[4]

The other side of the one-dimensional emphasis on development of highly subsidized intensive cultivation in lowland areas is the abandonment of mountainous and less favoured regions. This phenomenon also applies to other Member States in the EU. However, in Greece it is of particular significance due to the wide dispersal and size of such lands throughout the national territory. According to European institutional definitions as they have been adopted by the Greek administration,[5] mountainous and less favoured areas take up 82.6 per cent of the national total, 68.5 per cent of the cultivated area including fallow land, 91.5 per cent of forest land, 91.7 per cent of pasture land (private and communal), and 72.8 per cent of the land covered by water. Despite the adverse conditions in such areas, a significant share of the population (27.9 per cent) resides there, as shown by the national census figures. It should be remembered, however, that the figures tend to inflate the actual number who live in these areas, as family members who have already migrated to urban centres continue to declare residence in the areas of their origin so as to stave off the further decline in basic infrastructure and services provided by the state in such regions. The abandonment of marginal land to mountainous and semi-mountainous areas, already significant today, is expected to increase in the coming years. Compensatory allowances offered initially through the implementation of Directive 75/268 (which in 1985 was incorporated into Regulation 797/85, which was itself replaced by Regulation 2328/91 and, this, in turn, by 950/97) have reversed in large part the trend of desertion of mountainous and less favoured areas.

Recent development under the rubric of 'Action Programme 2000', Agenda 2000, seems to recognize the importance of ensuring the protection of mountainous and less favoured areas. More specifically, Regulation 1257/1999 regarding support of rural development from the European Agricultural Guidance and Guarantee Fund (EAGGF), while it does continue the regime of compensatory allowances based on prerequisites stipulated in Regulation 950/97, adds the prerequisite that environmentally compatible agricultural practices be used. In addition, the same regulation stipulates the use of selection criteria for compensation, so as to ensure efficient support, achieve the objectives of the regulation, and avoid over-compensation. Based on the implementation of Regulation 1750/1999, a further boost in compensation is provided for in order to achieve environmental goals. Most important for Greece, however, is the part in Regulation 1257/1999, mentioning that the EU aims to decrease the total number of mountainous and less favoured areas in all Member States so that they constitute no more than 10 per cent of the territory in each country. The targeting by the EU of more efficient policies is obvious, but the ramifications of this for countries with such widespread mountainous and less favoured areas such as Greece are not clear. At the same time, the decrease in income from cereals, due to the application of Agenda 2000, will to a large extent influence the holdings in the areas where cereals are cultivated. Given that cereal cultivation predominates in these areas, the rate of agricultural income will fall, with all the social consequences this may have, such as the abandonment of marginal lands. This abandonment may further reduce the self-sufficiency rate in the provision of the animal feed.

It is clear that the strategies for rural development do need to improve the options for supplementary income outside agriculture. This fortunate conjunction, however, does not automatically resolve the difficulties of the operation, although it means a turn away from agricultural policy as it is traditionally practised, toward the formulation of more realistic, multi-sectoral development policies in the countryside, emphasizing conservation and protection of the environment. Yet, in order to achieve this goal, policymakers must recognize that 'nature' is not simply a productive factor in agricultural practices, but a public good with specific ecological, aesthetic, and cultural value, and that agriculture and animal husbandry can make positive contributions to the management of these values. At the same time, the role being proposed for agriculture in the revaluation of 'nature' should not neglect the current processes of social and economic differentiation in the modern countryside. Such processes need to be taken into account, to ensure the widest possible approval and co-operation of individual and collective local actors. These actors are the key to the success of this new multi-sectoral rural development policy.

Agro-tourism: Successes and Failures

Agro-tourism in Greece has been promoted by two major developments (Iakovidou *et al.*, 1999): first, the individual initiatives which include various forms of accommodation ranging from small-scale hotels to rented rooms in farmers' houses located in agricultural areas; second, the establishment of the Women's Agro-Tourism Co-operatives.

There are two categories of agro-tourism included under private initiatives. The first category of agro-tourism, applied by the Ministry of Agriculture under Regulation 950/97 (see above), supports the economic heads of agricultural holdings. According to official data, a total of 960 agro-tourist accommodations provide 10 025 beds, most of which are first class. Out of these accommodations, which are not part of an overall development plan of a specific area, two-thirds are on islands and 9 per cent are located in coastal communities. These areas are not qualified as agricultural, either in terms of settlement and consumption patterns, or in terms of employment and composition of income. The second category of agro-tourism includes tourist enterprises being developed in agricultural areas, of the 'bed and breakfast' type, which are run chiefly by farmers who are permanent residents of the area but do not engage in agriculture as their main occupation. Most of these enterprises receive financial support from and are run under the auspices of the LEADER I and LEADER II communal initiatives.[6] In the words of the Geotechnical Chamber of Greece, 'agro-tourism in Greece covers mainly the coastal zones with developed tourism, and the consolidation of an agro-tourist conception has not gained authority over the dominant model of tourism in this region'. Similar criticism, focused here on the multi-sectoral dimension of development policy in mountainous and less favoured areas, is expressed by the director of the Institute for Mountainous Agriculture of the National Foundation for Agricultural Studies. He stated that the largest sums from the Mediterranean Integrated Programmes (IMP) and LEADER I, are being used for the development of agro-tourism and have solely involved the construction of accommodations. This observation applies to central Greece and particularly in mountainous Evrytania, which is an area where 65 per cent of agricultural family income comes from the primary sector, mainly from animal husbandry and forestry. According to estimates from the same author, 86.1 per cent of IMP are absorbed in Evrytania by tertiary sector activities, while only 5 per cent are channelled to the primary sector. Forty-one per cent of the total budget for LEADER I was dedicated to agro-tourism, but only 13 per cent to the primary sector (Katsaros, 1999).

The same criticism is adopted in the official review of the LEADER II programme (Ministry of Agriculture, 1999), in which it is stated that after three years of enacting the LEADER programme, 'we can speak of indices of differentiation in the agricultural sector of LEADER regions'. The review also states that 'serious weaknesses have been encountered in the various sectors and goals of the programme', among which are noted 'weakness in shaping policies for local products, non-existent initiatives for quality of life services, and feeble efforts at modernisation of agricultural activities'. Given all of the above, it would still be correct to say that

although the bed-and-breakfast form may be most appropriate for Greek conditions of small-scale enterprise...the functioning of agro-accommodation as merely
overnight shelter goes against the intention of agricultural tourism, and this form
can only play a limited role in furthering the goals of indigenous development (for
example, utilisation of products from local sources, widening of the sphere of
women's employment...) (Gidarakou *et al.*, 1997).

Finally it should not be underestimated that, according to the review referred
to above, 29 Local Action Groups (LAGs) and two collective bodies have
been formed under the rubric of LEADER II, and there is a projected 13 per
cent increase in accommodations from the initial number at the start of this
programme. The 29 LAGs, on average, each include 11 accommodations. Of
these lodgings 62 per cent are newly constructed and consist of at least 12
beds. These results, together with the projected 19 per cent increase of
infrastructure such as offices of organization and promotion, traditional tav-
erns, and food/wine tasting sites indicate that the LAGs programmes intend
to make up an integrated agro-tourist product. The majority of these activities
are being realized by private investors. Interestingly, 53 per cent of the 350
private investors were already involved in the agricultural sector, while the
remainder of private investors had previously been involved in the tourist
industry. The goal of the current policy is to lengthen the tourist season to 56
days (a 42.4 per cent increase from the current season) and increase the
occupancy rate of accommodations by 36 per cent. It is projected that 26
permanent and 29 seasonal positions will be created with the realization of
this policy measure, totalling 1595 positions.

The first Women's Agro-Tourism Cooperative (WAC) was established in
Greece in 1984, in the community of Petra. It is located on the island of Lesbos
in the Aegean Sea, and has an agricultural tradition, which already dates back
many centuries. The founding and functioning of the first agro-tourist co-
operatives were made possible by the stipulations of the Act regarding
Co-operatives 921/79, and later by Act 1541/85 (regarding 'Agricultural Co-
operative Organizations'). Today there are eight such co-operatives. Their
main activity is the running of guesthouses and rooms to rent. They function
along with 46 other WACs, which produce and standardize local products. Out
of the 54 total co-operatives, 10 are on the island of Crete, four on other
islands, and the rest are dispersed mainly in mountainous and less favoured
areas. There are also a few urban co-operatives which are active in rural areas
and of which 90 per cent are female farmers. Many of these do not and/or never
did function. In 1998 the WACs founded their Union as a national organization.
This organizational initiative was called to reverse the rather negative image
currently held of the WACs. Empirical data regarding agro-tourism and particularly co-operatives shows that, with the exception of the co-operatives of Aghios
Germanos of Prespes, and Sitia of Crete, which present a positive image, 'the

co-operatives remain stagnant and unable to attract new members, hindered by problems of interpersonal relations among current members, and are unwilling to reinvest profits as they continue to look to state bodies for financial support' (Tsartas and Thanopoulou, 1994).

ENVIRONMENTAL POLICY: AGRICULTURE UNDER RESTRICTIONS

It is well-known that the agri-environmental measures under Regulation 2078/ 92 might have major implications for farm management, and even the spatial distribution of agriculture in the medium and long-run. Before getting into the principal measures of this policy as it is applied in Greece, some preliminary comments are presented about environmental policy in Greece. Greece belongs to the 'lagging' states with regard to the application of environmental policy in the EU. In these states, there is no tradition of environmental policy; as a consequence, any levels of Community's protection constitute an innovation as compared to pre-existing gaps. In contrast, funding from structural funds plays an important role on a national policy for the environment. In spite of this, 'environmental specifications are often perceived as an obstacle for the rapid absorption of social resources or as a source of obligation for an administration that has not learned or can not enforce limitations on private action, and which has essentially resigned itself to "free riding" (Kazakos, 1999).[7] The Supreme Administrative Court of Greece, the Greek Council of State, has referred to the weakness of the political and bureaucratic process to produce and apply reliable environmental policies, as a determinant factor in such developments. 'The Council has been engaged in dynamic methods of constitutional and statutory interpretation and has reshaped Greek environmental law...these developments have caused a lot of institutional friction between the judicial and the political branches. The line of demarcation between judicial review and legislative authority has yet to be determined.' (Papaspyrou, 1999).

The implementation in Greece of the agri-environmental measures under Regulation 2078/92, and of certain key environmental directives, has been inscribed in this political framework. Before evaluating the significance of this package of policy measures for the integration of the environmental component into the new development policy for the countryside, a general comment must be made. Public opinion and the political order in Greece hesitate to dedicate public resources to these programmes. It has been shown elsewhere that the philosophy of the agri-environmental regulation corresponds to the reality of Northern and Central European Union countries, especially those that led the planning and adoption of this regulation (Billaud *et al.*, 1997). This explains why their implementation faced fewer difficulties in these countries. Second, the problem for Mediterranean agriculture is its low competitiveness, and as such, priority has been given so far to promoting modernization programmes among agricultural growth sectors so that they may deal with the new situation caused by the opening of world markets. Thus, societies in these countries, concerned with the problems of unemployment and stabilization of still uncertain economic improvement, do not exercise real pressure for public services to dedicate budget resources to these programmes or to their speedy application (Moyano and Garrigo, 1998).

Agri-environmental Policy

In Greece, the initial plan for Regulation 2078/92 did respond mainly to the key agriculture-related environmental problems. However, the programmes were changed during the process of its implementation. The most important programmes with respect to budgeted resources, which were recorded as the most urgent problems by public administration, were never applied; for example, the budget for the anti-erosion protection programme constituted 64 per cent of the total budget. Also typical was the absence of programmes for the maintenance of extensive production methods. Finally, even though this regulation was Greece's first implementation of an environmental programme, and gave principal importance to education and information, not a single programme was established for these purposes. However, we should note, this type of programme did not arouse interest in most of the Member States.

In December 1994, Greece submitted the following programmes for approval: a) 'organic farming' programme, b) programme for 'the reduction of nitrogen-pollution from agricultural sources in the Thessaly plain', and c) programme for 'protection and conservation of biodiversity and genetic diversity' which itself consists of two sub-programmes: 1) 'conservation of endangered breed of farm animals' and 2) 'conservation of local varieties of cultivated species'. In January 1995 the programme for 'Long term set-aside in the exploitation of farmlands' was submitted, and in June of that year also the programme for 'the Protection of habitats with special significance' was submitted.

The first two programmes were approved in July 1995, and their amendments were adopted during the summer of 1998. The part of the third programme on conservation of endangered breeds of animals was only approved in April 1997. The programme for long-term set-aside of agricultural land was approved in July 1996.

The first programmes in Greece were approved three years after the date of enactment of the regulation, while in other countries the first programmes had already been introduced in 1993 and 1994. Aside from the initial delay on the part of the Greek authorities in the submission of these programmes, there was also a delay in the process of approval on the part of the official bodies of the Community. As noted by the Ministry of Agriculture, the delay can be attributed to the fact that the European Commission did not designate an official to be responsible for Greek programmes (Ministry of Agriculture, 2000).

The overall progress of these programmes up to 1999, based on data supplied by the Ministry of Agriculture (Ministry of Agriculture, 2000), is shown in Table 9.1.

Table 9.1   Status of agri-environmental programmes under Regulation 2078/92 (1992–99)

Programme	No. of Producers	Extent of Programme (in ha)	Expenditure (ECU)	Share of total budget programme (%)
Reduction of nitrogen-pollution from agricultural sources in Thessaly plain	3,444	29,516	14,326,322	42.7
Long term set-aside in exploitation of agricultural land	125	21,579	11,628,661	34.6
Conservation of endangered breeds of animals	not available		733,224	2.1
Organic farming	1,305	6,502	6,855,994	20.4
Total	4,874	57,597	33,544,196	100

Source: Ministry of Agriculture, Department of Protection of the Environment and Natural Resources, data elaborated by the authors, 1999

It would be worthwhile to compare the programmes of this regulation as applied in Greece with the corresponding EU averages.[8] In Greece, then, the holdings participating in these programmes are 0.6 per cent of the total number of holdings, a figure which is far below the average 9.4 per cent of the EU of 11, or 13.4 per cent of the rest of the EU. The land included in Greek programmes is 1 per cent of the total agricultural land utilized in Greece, whereas in the EU as a whole the corresponding figure was 19.5 per cent. The approved credit, based on the projected budget for the application of the regulation, amounted to 160 million ECU from 1993 to 1997. The contribution of the European Agricultural Guidance and Guarantee Fund (EAGGF) was 120 million ECU (European Commission, 1997). The EAGGF expenses for Greece up to 1998 were 16.9 million ECU, and these expenses corresponded to 0.3 per cent of the total expenses in the EU (European Commission, 1998). Based on the data of the Ministry of Agriculture (see Table 9.1), the actual expenditure until 1999 was 33 million ECU, a figure which should give us an idea of the precision of these projected figures and the possibility of implementing new and complex programmes. It remains for us to note some interesting information regarding these programmes and their process of implementation.

Programmes for the reduction of nitrogen-pollution in the Thessaly plain
Agriculture in the Thessaly plain consists chiefly in the intensive irrigated monoculture of cotton. The goals of the programme are the significant reduction in the use of nitrogenous fertilizers in cotton cultivation, and stronger absorption of fertilizers by plants depending on the type of fertilizer and the manner in which it is added to decrease leaching. Farmers are obliged to execute a crop rotation programme with durum cereal, and to work towards a significant reduction in the amount of fertilizers applied. Furthermore, they are obliged to use specific methods of application and irrigation systems which reduce leaching of nutrients and control soil erosion.

The Ministry of Agriculture submitted an amendment to the programme for the first time in December 1996 and then again in 1997. The Commission approved this amendment in April 1999, resulting in the application of new measures for two years, under national monitoring and control. This amendment mainly extended the programme to include other intensive arable cultivations such as corn, processed tomato, sugarbeet, watermelon, honeydew, dry onions, dry garlic, dry beans and fresh green beans, and better incorporation of environmental objectives (plant hedgerows, set-aside). The programme for the reduction of nitrogen-pollution is conducted in certain zones and is of pilot type. Until now, and after the increase in demand that resulted from the amendment, 29 516 ha have been included in the programme. The Institute of Land Chartography and Soil Classification of Larissa has taken on the responsibility to monitor the programme. A committee of specialists, in which the monitoring body will also participate, will conduct the evaluation of this programme. The programme has essentially been completed, as the plain of Thessaly has been included among the vulnerable zones for the Nitrate Directive (Directive 91/676) and the mandatory measures arising from this directive make it ineligible for payments under the agri-environmental regulation. This measure has been applied to dispersed areas in only 5 per cent of the plain, and since there was no selection criterion for which exploitations would be included in the programme, either in terms of sensitivity to any environmental element, or based on contribution of certain exploitations to pollution, the programme is not expected to have beneficial consequences for water quality.

Organic farming programme
Methods of biological production were included in the agri-environmental measures of Regulation 2078/92, which took into consideration the beneficial effects of these methods for the environment and their reduction of yield levels, especially during the transition period in which these methods were given support. The Greek programme does not project support for the maintenance of biological production, as it considers that the market can ensure a sufficient economic yield. Recently, the Union of Professional Bio-cultivators of Greece vehemently protested against the decision of the Ministry of Agriculture to cut this support after five years under this particular programme: 'pioneering Greek cultivators need the support of the government, not its indifference'.[9] Organic livestock production does not receive compensatory payments, and farmers are obliged to place all of their resources in biological production. The main objective of the programme was to protect the environment from agricultural pollution. However, the programme turned to zonal development of ecologically sensitive areas, even though it was adopted on a national scale. Priority was given to areas in the Natura 2000 network and second priority was received by island, mountainous and semi-mountainous regions. An amendment was approved in January 1999, after three years of the programme's implementation. The implementation of the programme was only developed in three of the 52 prefectures of the country, and affected 60 per cent of the olive cultivation. The goal of targeting the programme towards ecologically vulnerable areas was only partially realized. Nevertheless, through the amendment, a more balanced and planned development was reached. In any case it is thought that agri-environmental measures gave incentives to farmers to transform their practice into organic farming. A total of 1305 holdings applied organic farming practices under the programme.

Long term set-aside in the exploitation of agricultural land
This programme includes two distinct measures. First, to create biotopes and ecoparks in areas of ecological interest, and second to protect water systems from agricultural pollution. Priority has been given to the application of the first measure. The projected area of application is 25 000 ha. Until now 20 000 ha have been included in the programme, 80 per cent of which land is in areas belonging to the Natura 2000 network, and the remaining 20 per cent

in areas bordering on the network lands, in riverside and other areas of ecological significance. The 20-year duration of the programme is too long to appraise the positive results in certain zones at this time.

Programme for the conservation of endangered breeds of animals
This programme has a duration of five years, and was introduced in Greece in 1998. The goal of the programme is the maintenance and increase in the number of animals belonging to breeds that are in danger of extinction or genetic erosion.

Environmental Directives

Agri-environmental regulation has shaped a reality in which public administration has already become involved with farmers. In contrast, Directives on nitrates (91/676/EEC) and on habitats (92/43/EEC) that deal with the agricultural sector are still in the preliminary stage of implementation.

Nitrates Directive
Directive 91/676 aims to protect water resources from pollution by nitrates from agricultural sources, and especially from livestock manure. Inorganic fertilizers constitute the major source of nitrogen applied in Greek agriculture. In contrast to the northern part of the EU, livestock manure is of limited significance. Eight years after the adoption of the Nitrates Directive in 1991, Greece has not implemented the measures demanded by the application time frame of the directive. Similar delays in implementing parts of the directive have been observed in most Member States. In any case, a recent acceleration in the taking of necessary measures is apparently related to the Commission's threats to take the country to the European Court. Already four vulnerable zones have been designated, although the scientific criteria for this designation provoke some debates (Louloudis *et al.*, 1999). These proposed zones are large in area and they are among the most agriculturally fertile. Programmes for action in three of these vulnerable zones have been submitted to the European Commission for the necessary deliberations before their approval, while plans for the fourth zone are in the preparatory stages. The Codes of Good Agricultural Practice set by the Ministry of Agriculture in 1994 are undergoing a process of review. Although application of the directive demands significant changes in agricultural practices as they currently stand, initiatives have not been taken to determine methods of informing and sensitizing farmers as to the importance of the directive with information and counselling.

Natura 2000 Network

Under the Habitats Directive (92/43), 264 regions will be included in the Natura 2000 network, representing in total some 2.6 million ha. This area corresponds to 20 per cent of the country, while on the level of the Union, in early 1999, the proposed areas correspond to 9 per cent of landed territory (European Commission, 1999). These areas also include agricultural zones, which are currently of unknown size but clearly not negligible. The successful application of the directive is dependent on the degree of acceptance and compromise among opposing interests in various social strata, such as farmers, environmentalists, those in the service of the Ministry of Agriculture and the Environment, local authorities, and so on, which are inevitably involved in such implementation. It does seem that the creation of this network has caused concern among farmers. Unfortunately, despite the self-evident significance of the directive (contribution to environmental education, possibilities for the creation of alternative employment in the countryside), the total lack of information of the farmers and the barely-existent communication between the latter and those agencies responsible for the implementation of the directive is obvious. The brief experience in applying agri-environmental programmes of organic farming and long-term set-aside of agricultural lands according to the priorities of regions belonging to the Natura 2000 network, indicates the strong interaction between both measures. The designation of agricultural practices in accordance with the maintenance of ecological values should reflect a will in society to protect and maintain these sites, and should provide farmers with compensation for the services they offer in the management of nature.

TOWARDS A REORIENTATION OF RURAL DEVELOPMENT POLICIES

Changes in the rural society of Greece have already accelerated during the 1970s, but mainly have taken place since the early 1980s. The rural population diminished drastically, and the following were consolidated: ageing of the male and female population, a tendency particularly among younger women to leave the countryside, and low literacy. In the context of employment, Greece faced a significant increase in the agricultural labour force living in urban and semi-urban areas. In these cases, agriculture has emerged as the most 'popular' second occupation. These two developments, in turn, pose the question to what extent the conventionally considered 'rural space' in Greece remains rural. The answer to this question lies in the planning of the new multisectorial rural policy, since it is obvious that its success depends on its ability to address realistically and convincingly the productive agencies and the social strata that make up the contemporary rural countryside. With equal urgency, the multisectorial development policies must face up to the most obvious proof of the up-to-present one-dimensional exercise of rural policy, that is, the expanding polarization of the dual development model of Greek agriculture, and its consequences in the economy, society, and the environment. The implementation of strategies under Agenda 2000 to maintain agricultural farm income and also to protect the physical environment of the semi-mountainous and plain areas would be rather complex. The examples of the application of measures for the promotion of agro-tourism and agri-environmental programmes indicate the difficulties but also the potential of the national rural development policy, for a turn towards a multisectorial, environment-friendly direction.

Agro-tourism has increased, which at least in part was due to the support from the LEADER programmes. Despite this, the declared strategic objectives of agro-tourism do not seem to have been fulfilled. Private initiatives exploited these programmes by increasing the number of lodging facilities in the already developed tourist areas, particularly along the extended coastline of the country. As for the mountainous and less favoured areas, the promotion of agro-tourism was not combined with a parallel push for agricultural modernization and, furthermore, with the production of quality products or products of designation of origin from the part of the primary sector or the process sector. Thus, with few exceptions, the entrepreneurial initiative based on agro-tourism remained fragmentary, without the integrated development dimension anticipated by its programmatic conception. Similarly, the participation of women in agro-tourism, which was particularly expected to keep young women from leaving the less favoured areas, does not seem to have had the results anticipated fifteen years ago with the establishment of the first women's co-operative. Yet, generally, in all cases, either from the private or from the social sector, there was undoubtedly much important experience gained towards the improvement of the present condition; moreover, there have been some successful examples of the strategy for the integrated development of the countryside, with the initiatives undertaken in the tourist sector as central.

Greece is one of the Member States that only established agri-environment programmes after the adoption of Regulation 2078/92. This presented significant gaps in the conception and application of programmes, as was the case in countries such as Italy and Spain, where agri-environmental programmes constituted an innovation. The delays in submission and approval of agri-environmental programmes led to their limited application and, by extension, to limited absorption of social resources. The goals regarding cultivated areas have remained very limited. In contrast to the other Member States, the number of agricultural holdings and the land that has been included in agricultural programmes is very small.

As noted in the report of the Commission (European Commission, 1998), considering the limited area covered by the application of this policy, it is very difficult to accept that the agricultural sector of the states with limited application of such programmes would be influenced by agri-environmental policy. This situation is likely to bring about a less efficient integration of environmental orders into the current agricultural policy. Greece, despite the fact that initial designs had corresponded to agricultural and environmental reality, could not in the end enact programmes that would incorporate the specific features of Mediterranean ecosystems, such as water shortage, forest fires, or soil erosion. The Ministry of Agriculture began to enact such programmes more because they were considered a supplementary source of income for farmers rather than because the Ministry was convinced of the necessity of such programmes. Moreover, most farmers considered the agri-environmental programmes as a solution to the difficulties they faced with the reductions of price support measures for some agricultural products. Here we must review the components of the regulation, which allowed for its divergent interpretations. Three goals have been defined, which are not always consistent with the achievement of environmental benefits. The programmes should cause least problems for farmers to adopt; they need to be capable of being implemented with limited public resources; and they need to incorporate a social dimension when distributing limited payments among a large number of recipients.

Regarding efficiency in the implementation of programmes, we must note the real difficulty presented by the lack of previous administrative experience, the well-known weaknesses of Greek public administration, and the underestimation of the need for political training and sensitizing on the part of farmers, all of which are basic prerequisites for the success of programmes. We should add also that the bureaucratic 'burden' was considered a difficulty by the farmers as much as by the managers of local agricultural programmes.

The implementation of policies also faced difficulties, but the elementary mechanisms of public administration did function, although such mechanisms were completely absent from the institutionally demanded process of appraisal. The relevant national monitoring and evaluation commissions that have been established have not yet met. In any case, the experience which has already been acquired should not be dismissed, but should be put to use as appropriate. In addition, effort should be made to make the process of appraisal, which increases the transparency of the political process, more substantive and for the results of this process to have a wider diffusion and more critical examination of the various works of appraisal which are employed. Today, although monitoring and appraisal have not been completed, the new reform Agenda 2000 brings new rules into agri-environmental policy, relegating the experience of agri-environmental programmes to the past, at least at the level of policy. Thus, national policies have turned to a new tool: development programmes. In other words, public administration has decided to foresee and set into action a new instrument, which takes inspiration from a still as yet incomplete experience.

It should not be forgotten, however, that the application of agri-environmental programmes would have been considered utopian only a few years ago, when intensive agriculture was at its apogee. Today it has become a constituent element of a policy deemed reliable by the new CAP orientations and the various measures which aim to encourage environmental initiatives and increased sensitivity towards the environment in society as a whole. Although a serious evaluation of the results of agri-environmental policies is not yet possible, it should be emphasized that, with these programmes, a new dynamic is being introduced into the interests of the Ministry of Agriculture. In addition, and more importantly, environmental protection is becoming an unavoidable parameter in the discussions of the agricultural policy network.

It is clear that any success to implement Directive 92/43 and Directive 91/676 is dependent mainly on the reception of such objectives by the greater social body and more specifically by the agricultural policy network, including policymakers, politicians, organized professional interests, co-operatives and individual farmers. However, until today the implementation of these directives has suffered at the hands of a bureaucratic worldview. Surely it is important for the country to fulfil its social obligations regarding protection of the environment, but it is equally important that the goals specified in the directives be accepted by as many citizens as possible, for this acceptance is the best guarantee for the success and efficient implementation of the directive.

The overall conclusion from the review of the main policies for the new type of rural development in Greece, is that the programmatically multisectoral and complementary character of their secondary objectives was not designed adequately, or, when this was the case, such as with the agri-environmental policy, they were not consistently adhered to during their implementation. The reasons for this inadequacy, or inconsistency, are many as the present chapter has attempted to show. The prevailing ones are the lack of political will at government level, the weaknesses of the 'Mediterranean syndrome' of public administration, the prevalence of economic interests of powerful lobbies related to the exercise of monosectoral agricultural policy, the lack of mechanisms for agricultural education and training, and, possibly, overall, throughout the whole network of national rural policy planning, a lack of a culture of creative adaptation to the new conditions of international competition, and of legitimization of the rural development policy. The quality of products, the protection of the environment, and the health of the European taxpayer and consumer, are, starting from the mid-1980s, and increasingly today, the imperatives to which the Greek agricultural policy network ought to adapt.

NOTES

1. I Kathimerini newspaper, 13 February, 2000.
2. However, the issue is controversial. It has been shown that the contribution of women to the rural economy is underestimated and very often invisible. For a recent in-depth analysis of the labour situation and strategies of farm women in Central Greece, see Efstratoglou (1998).
3. This is explained at least in part by the significant number of immigrants from the neighbouring countries in the Balkan region who are employed in the rural areas having a share of some 10 per cent of the national labour force. It should be noted that of the 225 000 of these immigrants who have applied for work and residence permits ('green cards') until April 1999, only 96 000 have been granted such permits; the others, along with those who have not submitted applications, continue to work illegally, often at very low wages.
4. A recent decision by the Minister of Agriculture has ordered a limitation in the land to be used for cotton cultivation. This affects around 75 000 producers. All farmers are allowed to maintain production, if the area to grow cotton does not exceed 6 ha. Farmers cultivating more land need to reduce their cultivation by up to 60 per cent. For instance, a cultivator with 50 ha can only cultivate up to around 20 ha. To determine the amount of land permitted, the average cultivation area for the last three years will be taken into account. This reform has advantages for small producers, but hampers the modernization of Greek agriculture.
5. See Directive 81/645/EEC, regarding the list of mountainous and less favoured areas in Greece as defined in Directive 75/268/EEC, and amendments 85/148/EEC, 89/158/EEC and 95/516/EEC.
6. Under the rubric of LEADER I, which was completed in 1995, agro-tourism received 41 per cent of the total funding for all measures. The remaining part was used for the valuation of agricultural products (16 per cent), SMEs-manufacturing (16 per cent), training (6 per cent), Local Action Groups (6 per cent), network (6 per cent) and other (6 per cent). The corresponding percentage in LEADER II, which was scheduled for completion in 2000, rose to 30 per cent. In the present study we do not refer to the contributions of Regional Operational Programmes (POPs) and of other programmes (for example, LIFE/EU, NOW Communal initiative, INTERREG, ECOS-OUVERTURE and so on), which indirectly secure investments for agro-tourism, but for which we did not have sufficient review data.
7. It is interesting to note that the environmental operational programme of the 2nd Community Support Framework shows, with 15 per cent, one of the lowest rates of absorption for the four-year period from 1994 to 1999.
8. In this comparison, information on Greece is based on the table included here, including the data from 1999, and data on the EU from the report of the Commission (European Commission, 1998, pp. 20–24), which include data from either April or the end of 1998. Given that the application of programmes in Greece was delayed, this time lag is not only justifiable, but also reflective of reality.
9. Eleftherotypia newspaper, 1 March, 2000.

REFERENCES

Beopoulos, N. and L. Louloudis (1997), 'Farmers' acceptance of agri-environmental policy measures. A survey of Greece', *Southern European Society and Politics*, **2**(1), 118–37.

Billaud, J.P., K. Bruckmeier, T. Patricio and F. Pinton (1997), 'Social construction of the rural environment. Europe and discourses in France, Germany and Portugal', in H. de Haan, B. Kasimis and M. Redclift (eds), *Sustainable Rural Development*, Aldershot: Ashgate, pp. 9–34.

Djurfeldt, G. (1999), 'Essentially non-peasant? Some critical comments on postmodernist discourse on the peasantry', *Sociologia Ruralis*, **39**(2), 262–70.

Efstratoglou, S. (1998), 'Fthiotis (Greece)', in *Labour situation and strategies of farm women in diversified rural areas of Europe. Research project funded by the AIR-programme of the European Commission (CT94–2414)*, Final Report, CAP Studies EC, DG VI, Luxembourg: European Communities, pp. 27–53.

European Commission, (1997), *Report to the European Parliament and to the Council on the application of Council Regulation (CEE) no. 2078/92, COM (97) 620*, Brussels: Directorate-General Agriculture to European Commission.

European Commission, (1998), *Evaluation of Agri-environment Programmes, DGVI Commission Working Document, State of application of regulation (EEC) no. 2078/92, VI/655/98*, Brussels: Directorate-General Agriculture to European Commission.

European Commission, (1999), *Agriculture, Environment, Rural Development: Facts and Figures – A Challenge for Agriculture*, Brussels: DG Agriculture, DG Environment, Eurostat.

Gidarakou, I., A. Xenou, K. Kazazis and K. Theofilidou (1997), 'The challenge of women's new roles in rural Greece – The case of Crete', paper presented at the XVII Congress of the European Society for Rural Sociology, '*Local Responses to Global Integration. Towards a new Era of Rural Restructuring*', MAICH, Chania, Crete, 25–29 August.

Iakovidou, O., Ch. Vlachou, A. Voltsou and M. Partalidou (1999), *Mountainous and Disadvantaged areas of Greece. Agrotourism*, Thessaloniki: Geotechnical Chamber of Greece (in Greek).

Kalantaridis, Ch. and L. Lambrianidis (1999), 'Family production and the global market: Rural industrial growth in Greece', *Sociologia Ruralis*, **39**(2), 146–64.

Kasimis, Ch. and E. Zakopoulou (2000), 'Social-demographic characteristics and employment in the agricultural sector', paper presented at the Ministry of Agriculture Conference Agriculture and Environment, 'Gaia' Museum of Natural History, Athens, 21–24 February (in Greek).

Katsaros, D. (1999), 'The mountainous areas of Greece under the vantage of new approaches', in the Proceedings of the 1st Conference on Market globalisation and Greek agriculture Challenges, threats and prospects, Agrotica, Thessaloniki 29–30 January, Thessaloniki: HELEXPO, pp. 113–24 (in Greek).

Kazakos, P. (1999), 'The 'Europeanisation' of public administration. The national environmental policy between internal factors and overnational bindings', *Hellenic Review of Political Science*, **13**, May, 84–122 (in Greek).

Louloudis, L., N. Beopoulos and G. Vlachos (1999), 'Policy for the protection of agricultural environment in Greece', in N. Maraveyias (ed.), *Greek Agriculture towards the Year 2010*, Athens: Papazisis editions – Agricultural University of Athens, pp. 309–59 (in Greek).

Louloudis, L., N. Beopoulos and G. Vlachos (2000), 'Greece: late implementation of agri-environmental policies', in H. Buller, G.A. Wilson and A. Höll (eds), *Agri-environmental Policy in the European Union*, Perspectives on Europe, Contemporary Interdisciplinary Research, Aldershot: Ashgate, pp. 71–93.

Ministry of Agriculture (1999), *Evaluation of national programme LEADER II*, Fourth evaluation report (review), Athens: Ministry of Agriculture, Directorate of Planning and Agricultural Structures, Volume 1, pp. 4–39.

Ministry of Agriculture (2000), *Description of public fiscal resources allocated to rural development in the frame of EAGGF during 1992–1999 programming period* (internal document), Athens: Ministry of Agriculture (in Greek).

Moyano, E. and F. Garrigo (1998), 'Acteurs sociaux et politique agri-environnementale dans l'Union Européenne', *Courrier de l'environnement de l'INRA*, **33**, 106–14.

Papaspyrou, N. (1999), 'A farewell to judicial passivity: The environmental jurisprudence of the Greek council of state', *Modern Greek Studies*, **17**(1), 63–84.

Spathes, P., K. Tsimboukas, G. Mermegas and T. Sklavos (1998), 'The impacts of AGENDA 2000 proposals in Greek farming exploitations. An appraisal based on RICA data', paper presented at the 5th Panhellenic Congress of Agricultural Economics, 'Reconstruction of agricultural space', Etairia Agrotikis Economias (Society of Agricultural Economists), Athens 11–13 December (in Greek).

Tsartas, P. and M. Thanopoulou (1994), *Women Agrotouristic Cooperatives in Greece – An appraisal study of how they work*, Mediterranean Women's Studies Institute.

Zakopoulou, E. (1999), 'Multi-employment and agriculture: towards a new conception of a multi-dimensional phenomenon', in Ch. Kasimis and L. Louloudis (eds), *Rural nation: Greek agricultural society at the end of the twentieth century*, Athens: EKKE/Plethron, pp. 115–47 (in Greek).

PART III

Mitigation and Regulation

10. Marketing public goods and externalities provided by agriculture and forestry

Maurizio Merlo

INTRODUCTION

In addition to traditional market commodities, agriculture, forestry and the related environment produce a large set of Environmental Recreational Goods and Services (ERGSs). Examples include pleasant landscapes, maintenance of rural lanes and footpaths, habitats for various kinds of flora and fauna, grounds for sports and other recreational activities. At the same time agriculture and forestry can produce Environmental Bads and Disservices (EBD). These ERGSs and EBDs are generally perceived by our societies as public goods and/or externalities of farming and forestry, as people cannot be excluded and rivalry is not greatly felt: everybody can enjoy and/or suffer from them without any market transaction taking place.

Failure to internalize the external effects of public goods supplied by agriculture and forestry typically is due to free riding. It subsequently provides fuel to 'tragedy of the commons' types of problems. The right signals are not perceived by producers and consumers: the provision of ERGSs is not sufficient to meet the demand, while the prevention of EBDs is not adequate.[1] The consequence can be a loss of welfare. Therefore, specific policy tools have been developed to cope with the issue aimed at achieving sufficient provision of ERGSs, and prevention of EBDs.

The main policy tools presented in Figure 10.1 include: (i) mandatory regulations; (ii) financial/economic interventions by the public sector; and (iii) market creation for public goods/bads and externalities. Complementary measures such as persuasion and communication are also considered to be essential for implementing all the above set of policy tools.

Mandatory Regulatory Tools

Mandatory regulations, that is the 'stick' approach, which may be softened by some form of compensation, have traditionally been applied to provide ERGSs, and prevent EBDs. Legally binding tools are often included within constitu-

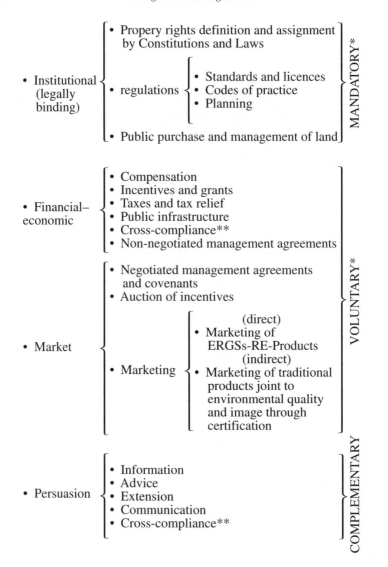

Notes:

* In certain countries the difference between mandatory and voluntary measures remains vague: certain mandatory measures should be understood as voluntary with powers of compulsion
** Cross-compliance can be considered as strongly persuasive, where the provision of ERGSs is conditional to the other financial measures (including income support).

Figure 10.1   Policy tools aimed at achieving provision of ERGSs and prevention of EBDs

tions and laws all over Europe. The framework of property rights, planning and programming, environmental standards and licences supported by codes of practice and indicators should be mentioned. Forest laws, soil conservation and water management are well established remarkable examples. The adoption of mandatory measures is now conceived as an essential part of any policy package aimed at conservation of natural resources.

Of course societies' changing ethical and cultural values, common understanding and consensus, have always been at the root of legal options. Obligations were conceived as a social commitment, and compensation was not generally considered. However, mandatory tools tend to be applied as remunerated 'voluntary means with powers of compulsion'.

A negative aspect of mandatory tools, often overlooked, is given by the high administrative transaction costs of policy implementation, requiring monitoring, control and policing (Whitby and Saunders, 1996); this is particularly relevant when social consensus is not widespread and administration and services are not well established. Economic instruments are in these cases considered the most viable alternative. However, recent evidence shows that consolidated policies and well established administrations give a reduction of transaction costs (Falconer and Whitby, 1999). Another problem with mandatory obligations, particularly in less productive marginal areas like the Alps and the Mediterranean mountains, has been land abandonment due to lack of profitability.

In these contexts purchase and management of land by public bodies like State and Regional Forest Enterprises has also been much used, for example in Italy, France and the UK, to guarantee the provision of ERGSs. The experience, in general, is positive whenever management is supported by effective administration. However, neither purchase nor management by public bodies are now considered efficient tools. Costs are generally too high. There are doubts on the efficiency of this provision.[2] Semi-public bodies, as shown by Figure 10.1, are now much more used and advocated, like trusts, consortia, even the old common properties, and various others Non Governmental Organizations (NGOs), provided of course these bodies can act without state support.

Financial–economic Voluntary Tools

Financial–economic tools, following Pigou's (1920) internalization approach, are based on the 'carrot' rather than on the 'stick', in other words positive instruments which are aimed at convincing farmers or landowners to implement certain measures in exchange for various advantages. According to OECD (1996), it is a 'state pays approach'. The Keynesian side must not be neglected, being often applied for creating jobs and activating depressed rural economies.

The CAP reform of 1992 introduced incentives through Regulation 2078/92 (agri-environmental measures) and Regulation 2080/92 (afforestation measures). Now they have been, even more vigorously, confirmed by the so-called Integrated Rural Development Incentives of Agenda 2000, and formulated under Regulation 1257/1999.

Financial–economic incentives vary according to their economic meaning and administration. First, compensation can be used to meet cost increases and/or income losses to maintain certain types of land uses and the related ERGSs, and prevention of EBDs. Incentives and investment grants are also widely adopted in various countries. Unlike compensation, the payments are geared to include something more – that is a surplus to stimulate the participation in a programme including non-productive environmental investments. It is interesting to stress that this extended view is fully accepted by Article 24 of Regulation 1257/1999 of Agenda 2000 at Chapter VI (agri-environmental measures).

Fiscal measures might also contribute to maintaining traditional farming/forestry systems and the related ERGSs, or preventing undesirable land uses (EBDs). Tax exemption is widely adopted in Less Favoured Areas and forests in countries like Italy and France. Taxes, perhaps the most commonly envisaged instrument to control land use, and therefore the environment quality, follow the much advocated, and little applied, Polluter Pays Principle.

Cross-compliance could be seen as an indirect financial instrument. It is widely debated after the Berlin Summit from the Head of States who reached agreement on Agenda 2000 in March 1999. The concession of existing payments, such as income support, is taken as conditional on the adoption of environmentally friendly techniques: that is eco-conditionality. In other words cross-compliance could be considered a type of strong persuasion supported by various kinds of payments, and as such is shown in Figure 10.1.

All Agenda 2000 'ordinary' payments, fully paid by the EU according to Regulation 1259/1999, should be conditioned to the application of environmentally 'good farming practice'. Unfortunately this condition is completely left to Member States. It is noticeable how agri-environmental measures of Regulation 1257/1999, merely financed by the EU for 50 per cent, are under EU direct control. The limited guidance offered by the European Commission in formulating such Codes of Good Agricultural Practices is probably one of the major shortcomings of the reform under Agenda 2000.

Payments, incentives and tax relief have also been granted throughout Europe by various states involving, for instance, millions of hectares for reforestation in Central and Southern Europe. Timber production objectives were often declared, while environmental objectives were thought to be implicit.

Certainly it should be acknowledged that policy failure is an intrinsic risk of financial means as shown by several cases around the world (Paveri and

Merlo, 1998). For instance the various shortcomings of post-war reforestation policy in Southern Italy should be acknowledged, and may start to
become recognized in other countries. Whitby and Saunders (1996), with
reference to agri-environmental policies, have shown British cases where
landowners and farmers have been overcompensated by 'standard payments',
undermining an ethical commitment to stewardship. Meanwhile, where public goods and positive externalities were more demanded, and needed,
appropriate incentives could not be made available. Of course, this kind of
reflection on the intrinsic danger of intervention policies can be extended to
the overall CAP.[3]

Market Tools

Marketing ERGSs by their transformation and development into Recreational
Environmental (RE)-Products is a relatively new policy tool, which is currently envisaged by the EU [4] and various Member States as a means to
increase the provision of ERGSs, prevent EBDs, and to create additional
income for the farming industry. The approach, based on the Beneficiary
Pays Principle of the OECD (1996), is, to a certain extent, the one theorized
by Coase (1960), advocating that the best way to cope with public goods and
externalities is through the provision of free market arrangements and solutions amongst the concerned parties, bypassing the various pitfalls inherent in
regulations and internalization through state payments.

As shown by Figure 10.1, management agreements providing payments
subject to negotiations between land owners or farmers and the responsible
public authorities can be considered the first step towards the market (Bishop
and Philips, 1993). It is still the State Pays Approach (OECD, 1996), however
mitigated by the negotiation process. The provision of standard payments
should avoid possible excess payments, resulting in owners or enterprises'
rent (Whitby and Saunders, 1996). A more extended view of management
agreements, requiring registration of contracts, is given by the so-called
covenants, or *servitutes praediorum* of Roman law, legally attached to the
land. From the community's point of view they represent a stronger commitment to the provision of ERGSs, or prevention of EBDs.

Auctions of incentives is another market-led tool based on competitive
bidding directly submitted by landowners wishing to provide ERGSs under
specific programmes financed by the public sector (Latacz-Lohmann and Van
der Hamsvoort, 1997). Bids represent the amount of money for which landowners or entrepreneurs are willing to start the scheme and/or accept its
restrictions.

It is, however, with marketing of ERGSs, more or less transformed into
real RE-Products, that the market approach reaches its full extent and poten-

tial. Cases are now spreading all over Europe under different situations, institutions, managerial skills, and RE-Products typology.

In order to document this development a specific survey has been undertaken and reported in this chapter. This chapter first offers a theoretical background based on public and private goods theory to be followed by the type of surveyed ERGSs and RE-products. The empirical evidence of transformation and development is outlined, and the underlying economic and institutional mechanisms are described. Paths of transformation and development are shown with reference to the various area conditions and case studies deriving a synthetic view of the market approach. The chapter concludes with policy and management implications, stressing, however, that the market approach to agri-environment issues must be seen in the context of an appropriate policy mix and area packages of measures including regulatory and financial means, as well as information and communication.

THEORETICAL BACKGROUND FOR TRANSFORMATION OF ERGS INTO RE-PRODUCTS

Following the work of Samuelson (1954) and Musgrave (1959) goods can be defined in terms of rivalry and excludability, two terms much discussed, though sometimes with various degrees of misunderstanding (Randall, 1987). Pure public goods should be non-rival and non-excludable in consumption, therefore fully available to the public. In contrast to this feature, pure private goods should be fully rival and excludable.

ERGSs provided by agriculture and forestry generally appear, and are perceived by our society, as public goods and/or externalities implying low excludability and rivalry. The degree of excludability can, however, vary according to the property rights of each particular ERGS and are sometimes very different across Europe as are the local customs and the transaction costs to enforce exclusion. The degree of rivalry is equally variable according to each particular ERGS: for example a landscape visible from a public road does not generally have a high level of rivalry while the access to a nature reserve can create congestion and rivalry.

The two concepts of rivalry and excludability are presented in Figure 10.2. Excludability ranges from 0 to 10 along the horizontal axis and rivalry, again, from 0 to 10 along the vertical axis. Examples of similar presentations can be found in Buchanan (1967, p. 188), perhaps the first author to propose the diagram and Brosio (1986) who added a third dimension from local to global goods.

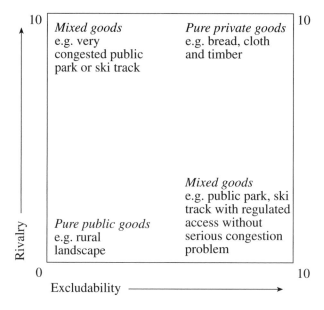

Figure 10.2   Public, private and mixed impure public goods

The Continuum from Public to Private Goods: Mixed Cases

Pure public goods and pure private goods are 'polar' cases, as termed by Samuelson (1955). The actual situation is, in fact, much more differentiated and varied as argued by various authors trying to criticize and complete Samuelson's model. Buchanan (1965) introduced the new category of 'club', collectively shared goods, which are offered by an organization to its members, defraying the cost of the good from member payments (McGuire, 1987). These goods with various degrees of rivalry and excludability are defined as mixed impure public goods. In addition he had a dynamic view, making clear that the group of users can be enlarged or restricted according to property rights (Buchanan, 1967, pp. 190–191). It was also shown that goods and services could move around the diagram according to rivalry and excludability: the allocation of hunting rights and their enforcement (p. 191) being a given example. Other examples of mixed goods were previously given by Tiebout (1956) making reference to local public goods like hospitals and other services that are also characterized by various degrees of rivalry and of excludability.

The Marketability of ERGSs and RE-Products

The theories of local public goods (Tiebout, 1956) and club goods (Buchanan, 1965), have assumed momentum in the last decades regarding the environment and the related ERGSs and RE-Products like those provided by agriculture, forestry and the rural environment in general. Some people have started to question the State Pays Approach (OECD, 1996), resulting in a mere Provider Gets Principle (PGP) (Blöchliger, 1994), while the Beneficiary Pays Approach based on market transaction was so much neglected (OECD, 1996). In particular it is striking that several research efforts across Europe observed a high willingness to pay for ERGSs (Dubgaard *et al.*, 1994). Hanley (1995), in a review of case studies from various countries, found a high level of use of the State Pays Approach, in practice a Provider Gets Principle, but very limited use of the Beneficiary Pays Approach. On the other hand, an extensive research on countryside stewardship policies around the EU analysing some 351 policies in eight Member States could show that 12 per cent of the available ERGSs were already marketed, while 27 per cent were potentially marketable (Gatto and Merlo, 1999).

The marketability concept already shown by Ferro *et al.* (1995) has been formally introduced by Mantau (1995) in the excludability/rivalry diagram by drawing an arrow from public to private goods (Figure 10.3), what is called the 'marketability arrow'. The feasibility of this hypothesis, regarding the applicability of ERGS marketing tools, has been tested surveying 98 case studies in different countries of Europe. Some main findings of this analysis are presented in this chapter.

THE LIST OF CASE STUDIES (ERGSs) AND THE TYPOLOGY OF RE-PRODUCTS

The 98 case studies investigated are grouped in Table 10.1 under the headings of each country: Austria (21 cases), Germany (28), Italy (29) and the Netherlands (20). The RE-Products supplied by, or linked to, agriculture and forestry have been classified in three broad categories of recreational, environmental and traditional products. Occasionally, it was not possible to assign a case study to a precise category, because of the complex structure of RE-Products. Therefore, the mixed categories of environmental/recreational, traditional/recreational and traditional/environmental products have been included in addition to pure recreational and pure environmental as shown in Table 10.1.

Remarkably, the majority of RE-Products had a recreational component and fell, at least to a certain extent, in the category of recreational goods and services: 71 products out of 98. These were mainly 'structured' activities

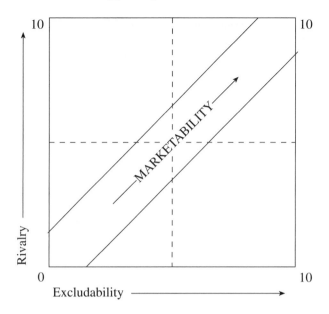

Source: modified from Mantau (1995)

Figure 10.3   The marketability arrow: from public to private goods

Table 10.1   Typology of RE-Products

	Austria	Germany	Italy	The Netherlands	Total
One category					
Recreational	9	10	16	7	42
Environmental	6	4	1	5	16
Mixed categories					
Environmental/Recreational	3	10	8	4	25
Traditional/Recreational	1	3	–	–	4
Traditional/Environmental	–	1	4	4	9
Not classifiable	2	–	–	–	2
Total	21	28	29	20	98

giving added value to the ERGSs and taking advantage of the forest environment. RE-Products with an environmental component (50 out of 98) included case studies that were strictly dependent on the place where they occurred. Sponsorship provides a good example: the real product is an 'environmental image' helping the promotion and/or the business undertaken by the sponsor. Traditional products with a recreational/environmental component (13 cases out of 98) were marketable products, normally produced by agricultural and forest enterprises like timber and meat. Such products were transformed to remunerate for the quality of the environment and for possible recreational activities taking place where they are produced.

INSTITUTIONAL CHANGES AND/OR MANAGEMENT AND MARKETING TECHNIQUES?

Quantification of Excludability and Rivalry

Throughout the survey, questions on excludability and rivalry dealt primarily with the modifications before and after transformation of the ERGs into RE-Products. The following evaluation procedure was undertaken:

i.   a scale of 5 grades was adopted, both for excludability and rivalry (0; 2.5; 5; 7.5; 10). This distinction is made in order to plot ERGSs and RE-Products in the public–private goods diagram;

ii.   rivalry and excludability were evaluated independently, before and after transformation/development;

iii. initially excludability and rivalry were equal to zero when the RE-Product was newly established and the existing ERGS had free access without rivalry/congestion;

iv.   after transformation/development of the ERGSs into RE-Products, excludability was evaluated according to the combined effects of actions undertaken in terms of institutional changes and management/marketing techniques;[5]

v.   again, after transformation/development, rivalry was valued at the highest level, scoring 10, when transformation was related to, or brought to, a fully rival good (for example house lease and product certification) where it is compulsory to pay a price for the RE-Product and the attached ERGSs.[6]

The valuation of rivalry could be biased by subjective judgement. The following criteria have been adopted taking into account that, for club goods, rivalry by definition can not score 10:

a.   rivalry = 2.5, means the availability of a club good without any problems of rivalry among users (internal and external);

b.   rivalry = 5, is the standard club good. It occurs in cases that congestion problems may arise accidentally or temporarily at some periods of the year, week, or day;

c.   rivalry = 7.5, when there is a declared problem of congestion (high internal rivalry) and/or a demand greater than supply (high external rivalry).

The State of ERGSs (and Potential RE-Products) before Transformation

In most cases (Tables 10.2 and 10.3) ERGSs, before transformation (and the potential RE-Products taking place) were characterized as public goods, without excludability or rivalry. This was sometimes due to the physical constraints to forbid use or access to the ERGSs. There were only a few existing pure private goods, which did not require transformation. In these cases, the development of RE-Products dealt mainly with management and marketing.

The few existing pure private goods and services were mainly found in Austria, where in 9 out of 19 cases (Table 10.2) the ERGSs were already

Table 10.2   Excludability before transformation[a]

Excludability	Austria	Germany	Italy	The Netherlands	Total
No (0)	7	25	23	15	70
Very low (2.5)	–	–	–	–	–
Low (5.0)	3	–	2	1	6
Relevant (7.5)	–	–	1	–	1
Very relevant (10)	9	3	2	4	18
Total	19	28	28	20	95

Note: a   Not applicable to 3 case studies

Table 10.3   Rivalry before transformation/development[a]

Rivalry	Austria	Germany	Italy	The Netherlands	Total
No (0)	14	22	14	12	62
Very low (2.5)	1	1	3	2	7
Low (5.0)	1	2	9	1	13
Relevant (7.5)	–	2	2	4	8
Very relevant (10)	3	1	–	1	5
Total	19	28	28	20	95

Note: a   Not applicable to 3 case studies

subject to very relevant exclusion before transformation. Examples included the use of forest roads, spring water and fishing. In some cases this was due to a precise definition and assignment of property rights: for example in Austrian legislation water rights are private. In most cases, however, the ERGSs that were to be exploited through RE-Products were non-excludable, or at least excludability was not clearly defined. It applied to 70 cases out of a total of 95. It also applied to traditional products such as those transformed into RE-Products, exploiting their environmental image and origin. In general, before transformation the image was that of a public good, as everybody could claim that a certain product came from a certain area where certain agriculture practices were employed.

The concept of rivalry overlaps with that of congestion. In fact a good is rival when the consumption by one individual detracts all the opportunities of consumption of the same unit of the good to other consumers. Congestion can be considered as 'the situation in which one individual's consumption reduces the quality of service available to others' (Cornes and Sandler, 1986). Randall's (1987) congestable goods are those 'that can be enjoyed by many individuals but are subject to a capacity constraint and for which the fixed cost of provision far exceeds the marginal cost of adding additional users until the capacity constraint is approached'. From this definition, most club goods can be regarded as congestable. It is clear that congestion, diminishing the possibility of consumption by other people, causes an increase in rivalry. Rivalry, however, can exist independently from congestion, as long as a certain good is divisible and consumption by an individual excludes any other.

As far as it was possible, rivalry due to congestion (internal and linked to indivisibility amongst people entitled to use a certain good) and to the good's intrinsic nature (external) were evaluated separately and summed up in the final assignment of rivalry level. It should be underlined that before transformation it was the rivalry concerning the ERGSs, and not the potential RE-Products that was valued, although the two identify themselves to a lesser or larger degree according to the level of their consumption complementarity.

The State of RE-Products (Previously ERGSs) after Transformation

The situation of RE-Products (previously ERGSs) after transformation can be very different, as shown in Table 10.4, with various levels of excludability, as in some case payment for the use of the RE-Product is voluntary, and not compulsorily linked to the related ERGSs.

Measures were taken to prevent free riding and to enforce excludability or to regulate access to the RE-Products in 40 cases out of 83 (Table 10.5). These measures have been adopted in more than half of the Austrian and Italian cases. Only in Germany were measures to prevent free riding rather rare. The adop-

Table 10.4 Excludability after transformation/development[a]

Excludability	Austria	Germany	Italy	The Netherlands	Total
No (0)	–	–	–	–	–
Very low (2.5)	–	1	2	–	3
Low (5.0)	1	2	–	–	3
Relevant (7.5)	–	–	–	1	1
Very relevant (10)	18	25	26	19	88
Total	19	28	28	20	95

Note: a Not applicable to 3 case studies

Table 10.5 Adoption of measures to prevent free riding[a]

Measures to prevent free riding	Austria	Germany	Italy	The Netherlands	Total
No	7	16	9	11	43
Yes	13	3	17	7	40
Total	20	19	26	18	83

Note: a Not applicable to 15 case studies

Table 10.6 Relevance of costs to prevent free riding (cases where measures have been taken)[a]

Costs to prevent free riding	Austria	Germany	Italy	The Netherlands	Total
No	6	–	2	2	10
Very low/low	6	1	11	2	20
Very relevant	1	2	4	3	10
Total	13	3	17	7	40

Note: a Not applicable to 58 case studies

tion of these measures seems to depend upon RE-Products typology. Products like access to forest roads by bike, or mushroom picking need more control than a Christmas market or cabin leasing. However, the costs of these measures were considered relevant in only a few cases (Table 10.6). This can be due to the nature of the goods paid for by the consumers, which are usually familiar market products – for example car parks, guided visits and accommodation. In addition in many cases (58) the issue of costs to prevent free riding was not even considered in the case studies analysed, mainly being a matter to protect common activities of the public. This was particularly evident in Germany and the Netherlands where the issue rarely arose in the course of the survey.

Table 10.7   Rivalry after transformation[a]

Rivalry	Austria	Germany	Italy	The Netherlands	Total
No (0)	–	–	–	–	–
Very low (2.5)	4	6	4	1	15
Low (5.0)	6	5	5	6	22
Relevant (7.5)	1	2	13	3	19
Very relevant (10)	8	15	6	10	39
Total	19	28	28	20	95

Note: a   Not applicable to 3 case studies

Rivalry after transformation into RE-Products generally increases (Table 10.7). Reduction is, however, also evident. Therefore it is difficult to identify a clear trend. Rivalry depends, to a certain extent, on congestion, since if there are too many users the enjoyment of the good or service decreases. RE-Products can therefore have different and opposite effects on the congestion of ERGSs:

i.   a promotion of access and use, due to the attraction of a larger number of users, increasing congestion;
ii.   a more regulated use of the ERGSs, due to zoning and the introduction of entrance fees or permits, reducing, or at least controlling, congestion.

It is interesting to note that, when rivalry was originally low, it tended to increase after transformation or development, while it increased very little or decreased when the level was already high – as in three Dutch cases. A low level of rivalry before transformation indicates that a certain ERGS is a typical public good with no congestion problems and so the aim of transformation or development is to increase the use. Where there is already a high level of rivalry the product transformation or development consists mostly of an increase of regulation and production efficiency. Finally, when there is a serious problem of congestion, transformation or development can often decrease congestion through market regulation, that is exclusion given by the price, as shown by the experience of well-consolidated RE-Products.

In summarizing excludability and rivalry aspects of transformation or development, it is clear that excludability has been successfully achieved in most cases – 88 out of 95 (Table 10.4). There are fewer cases that achieved a high level of rivalry – 39 cases out of 95 (Table 10.7). Overall about half the cases have shown full transformation into pure private goods when considering both rivalry and excludability.[7] Rivalry was the criterion most difficult to achieve. In general terms, development mainly led to club local goods, rather than private goods, due to the intrinsic characteristics of the goods and services offered – for example car parks, picnic sites and cross country skiing.

Mechanisms of Transformation or Development

The transformation of ERGSs into RE-Products can be divided into two stages. The first stage reflects a real transformation concerning institutional factors such as legal status and property rights, planning and permissions or contractual arrangements. The second stage concerns development, mainly linked to management and marketing, above all the provision of complementary/additional goods and services, promotion and information.

Institutional factor changes can be listed as:

i.   legislative changes concerning state and regional laws, often representing the first step towards transformation, creating the base for the RE-Products market niche: for example the Italian law on mushroom picking obliging pickers to buy a permit, or the EU Regulations on product origin certification (Food Geographical Origin – FGO) obliging producers to get approval and follow a code of practice (Regulation 2081/91);

ii. planning changes, concerning regional and local actions, which can again initiate the transformation of an ERGS into an RE-Product. Land use and environmental planning including zoning, the designation of parks and protected areas, for example, create new opportunities for RE-Products;

iii. administrative changes, at an even lower level, implying local planning standards, licences and other regulations, again making possible the first step towards the establishment of RE-Products on the basis of existing ERGSs.

Therefore institutional changes, or at least compliance with a certain administrative procedure, often represent the first step towards the transformation process triggering the following developments possible through management and marketing. Notable differences do exist among the four countries de-

Table 10.8   Occurrence of legal changes

	Austria	Germany	Italy	The Netherlands	Total
No	12	24	10	12	58
Yes	9	4	19	8	40
Total	21	28	29	20	98

pending upon existing property rights and, above all, RE-Products typology. Only a few German cases required a true legal change, while in several Italian cases such a change was required (Table 10.8). This certainly has to be related to products typology being prevalent in German and Dutch cases, with the development of products like farm hospitality, Christmas market, organic meat, and so on, always supported by clearly defined property rights. Complex types of RE-Products have been developed in Italy, and to a lesser extent in Austria as well. Examples in these countries include access to private land, cross country skiing, biking on forest roads, Food Geographical Origin (FGO), in a context where, at least in Italy, property rights are affected by a heritage of communal rights, quite obviously more difficult to be modified and regulated.

Management and market developments were generally based on the relationship between the ERGSs and the RE-Products actually sold in the market – a relationship often given by consumption complementarity. In order to appreciate the environment (the ERGSs) one must use appropriate infrastructures and equipment – RE-Products. This complementarity can also be seen as the RE-Products giving added value to the ERGSs. The relationship of complementarity and the additional value of the equipment and infrastructure therefore represents a final step for making a market value of ERGSs through the RE-Products.

Usually, both institutional and management or market approaches are needed to achieve remuneration of ERGSs through RE-Products. The institutional approach builds the base for transformation, for example new regulations are introduced for using the ERGSs. However, it is management and marketing that give the core for the development. In fact the availability of additional goods and services is necessary to create a market for the ERGSs through the RE-Products. Figure 10.4 exemplifies the transformation process. The figure shows that the ERGSs for which institutional status is slightly changed (continuous line), are enveloped within conventional complementary market goods such as car parks, tourist and sport facilities (dotted line). In addition, they also include traditional farm/forest products, whose quality and image is linked to the environment and the landscape (ERGSs) where they are produced.

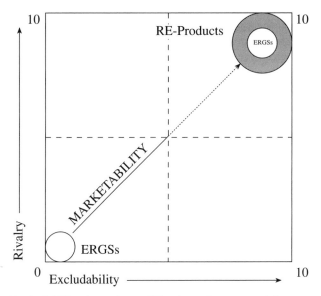

Excludability through modification of property rights: transformation
Excludability through provision of additional services, management
and marketing techniques: development

Figure 10.4   Transformation and development paths from ERGSs to RE-Products: the two components of the 'marketability arrow'

The possible level of complementarity between ERGSs and RE-Products is variable, as shown by Figures 10.5 and 10.6: for example, there is a high complementarity between the pure environment and the footpaths to gain access to the environment, while it is lower with restaurants and shops. At the limit, when complementarity is very high the ERGSs and the RE-Products overlap almost completely, as shown by Figure 10.5. The case studies have also shown that it is almost always the RE-Products that are paid for in the market, not the ERGSs.

In addition to the 98 cases surveyed, some 20 cases of failures were also recorded. Causes were rather different; however, in general it was mainly a case of property rights violation arousing protest by the public. In other cases it was lack of demand and/or poor management or poor communication with consumers.

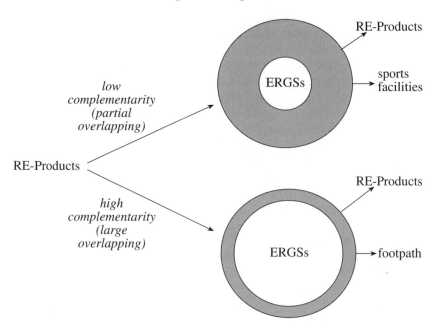

Figure 10.5   Degree of complementarity between ERGSs and RE-Products

LINKS BETWEEN RE-PRODUCTS AND REGIONAL/ LOCAL CONDITIONS DURING THE TRANSFORMATION/ DEVELOPMENT

Reference to Country Case Studies

It appears that the transformation or development involves both institutional and management and market based approaches. The case studies examined indicate that the two approaches can be applied alone or simultaneously helping each other towards the marketability of the RE-Product. Both approaches, however, aim at increasing excludability while rivalry may or may not be increased.

Tables 10.2 and 10.3 (before transformation) and Tables 10.4 and 10.7 (after transformation), show the transformation or development for the four countries surveyed. The cases demonstrate that changes in the transformation or development 'paths' can be very different in terms of excludability or rivalry. However, the 'marketability' arrow of Figure 10.3 remains a common feature. It is also evident that transformation and development can either be applied separately or together according to the different case studies.

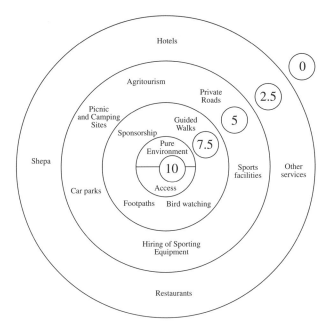

Note: a.   The numbers 0, 2.5, 5, 7.5 and 10 indicate the level of complementarity between the RE-Product and the related ERGS

Source: elaborated from Mantau (1995)

Figure 10.6   Complementarity between the pure environment (ERGSs) and the means to make use of it (RE- Products)

The interdependency between institutional and management and marketing means is particularly evident for Italy. In Germany and Austria management and marketing means are already frequently applied and sufficient alone, while initial support and gearing by institutional changes is less evident and less needed. This applies also to the Netherlands where, however, similarly to Italy, paths often move from a higher degree of rivalry/congestion to a less evident one, meaning that marketing of RE-Products is also aimed at reducing pressure on the environment. As a consequence Austria and Germany show transformation or development paths more similar to the 'marketability arrow' of Figure 10.3 compared to Italy and the Netherlands where they are more dispersed in the diagram. The differences in paths can be linked to Austrian and German property rights for ERGSs, which are better defined and assigned by consolidated legislation particularly in forestry, which represents the largest number of case studies. Traditionally, in Austria and Germany forest owners are also more business-minded both for timber and tourism services linked to farming and forestry. The lack of business tradition in Italy can also be seen in terms of 'late economic development' and inheritance law, which has left a legacy of fragmentation. Property rights are not always well defined and assigned, including communal rights on rural land. The present situation, which is characterized by a rather affluent and environmentally sensitive society, makes it difficult to apply unpalatable land policies that were easily applicable centuries ago. Therefore, other more socially acceptable means have to be applied. In the Netherlands meanwhile it is striking to observe the high rivalry/congestion of ERGSs before transformation or development into RE-Products with private and/or club connotations. This helps to explain the complicated mix of institutional, management or marketing approaches as shown by the Italian and Dutch case studies. These two countries also both experience high pressure on rural resources determined by high population density, which, however, allows more opportunities to farmers and land owners.

TOWARDS A SYNTHESIS OF TRANSFORMATION/ DEVELOPMENT PATHS

The different case studies can be grouped to give six significant paths of transformation or development of ERGSs into RE-Products as illustrated by Figure 10.7. To simplify the diagram, only paths consisting of two or more cases are shown. These paths are detailed below:

1. re-launch of an already private RE-Product. In these cases there was not any variation in the excludability/rivalry criteria;
2. from a public ERGS (pure or rival to various degree) to a pure private RE-Product;
3. from a public ERGS (pure or rival to various degrees) to a club RE-Product with partial excludability;
4. from a public (rather rival) or a club ERGS with partial excludability to a club good with a decrease in rivalry;
5. from an excludable club ERGS with low rivalry to a club or private RE-Product with partial and high rivalry;
6. from a public ERGS (pure or rival to a certain extent) to a club RE-Product with high excludability. Path 6, the most common, consists of several paths that are all within the shaded area given various excludablity/ rivalry levels before and after transformation/development.

The simplification of Figure 10.7 allows the following common features to be pointed out:

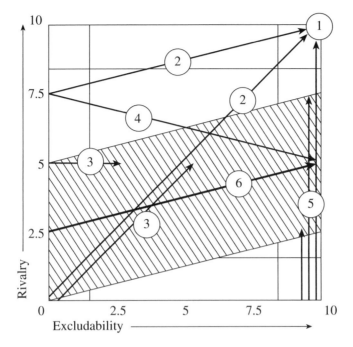

Note: The numbers 0, 2.5, 5, 7.5 and 10 indicate the level of complementarity between the RE-Product and the related ERGS

Figure 10.7   The main transformation/development paths

i.   transformation or development paths mainly move from left to right and usually from down to up as this is the result of the fact that the main purpose of transformation or development actions is to obtain private goods where remuneration is easier;

ii.   some areas of Figure 10.7, characterized by high rivalry and low excludability do not have significant paths to indicate that these positions are difficult to deal with, meaning that 'free riding' and 'tragedy of the commons' can easily take place;

iii.   the key issue for transformation or development is the increase in excludability, while changes in rivalry mainly result from this modification. In path 4 in particular the goal is rivalry reduction, obtained through an increase in excludability;

iv.   transformation or development usually leads to private or club goods, depending on the products' intrinsic characteristics. Path 3 is quite unusual, it corresponds to the use of voluntary contribution/donation as a means of payment, and it could be considered as an incomplete transformation or development – the RE-Product remains in the central undefined area of mixed goods, potentially club/private goods;

v.   path 4 is the only path, including cases in the Netherlands, which goes between goods with low excludability and high rivalry to club goods with reduced rivalry. More paths of this type could have been expected, as it seems a logical further development of path 3, which is more common with 7 cases observed in all countries. The likely reason for this is that the change from voluntary donations to compulsory payments is often unpalatable to the public and it is often unwise to disturb or upset people;

vi.   it must finally be underlined that the most common case of transformation or development is given by path 6, grouping 32 cases where transformation or development is mainly aimed at the creation of club/local goods with full excludability and various levels of rivalry.

CONCLUSIONS

The following points can be underlined with reference to the potential markets open to ERGSs and the related RE-Products:

i.   recreational products, requiring various types of facilities and structures in addition to the pure environment, can be transformed and developed rather easily. This type of product offer good opportunities for several ERGSs, particularly those located in regions where less intensive types of farming systems prevail, and for forestry where tourism is more important, particularly on coastal and mountainous areas. Meanwhile, the environment alone cannot be easily marketed; however, traditional quality products labelled according to the environment/geographical area they come from like FGO, the well established *appellation d'origine* of wine and cheeses, and in general production processes certification, and also sponsorship of a certain environment, represent viable opportunities that can be exploited in order to capture consumers' willingness to pay for the environment;

ii.   public and private land ownership both give opportunities for the development of RE-Products. It is important to note, however, the role played by landowners' associations, consortia, even the traditional common properties of forests and the modern trusts and environmental societies. In the meantime specialized contractors must not be forgotten as they often represent the easiest way towards transformation or development, because they can reach the adequate land base necessary for RE-Products development more easily than individual landowners;

iii. institutional changes are certainly needed for triggering transformation of ERGSs into RE-Products. However, various case studies have shown that dramatic changes of property rights are not feasible as they are unpalatable to the general public, and in any case they are not so necessary, as management and marketing approaches aimed at achieving 'exclusiveness through additional services' are often sufficient. Generally speaking, it is a matter of both institutional and management and marketing changes to achieve transformation as outlined in Figure 10.4. According to Italian case studies, one third of the paths, measured according to the already mentioned scale of excludability/rivalry before and after transformation[8] the result of institutional changes often granted by Local Authorities (permission, licences, etc) and two thirds were down by management and marketing;

iv. a positive relationship was also found, particularly in Italy, between the different ERGSs, the related RE-Products and other local market products. The term 'area product mix' can be used to describe the situation where RE-Products related to farming and forestry have been more successful because of the regional system to which they belong. Marketing of RE-Products is easier in an area where various infrastructures and other products are already available;

v. finally, the most evident shortcoming of any transformation or development strategy which was particularly clear in Italy, but also applies to other countries, is demonstrated by the fact that those producing the positive ERGSs are not always those involved with the management and marketing of the RE-Products; in fact it can be quite the opposite. The result is market distortions and inefficiency. Compensation amongst economic actors at area level must therefore be considered and represents the most challenging task for market based environmental policies.

Concerning the various policy tools for promoting ERGSs and RE-Products, all of them have both advantages and disadvantages. However, it is clear that they cannot be seen, and conceived, separately, and this is a common feature of environmental policies aimed at increasing the provision of ERGSs and RE-Products (Glück, 1998). Mandatory legally binding instruments, new and old, should be applied together with economic–financial and market-led tools. The sustainable provision of the various ERGSs, RE-Products and the prevention of EBDs, goes through jointly devised and applied policy tools, integrated and permeated by the 'transparency' of information, including measures of persuasion and communication as outlined in Figure 10.1. After all the various ERGSs are given by different value-types: from use-value (direct and indirect), to option, to existence and non-use value. It appears rather obvious that an effective and efficient agri-environmental policy needs various possible tools and measures.

It also seems important to stress that the policy mix should be devised area by area according to the 'subsidiarity' principle, developing specific packages of policy measures and tools. The concept is not new, being for instance demanded by the Structural Funds. It represents, however, a general meaning, being also related to compensation amongst local forest actors, taxation, devolution, indeed, an autonomous status (Rojas Briales, 1995), of each area able to guarantee local responsibility over farming, forestry and more generally over the environmental resources.

NOTES

The present chapter reports results of EU financed research on 'Niche Markets for Recreational and Environmental Services – RES' (FAIR – CT95–0743) undertaken in 1996–1999 at Padua University (Prof. Maurizio Merlo) in collaboration with the University of Hamburg (co-ordinator Prof. Udo Mantau), the University of Vienna (Prof. Walter Sekot) and IBN – DLO – Wageningen (Dr. Kees Van Vliet). Part of the results of the above research, specifically focused on forestry, have been published in: Forest Policy and Economics, 1 (2), 2000, Elsevier journal, ISSN 1389–9341 quoted in the references as Merlo M., Milocco E., Panting R. and Virgilietti P. (2000). Other versions of the same research are forthcoming in the following two books: 'Recreational and Environmental Markets for Forest Enterprises' eds U. Mantau, et al, CABI Publishing, Oxford, OX10 8DE, UK 'Economic studies on Food, Agriculture and the Environment' eds M. Canavari, Kluwer Proceedings, 233, Spring Street, New York 10011.

The author is indebted for the broad help received from E. Milocco, P. Virgilietti, R. Panting and other collaborators and PhD students.

1. The price support measures that are offered under the Common Agricultural Policy (CAP) during the past 30 years are often recognized for having systematically helped intensive farming, rather than extensive and environmentally friendly farming practices and their related ERGSs.
2. For instance in Italy costs have been estimated at around 200 euro/ha for State forests; 150 for regional forests; 90 for communal and common property forests and 40 for private forests. Of course it must be noted that public forests generally provide a larger share of ERGSs (Centro Contabilità e Gestione Agraria, Forestale e Ambientale, 1998).
3. Support has been given above all to the high productivity areas, which have been over compensated, while the low productivity areas (naturally disadvantaged) have been neglected. According to 1992 CAP reform premises, 20 per cent of the farmers were draining 80 per cent of the subsidies.
4. For example, chapter IX, Article 33 of Regulation 1257/1999 is considered as a means to achieve rural development. This article includes measures for farm diversification, rural tourism and environmental conservation.
5. Excludability was valued at 10 whenever the 'price' of RE-Products was the only possible way to use the ERGS. However, if paying the price for the ERGS could be avoided, a reduction in excludability was accounted (for example voluntary contribution for a picnic area) and excludability was valued around 5.
6. For club goods and services two types of rivalry were distinguished as either (a) internal rivalry among people already entitled (that is club members) to use the good where congestion could be a problem, or (b) an external rivalry among potential users. For example, for admittance to a park, there can be rivalry to obtain the entrance ticket if the number of admitted persons is regulated and demand is greater than supply (external rivalry). Once tickets have been issued, rivalry can exist among the admitted persons, due to congestion within the park (internal rivalry).

7. In Italy, however, only a quarter of RE-Products were completely transformed into pure private goods with full excludability and rivalry.
8. For Italian cases respondents were also asked to separate the role of institutional means (legal changes including property rights, permissions granted by Local Authorities, and so on) from the managerial and economics aspects.

REFERENCES

Bishop, K.D. and A.P. Philips (1993), 'Seven steps to market: the development of the market led approach to countryside conservation and recreation', *Journal of Rural Studies*, **9**(4), 315–18.

Blöchliger, H. (1994), 'Main results of the study', in *The contributions of amenities to rural development*, Paris: Organization for Economic Co-operation and Development (OECD), pp. 71–86.

Brosio, G. (1986), *Economia e finanza pubblica*, Roma: NIS (Nuova Italiana Scientifica).

Buchanan, J. M. (1965), 'An economic theory of clubs', *Economica*, February, 1–14.

Buchanan, J. M. (1967), *The Demand and Supply of Public Goods*, Skokie, Illinois, USA: Rand McNally.

Centro Contabilità e Gestione Agraria, Forestale e Ambientale – Università di Padova (1998), unpublished data.

Coase, R. (1960), 'The problem of social cost', *Journal of Law and Economics*, **3**, 144–71.

Cornes, R. and T. Sandler (1986), *The Theory of Externalities, Public Goods and Club Goods*, Cambridge: Cambridge University Press.

Dubgaard, A., I. Bateman and M. Merlo (eds) (1994), *Identification and Valuation of Public Benefits from Farming and Countryside Stewardship*, Kiel: Wissenschaftsverlag Vauk.

Falconer, K. and M. Whitby (1999), 'The invisible costs of scheme implementation and administration', in G. van Huylenbroeck and M. Whitby (eds), *Countryside Stewardship: Farmers, Policies and Markets*, Amsterdam: Pergamon, pp. 67–87.

Ferro, O., M. Merlo and A. Povellato (1995), 'Valuation and remuneration of countryside stewardship performed by agriculture and forestry', in G.H. Peters and D.D. Hedley (eds), *Proceedings of the XXII International Conference of Agricultural Economists, Harare, Zimbabwe,* London: Dartmouth, pp. 415–35.

Gatto, P. and M. Merlo (1999), 'The economic nature of stewardship: complementarity and trade-offs with food and fibre production', in G. van Huylenbroeck and M. Whitby (eds), *Countryside Stewardship: Farmers, Policies and Markets*, Amsterdam: Pergamon, pp. 21–46.

Glück, P. (1998), 'The task of research in evaluation of multifunctional forestry', II International Forest Policy Forum', Solsona: Centre Tecnológic Forestal de Catalunya vol. IV, 215–27.

Hanley, N. (1995), 'Synthesis report, observation concerning the implementation of amenity policy', in N. Hanley (ed.), *Amenities for Rural Development: Policy Examples*, Paris: OECD, pp. 9–28.

Latacz-Lohmann, U. and C.P. van der Hamsvoort (1997), 'Auctioning conservation contracts – A theoretical analysis and an application', *American Journal of Agricultural Economics*, **79**(2), 407–18.

Mantau, U. (1995), 'Forest policy means to support forest outputs', in B. Solberg and

P. Pelli (eds), *Forest Policy Analysis – Methodological and Empirical Aspects,* Joensuu: EFI Proceedings 2, pp. 131–45.

McGuire, M. (1987), 'Clubs', in J. Eatwell, M. Milgate and P. Newman (eds), *The new Palgrave: a Dictionary of Economics*, London: McMillan Press, pp. 454–5.

Musgrave, R.A. (1959), *The Theory of Public Finance. A Study in Public Economy*: New York: McGraw-Hill.

OECD (1996), *Amenities for Rural Development*, Paris: Organization for Economic Co-operation and Development.

Paveri, M. and M. Merlo (1998), 'Formation and implementation of forest policies: a focus on the policy tools mix', FAO XI World Forestry Congress, Rome: **5**, 233–54.

Pigou, A. C. (1920), *The Economics of Welfare*, London: MacMillan.

Randall, A. (1987), *Resource Economics – An Economic Approach to Natural Resource and Environmental Policy*, New York: John Wiley.

Rojas Briales, E. (1995), *Una Política Forestal para el Estado de las Autonomías*, Madrid: Editorial Aedos.

Samuelson, P. (1954), 'The pure theory of public expenditure', *Review of Economics and Statistics*, **36**, 387–9.

Samuelson, P. (1955), 'A diagrammatic exposition of a theory of public expenditure', *Review of Economics and Statistics*, **37**, 350–56.

Tiebout, C. M. (1956), 'A pure theory of local expenditures', *Journal of Political Economy*, **5**, 416–24.

Whitby, M. and C. Saunders (1996), 'Estimating conservation goods in Britain', *Land Economics*, **72**(3), 313–25.

11. Co-operative agreements to improve efficiency and effectiveness of policy targets

Ingo Heinz

INTRODUCTION

The adverse impacts of agriculture on nature include degradations of water resources and decreasing levels of biodiversity. However, in the last decades a growing number of environmental policies have been introduced in the individual EU member states, and subsequently have led to a change towards a more extensive and sustainable agriculture. On the other hand, the cost-effectiveness of policy measures becomes more and more an important criterion for assessing this development. Many environmental economists are of the opinion that the cost-effectiveness of a rigid command and control policy as well as of economic instruments applied in agriculture, especially with regard to water protection and nature conservation, is limited (OECD, 1998). The argument is that the specific conditions in vulnerable areas will not be adequately considered. Since the impacts on the environment are typically diffuse due to the complex processes in water and soil, it is very difficult to control compliance with compulsory regulations and ensure the requirements for the application of economic instruments, such as for example charges on pollution. In particular, the level of water pollution resulting from a certain farmer is often very difficult to identify. This situation differs from that in industry where the authorities can find out more easily the sources and also the level of this type of pollution. As a consequence, in recent years voluntary approaches to influence farming practices have been increasingly adopted in some EU member countries (Brouwer et al., 1999). In most of these cases, co-operative agreements between farmers and water suppliers and/or nature conservation groups have been supported by authorities who have recognized that the enforcement of environmental regulations can be facilitated by voluntary approaches.

Below, the principles of co-operative agreements in agriculture and the linkages to other agri-environmental policy instruments will be highlighted.

Moreover, the occurrence and reasons for establishing co-operative agreements, especially in the EU member countries, are discussed. A further aim is to show that legislation opens itself increasingly to voluntary approaches and that in some cases compulsory rules have been replaced by co-operative agreements. Here the authorities give priority to voluntary negotiations with farmers over a rigid enforcement of obligatory rules as they have observed that this approach has some advantages in terms of environmental effectivity and economic efficiency. In the following, a co-operative agreement (CA) is principally understood as the result of voluntary negotiations between groups or individual agents who use the same environmental resources but with divergent intentions, while governments refrain from using direct compulsory rules, even though they provide a legal framework to protect these resources. Consequently, such CAs are typically characterized by their self-regulation and bottom-up processes.

OVERVIEW ON AGRI-ENVIRONMENTAL INSTRUMENTS

The main purpose of this overview is to clarify the meaning of CAs in agriculture and the key features of such agreements relative to the other agri-environmental instruments. A growing literature exists which deals with different types of agri-environmental instruments (Oskam *et al.*, 1998; van Zeijts, 1999; Wossink *et al.*, 1998; Brouwer and Lowe, 2000; Buller *et al.*, 2000). In a recent publication (Just and Heinz, 2000) a typology can be found where such instruments are classified by means of various criteria such as for example 'statutory', 'compulsory', 'economic', 'communicative', 'self-regulatory' and 'voluntary'. The different implementation forms include statutory norms, acts, prohibitions, permits, taxes, subsidies, education, voluntary associations and contracts. These instruments are ranked in accordance with the degree of state intervention and voluntary self-regulation, respectively.

CAs, typically a bottom-up approach and integrated in a legal framework of obligatory environmental standards, are self-regulatory and voluntary, and are often implemented by contracts, so that they differ clearly from statutory rules and taxes which are compulsory. Taxes (or levies, charges, and so on) on the use of pesticides, nitrogen or phosphorous fertilizers, usually known as economic and market-based instruments, are not so rigid as is often assumed. Farmers are in the position to influence the level of the tax by decreasing the use of pesticides or fertilizers. Subsidies, as one of the most important instruments of the EU agri-environmental policy (as especially the 2078/92 regulation replaced by the 1257/1999 regulation) are also based on voluntary and contractual agreements, but they are not self-regulatory (Table 11.1). Educational or advisory measures are typically voluntary and are often connected with CAs.

Table 11.1   Various instruments influencing farming practices

Approaches to meet environmental policy targets	Key features
Statutory rules, prohibitions, permits	Compulsory, high degree of state intervention
Taxes, levies, charges, tradeable permits	Compulsory, high degree of state intervention
Subsidies (for example 2078/92 regulation)	Voluntary, non-compulsory state intervention
CAs	Voluntary, self-regulatory, bottom-up approach, and frequently based on a legal framework of compulsory standards

An important characteristic of CAs is that they usually go beyond the re-quirements of good agricultural practice laid down in the legal framework. The victims of the pollution caused by agriculture, namely water suppliers and/or nature conservation groups are ready to compensate the farmers, because they expect to gain from it. The exclusive pursuit of the Polluter Pays Principle (PPP) in agriculture has often not lead to the desired environmental effects due to the excessive cost of its enforcement (Heinz, 1998), which might be in part because the constraints applying to farmers did not give sufficient incentives to meet the targeted requirements on quality of water and nature in specific areas. This can be proved by the fact that in many environmentally vulnerable areas the agricultural pollution of soils and waters exceeds limit values, although an increasing number of regulations have come into force during recent decades. In many cases, breaching of compulsory rules cannot be proved either by the victims or by the authorities. The main reason is that in agriculture diffuse and long-term processes of contamination prevail (compared with for example power plants as point sources of pollution). Consequently, it is often difficult to make individual farmers responsible for using excessive quantities of pesticides and fertilizers, especially in periods with frequent rainfall and runoffs. This is also true where the contamination of pumped water was caused by pollution incurred many years ago. However, in the framework of CAs it is easier to cope with these problems, because the incentives for the farmers to get round obliga-tions are generally fewer than in the case of compulsory rules, and the willingness to change farming practices is considerably greater.

As explained below, each of the participants in CAs could be better off by fulfilling the voluntarily agreed obligations. This effect can also be the result of agri-environmental measures, offering support for measures taken by the farmers. In the case of CAs, however, the compensation payments and advisory measures are the outcomes of mutual negotiations between the involved actors on the basis of self-interest and self-determination. Consequently, the incentives to find out the most cost-effective measures play a major role relative to agri-environmental programmes whose financial volumes are usually not a result of site-specific negotiations or direct public payments that may be of a more generic nature (by area or head of livestock).

There are various hydro-geographic, institutional and socio-economic factors which can hamper or facilitate the establishment of CAs. For instance, in large water catchment areas it is difficult to enter into negotiations with individual farmers. Since groundwater catchments are generally more contained, such negotiations are more likely at these sites than in areas where the share of surface waters is high. The co-operative approach will hardly occur in countries where the water suppliers cannot pass on the costs of such agreements to the customers. CAs are more likely where farmers can expect economic gains from changeover to more efficient farming management, especially in cases where there is a high level of inefficiency at the farm level as significant savings can be achieved without large payments for advice and compensation (Heinz *et al.*, 2000).

In reality, there is a great variety of different types of voluntary agreements between farmers and water suppliers. They differ with regard to the participants, objectives, geographical scope, legal conditions and source of funds. In some cases the authorities participate in the supervision of the procedure of the CAs. At the local level CAs prevail in groundwater catchment areas; however, such agreements can also be found at the regional level in river basins. The outcomes of the agreements are also influenced by whether or not statutory water or nature protection zones are established. Moreover, there are cases where the compensation payments and advisory programmes are partly financed by the government, for instance from the revenues obtained from water abstraction charges.

METHODOLOGICAL IMPLICATIONS OF CAs

The Basic Model

The Coasean theorem (Coase, 1960) is often used to show under which conditions voluntary arrangements between polluters and victims lead to environmentally effective and economically efficient outcomes without direct state intervention (Glachant, 1999). The aim of this theorem is to prove that in special cases, such as for example a relatively small number of participants, the problem of externalities can be solved by self-regulation. The only state regulation needed is that property rights are properly defined by law. Since the externalities are generally seen as being caused by the lack of defined property rights, the simple conclusion is to establish those by government regulation. Compulsory rules, such as prescriptions and prohibitions, or economic policy instruments, such as taxes or subsidies, are, from the viewpoint of self-regulation, less efficient than voluntary arrangements. Typically, Coase originally developed his theorem in the agriculture sector. Obviously, agriculture seems to have features that make this sector suitable for demonstrating this theorem. The example used by Coase is simple. The cattle of a stock breeder reduces the corn harvest of a neighbouring farmer because there is no pasture fence.

What Coase tried to show was that a clear rule of liability is a crucial requirement regardless of to whom the protected right is allocated. Consequently, obliging the stock breeder to build a fence or compensating the farmer for his yield losses do not present the only solution. To protect the stock breeder against the claims of the farmer might also be a solution (especially in the case where the cereal cropping on adjoining land was established after the settlement of the stock breeder). The decisive question is how the total costs of the two parties could be minimized, so that at least one of them becomes better off without the other suffering. The best way to achieve this is to enter into mutual negotiations. The Coase Theorem tries to prove that under certain conditions such negotiations lead to optimal outcomes in terms of an efficient level of damages (or externalities) prevented regardless of the allocation of the property right. Apart from the existence of a clear rule of liability, one of the most important conditions is that the costs of negotiation (transaction cost) are not excessively high.

If the right is assigned to the stock breeder, the neighbouring farmer will be interested in compensating him for preventative measures. The farmer's readiness to pay will be dependent on the benefits obtained from these measures, but he will try to gain from trade by paying less than these benefits. On the other hand, the stock breeder will not spend more money for preventative measures than he will be compensated for by the farmer. This behaviour of both ensures that prevention will be realized only to an extent to which the difference between costs and benefits (that is the total net-benefits) is maximized. Assuming that the property right is assigned to the farmer, the same outcome can be expected. The stock breeder will only spend additional money on preventative measures if the compensation he would otherwise have to pay to the farmer exceeds the costs of these measures.

Generally speaking, this theorem refers to mutual negotiations between two actors outside the public domain, each of them having their own private interest. Apart from the example used by Coase, CAs between farmers and water supply companies are obviously such cases as well. Moreover, to some extent the theorem appears to be suitable to explain negotiations between private actors and members of public agencies who represent special interest groups, such as, for instance, nature conservation or regulating industrial pollution (Glachant, 1999). Again, in some of those cases, assigning the property rights to polluters might be advantageous, where public subsidies additionally play an important role (Polman and Slangen, 1999). Mixed forms of private and public arrangements can be found, such as CAs between farmers and water supply companies where nature conservation bodies are participating (Bahner, 1996).

The Bargaining Model in the Water Sector

Of course, the further discussion of the theorem by Coase himself and in the literature is far more sophisticated. One important issue concerns the costs of negotiation (transaction cost), which diminish the net-benefits from trade or are even prohibitively high, so that bargaining does not take place. This occurs if the cost of bargaining for at least one of the parties exceeds the gains from trade (Carlson *et al.*, 1993, p. 221). But under certain conditions it could be worthwhile if the government subsidizes these costs.

Since excessive transaction costs indicate that bargaining may not necessarily lead to net-benefits, so that a trade should consequently not take place on efficiency grounds, further gains must be obtained as a result of the agreements in terms of environmental or other social benefits. One example is the conservation of ecosystems achieved by more environmentally friendly farming. Of course, the extent by which the transaction costs should be subsidized depends, for instance, on the value of the special ecosystems located in a certain water catchment area. Even though it is difficult to find appropriate indicators and to assign values to ecosystems, an assessment of these side-effects should be carried out. Otherwise the total benefits resulting from the CAs would be underestimated. One example is to switch over from cropping to grassland farming, leading to an increasing biodiversity. However, these values are often not taken into account. If this were to be done, turning farmers to more environmentally friendly production methods would possibly be intensified. In order to achieve an extension of the altered farming practices, the farmers are to be paid additional compensation or the extension services offered are to be intensified. The water suppliers are probably interested in promoting such an extension by contributing to these additional costs, because they may further increase their gross margins. As a result, the total net-benefit gained from the CA would be considerably higher compared with an agreement without considering nature conservation. In reality, cases can be found where nature conservation groups are involved in

CAs between farmers and water suppliers. Other reasons for subsidizing transaction costs of bargaining between farmers and water suppliers include supporting further agri-environmental policies, such as protection against erosion and water overexploitation, and maintaining the socio-economic sustainability of agricultural production in the areas concerned.

The transaction costs can differ depending on the allocation of the property rights. Typically, in the case of water pollution caused by intensive agriculture the water suppliers have the right to be protected. If this legal condition were really to be implemented, the farmers would be obliged by law to pay compensation to the water suppliers for causing additional costs and/or would be punished because of breaching of environmental rules. However, the efforts by authorities needed to prove a certain water pollution caused by an individual farmer are often great, so that in reality the enforcement of the protected rights is rare. Moreover, there is hardly a possibility for the single water supplier to trade with the farmers in order to get compensation payments for polluting the water. Usually no voluntary bargaining occurs to induce the farmers either to reduce the pollution or to pay. Again, the transaction costs are prohibitively high (the cost of establishing and enforcing the property rights is to be considered as a part of the transaction costs). Of course, the transaction costs are also influenced by various other factors, such as for example the size of the water catchment areas, the number of participants and the complexity of voluntarily agreed rules.

On the other hand, if the water supplier were to be ready to pay the farmers for reducing pollution the situation would change, because the farmers are not obliged to pay if they pollute the water. In this case the transaction costs might be expected to be moderate and a trade could take place. The incentive of the farmers to conceal the use of pesticides or nitrates is smaller because they do not gain much from it. On the contrary, they will be motivated to reveal their farming practices since this a prerequisite for getting compensation payments and/or free advice as to how they can improve farm management. Both parties will gain from negotiation. The water supplier's total expenditure for negotiations, compensation and advisory programmes might be less than the costs of water treatment or water development saved. The compensation payments will decrease in direct relation to the farm management's increased efficiency brought about by the advisory programmes.

A further limitation of the bargaining model might be the risk that the parties would try to cheat one another by giving wrong information about their true costs, so that the outcome of the negotiations would not be efficient. However, each of the parties must fear the retreat of the other if they claim excessive compensation payments or exaggerate their costs. Both parties are interested in finding out the most efficient measures because they will be better off. It can be assumed that exactly those changes of farming methods will be chosen which reduce water pollution as far as possible by taking into account the local site-specific conditions and by avoiding unnecessary expenditures. The more they can trust each other, the more likely that this result can be achieved. This appears to be true, although it can be argued that there is typically a negotiating advantage of farmers against the water suppliers due to the application of more efficient farm management promoted by the agreement. The compensation payments received would tend to exceed the farmers' economic losses by an unreasonable amount. However, this particular effect makes the bargaining an especially efficient agri-environmental instrument. The water suppliers are keen to keep their expenses for compensation and other measures to protect the water against pollution (for example purchasing land) as low as possible. The farmers are trying to maximize the difference between the costs of changing to more environmentally friendly farming and the compensation payments they receive. Consequently, there is a strong incentive on both sides to agree on measures to change farming methods as efficiently as possible. As mentioned already, as soon as more efficient farming management takes place on a larger scale, leading for instance to savings of mineral fertilizers following a better application of manure according to the requirements of every field, the payments to compensate the farmers can be continuously reduced.

CAs, TAXES AND OBLIGATORY RULES

In contrast to compulsory regulations, such as prohibitions, restrictions or taxes on farm inputs, CAs between farmers and water suppliers are based on self-interest, self-determination and are voluntary. Even though taxes on the use of fertilizers and pesticides give some incentives to apply economically efficient farming practices, they do not sufficiently take into account the locally different conditions with respect to the vulnerability of the environment and to the site-specific cost–benefit relationships in the water sector. In contrast, CAs focus on the specific geographical and temporal variations, among other variations in climate, soil, groundwater level, and river stage. In particular, unit taxes on farm inputs can lead to inefficient changes of farming production methods if the inputs are reduced more than necessary due to favourable local environmental conditions or if they are not sufficiently reduced at more vulnerable sites.

In particular, charging for the use of agro-chemicals can lead to a deviation of a bargaining's outcome from the optimal solution or can hinder the establishment of such agreements, especially if they sap the potential economic gains of the farmers from CAs with water suppliers. Under certain circumstances, however, taxes on water use can promote such agreements, especially if small-sized water suppliers are surrounded by large farmlands, and if the revenues from this tax are used to support the establishment of CAs.

It can be shown that if the property right is assigned to the polluter – given the farmer has to comply with minimum requirements for a sustainable agriculture – paying taxes according to the externalities (Pigouvian tax) might result in bargaining which leads to higher expenditure for reducing the pollution than the losses thereby prevented (Carlson *et al.*, 1993, p. 229). Obviously, this outcome is not efficient in terms of applying the most appropriate agri-environmental measures. Moreover, CAs can be hampered if the farmer has to pay a tax which does not induce him to an essential reduction of agro-chemicals. In this situation the compensation payment needed to entice the farmer to reduce pollution might be greater than the amount the water supplier is willing to pay. Generally speaking, the parties should be allowed to work out agreements that will ensure that all possibilities aimed at achieving efficient solutions are exhausted before government intervention through taxation takes place. In those countries where taxes on the use of pesticides or fertilizers exist, an exemption of farmers participating in CAs with water suppliers and/or nature conservation groups should therefore be considered. This should also be done with respect to certain rules of the regular legal framework, as practised already in some regions in Germany where CAs have priority to compulsory rules (see below).

As mentioned already, under special conditions charging water suppliers with an abstraction tax can, however, promote CAs in agriculture. This is the case if many small water suppliers are located in catchment areas where agricultural lands prevail. If the revenue of the tax were to be available for promoting such agreements, it could be used to initiate bargaining and to establish the agreements by reimbursing water suppliers for paying compensations to farmers. Without such a regulation CAs would hardly occur on a larger scale due to the lack of preconditions for mutual negotiations. Also in such a situation the transaction costs can be considered as prohibitively high. However, in those regions where CAs have already been established, the introduction of an abstraction tax might be counterproductive since the water suppliers would no longer be ready to spend money on changing farming practices, because of the double financial burden. This consequence increases in likelihood if the water suppliers feel that they do not benefit from expending the revenues, for instance, if they are spent partly for other public purposes. Moreover, they would possibly withdraw from CAs due to the loss of self-determination resulting from a stronger intervention by the authorities, even though they would be reimbursed. Indeed, in Germany (especially in Bavaria and North Rhine-Westphalia) many contracts between water suppliers and farmers contain a passage which regulates that the agreements would be annulled in the event of introduction of such a tax. The water suppliers fear that funding CAs via an abstraction charge would lead to a less efficient use of the money because of their reduced influence in the negotiations.

Of course, state regulations are indisputable, such as prohibitions of hazardous agro-chemicals or limit values for maximum allowable concentrations of pollutants in drinking water. In addition to those regulations, a 'Code for Good Agricultural Practice' is necessary to define minimum requirements for which a farmer should pay his own costs. Furthermore, sanctions are needed for breaching of environmental laws. Those regulations are the necessary legal framework of CAs. However, by using the voluntary approach environmental targets can be achieved more efficiently than by using exclusively compulsory rules. The most important reasons are that such agreements focus especially on site-specific agri-environmental requirements, which are specifically relevant to the actors involved, and that all the participants are highly motivated to find out the most appropriate actions to change the farming practices.

State regulators can promote those co-operative arrangements by giving priority to the voluntarily agreed obligations to compulsory rules so that the participants can work out solutions which in many cases go beyond the legal requirements laid down, for instance, in ordinances for statutory water protection zones.

CAs IN PRACTICE

Occurrence and Reasons for Establishing CAs in some Member States

CAs with farmers have mostly been initiated by water suppliers, especially in those catchment areas where excessive pollution by pesticides and nitrates were found and in those areas where water pollution caused by agriculture should be prevented. Typically, many water suppliers came under pressure from the EU water legislation, especially the Drinking Water Directive (80/778/EEC) of 1989 which prescribed more rigid limit values for pesticides and nitrate in potable water. Some of them tried to force the farmers to reduce water pollution by law. However, due mainly to the diffuse character of the agricultural pollutants, the authorities were in most of the cases not in the position to check if the farmers were complying with the legal regulations. Moreover, law implementation by the authorities has been hindered since the requirements according to the 'good agricultural practice' appear not to be defined clearly enough. In addition, due to the long detention periods, changing the water quality takes many years even when farming practices have changed. In many cases it was no longer possible to meet the prescribed limit values by only blending water. Consequently, it was crucial for many water suppliers to start negotiating with farmers in order to avoid treatment measures. This reaction is especially prevalent in Germany.

For many water suppliers in the Netherlands water treatment was, at first, the only way to comply with the new MACs, especially for pesticides. The response of the water suppliers was to ensure water quality by measures which were under their own control and which were effective in a relatively short time. Also in other EU member states such as in France, Italy and Great Britain the treatment approach was mostly chosen by those water suppliers who faced excessive concentrations of pesticides or nitrates in drinking water. However, in the Netherlands more and more water suppliers decided to enter into agreements with farmers. A great number of CAs (for instance, more than 50 'Ferti-Mieux' actions which can be translated as 'fertilize better') have been established in France, especially between farmer groups and water agencies. The aim is to change the attitude of farmers towards the environment, mainly based on advisory programmes. In the EU, the largest number of CAs between water suppliers and farmers exists in Germany (more than 400). In the Netherlands a reasonable number of agreements have been established (between 5 and 10). In Great Britain one case is in an initial state. Also in Austria, Denmark and Sweden preliminary cases can be found. In each of these countries there are various types of such agreements with respect to the role of authorities and funding. All of the agreements are characterized by specialized contents as a result of mutual negotiations.

In the Netherlands, since 1989, the establishment of groundwater protection areas has been possible where restrictions have been regulated concerning the application of nutrients and pesticides. Whereas in the first years of this regulation the farmers had been paid on the basis of legal right to claim compensation for restricted standards in protected areas, there is currently an increasing tendency to apply the payment-by-result principle. This principle is a crucial feature of CAs in contrast to payments provided in connection with the legal right to claim compensations. It is of special interest in this concern that in the Netherlands the gaps between rules in groundwater protection areas and outside of these areas tend to narrow down. Consequently, the fixed compensation payments are gradually reduced with the rising requirements outside groundwater protection zones. A further specific feature of the CAs in this country is the involvement of nature conservation groups in several cases. As in Germany particularly, CAs can also be found in the Netherlands which aim to prevent a further deterioration of water quality due to harmful practices in order to avoid measures, such as closing wells, water treatment, and so on. A further measure to achieve this is to purchase agricultural land. Obviously, the outcomes of the agreements cannot be directly observed by amendments to the water quality and the economic benefits to be achieved in the future can only be estimated. Apart from the uncertainties involved here, proving the cost-effectivity of such agreements is only possible in the long-term perspective.

The reasons for the rare occurrence of such agreements in Great Britain are manifold. Apart from institutional factors (for example strict governmental control of water charges and investments of the water suppliers, no possibility to pass costs of compensations through to customers, short-term planning, and so on) the natural conditions, such as large river basins and a low share of groundwater abstraction, appear to play the main role. It seems that especially in this country the transaction costs are prohibitively high in most of the regions. In Italy one important reason for the lack of CAs is obviously the reluctance of the water suppliers to enter into negotiations with farmers and the preference for treatment measures. In France, where many CAs exist initiated mostly by farmer bodies (for example Chamber of Agriculture), the water suppliers generally play a minor role. Although the municipalities are responsible for the drinking water supply, in most cases the supply services (about 75 per cent of the customers) are delegated to private companies which run the equipment. These companies are not leading participants in the CAs, because they are not authorized to enter directly into negotiations with farmers. In addition, they expect fast results from the agreements. However, it usually takes a long time until improvements to the water quality occur as a consequence of changing agricultural practices. Furthermore, the companies consider measures to reduce or prevent water pollution not as their own task, since the authorities are responsible for that.

In Germany, about 95 per cent of the agreements occur in four of 16 States. It is difficult to explain this imbalance. Common features of these four German states are the relatively high volumes of groundwater abstraction and the large agricultural areas. In addition, the water monitoring systems do not cover the catchment areas very densely (as is the case in Baden-Württemberg, a German State with a large total farmland), so that the authorities only partly control farmers' compliance with agri-environmental rules and therefore promote the establishment of CAs. With regard to the four German states (with about 50 per cent of the total drinking water demand in Germany) it is typical that in Bavaria and in North Rhine-Westphalia the authorities intervene in the CAs to a minor extent, whereas in Lower Saxony and Hesse the government agencies play a more dominant role. In these two states the revenue of a water abstraction charge is used partly to promote the establishment and operation of CAs – one of the main reasons for the state interventions into CAs.

One of the reasons for the overwhelming occurrence of CAs in Germany is certainly the difficulty in enforcing regulations. Another important reason is the opinion of the water suppliers and their customers that drinking water should not be treated whenever possible. Further influencing factors are the highly decentralized organization of the water supply and the high share of groundwater abstraction in many of the German states. Last but not least, in most of the cases the payments for compensation and advising farmers are lower than the costs of treatment or development of water resources. Especially in the case of 'preventative' agreements, these cost-effectivity considerations are, as mentioned already, only achievable in the long run. But in the other cases where improvements of the water quality are expected, the long-term impacts of altering farming practices require long-term planning as well. Typically, in Great Britain difficulties occur due to the short-term (5 years) nature of the water suppliers' planning system.

The hypothesis that CAs are a useful instrument to implement agri-environmental targets especially in vulnerable areas can be proved by many cases where farming practices have been turned over to a more sustainable agriculture. There are several indicators showing the higher requirements which have been contractually agreed between farmers and water suppliers. For instance, the periods during which the spreading of semi-liquid manure is not allowed are in nearly all of such agreements longer than as prescribed in legal regulations. Other examples are the larger capacities for livestock manure storage and the reduced amount of fertilizers applied on a per hectare basis. The main advantage of CAs, as a self-regulatory interactive process, is that the individual measures to change the farming practices can be adapted to the manifold local differences in agricultural land, climatic situations and water resource characteristics, including aquatic ecosystems. Furthermore, the contents of the agreements can be modified very quickly if one of these conditions changes. Since the actions undertaken are suitable at the right site and time, CAs can contribute essentially to implementing environmental targets in an environmentally effective and economically efficient way.

The Role of CAs for Regulations and vice versa

Conditions that are agreed between water suppliers and farmers on a voluntary basis, seem to be opposed to compulsory measures in environmental policy. However, in reality those CAs help to enforce mandatory measures. As already mentioned, in most of the cases the outcomes of the agreements go beyond the requirements laid down in compulsory rules. Furthermore, as already mentioned, the contents of the agreements are better adapted to changes of local conditions, for example type of cultivations. Last but not least there is self-control among the farmers. These insights have induced several governments, particularly in Germany, to revise laws and ordinances by incorporating the voluntary approach into legal regulations. This new element brought in the legislation relating predominantly to water catchment areas which must be protected against agricultural pollutants.

One prominent example can be found in the German state Hesse, where the Water Law allows the authorities to accept CAs as an appropriate arrangement to protect water resources instead of statutory water protection zones. CAs can take the place of compulsory rules under the condition that fundamental requirements laid down in a framework ordinance for water protection zones are acknowledged by the farmers (§ 13 Muster-Wasserschutzgebietsverordnung). According to this regulation, the government subsidizes the costs for advisory programmes only during the first three years since the foundation of a CA in order to initiate negotiations between the water suppliers and farmers. The advisory programmes aim to develop site-specific advisory programmes and concepts for switching over to more sustainable farming practices. To ensure that the bargaining is fair, authorities are involved in the negotiations.

In the German state Lower Saxony the government plays a stronger role in CAs to ensure that the subsidies granted to the farmers are used efficiently. A main part of these public funds is used to offer a wide range of extension services. Farmers can make contracts directly with water suppliers or with authorities. Public funds are used in each of the two cases, and water suppliers are compensated for that. The revenue from water abstraction charges makes this possible.

Another regulation exists in the German State North Rhine-Westphalia where CAs have, in some cases, priority over compulsory rules enforced by authorities. This principle is practised especially in statutory water protection zones, but more and more it is also applied outside of such areas. In particular, those farmers who participate in voluntary agreements are no longer controlled directly by the authority but by the executive committee of a local CA. This body consists of members of the water suppliers and Chamber of Agriculture. In addition, an agricultural advisor participates in the meetings where advisory programmes and site-specific rules for more environmentally friendly farming are developed. The authorities believe in the results of these activities, especially with regard to the impacts of advisory programmes. Those farmers who do not sign the agreement are thoroughly checked by the authorities who demand periodic reports on the use of pesticides and on nutrient balances. The water suppliers pay the agricultural advisors and the farmers are compensated, at least in part, for the income losses they face. The government offers support for special measures taken by the farmers, such as for example purchase of manure capacity or abstaining from using agrochemicals in areas near brooks and lakes. All these privileges exist only for the farmers who entered into an agreement. Since in this German state water abstraction is free of charge, the government does not intervene directly in the arrangements. However, it has the authority to declare such an arrangement to be a CA, provided the conditions are fulfilled. These conditions include the compliance with environmental regulations, for instance, the limit values for pesticide and nitrate concentrations in drinking water.

In the German state Bavaria the government nearly refrains almost completely from direct intervention in CAs, provided the requirements of the environmental laws are met. The majority of the approximately 2600 mostly very small water suppliers in this state (which make up about 40 per cent of the total number of water suppliers in Germany) are protected by statutory water protection zones. Nevertheless, CAs have proved to be an effective tool in maintaining good drinking water quality. The main reason for this situation is the difficulty of enforcing rules laid down in the ordinances of the protection zones, the lack of controls and the lack of attractiveness of obligatory compensation regulations in these zones. In addition to or instead of these regulations, the farmers receive compensation payments on the basis of CAs with water suppliers. According to a governmental decree, such voluntary arrangements are treated preferentially because of the easier management of compensation payments (flat rate instead of individual compensation prescribed in protection zones). Apparently, CAs are more or less indispensable in achieving drinking water quality standards or in preventing a further deterioration of water quality. In addition to public payments, mainly based on Regulation 2078/92, the water suppliers bear an essential part of the financial burden necessary to protect the waters against agricultural pollutants. It is remarkable that also in Bavaria no water abstraction charges exist. Consequently, in this German state the government – like in North Rhine-Westphalia – does not intervene in the CAs. (In 11 of 16 States such a charge has been introduced (Meyer, 1999).)

The most important feature common to all of these different co-operation models in Germany is that the legislation opens itself up to voluntary approaches in contrast to the hitherto usually practised rigid command and control policy. Mandatory measures are replaced or at least complemented by co-operative arrangements, because the authorities have acknowledged their advantages. Such agreements increasingly take the place of legal prohibitions or restrictions laid down especially in ordinances of statutory water protection zones. In many cases, voluntarily agreed obligations have been added to compulsory rules. This development is obvious first of all in Germany (also in the Netherlands on a smaller scale), where compensation payments to farmers are based increasingly on the 'payment-by-result' principle instead of legal claims to be paid due to stricter requirements in protected zones. A more efficient compliance with water quality standards both from the environmental and economic point of view is considered as the result of this development. Farmers and water suppliers jointly decide on the actions which best fit local conditions in protecting the waters. Following this insight many water authorities give the voluntary negotiations priority over rigid command

and control measures as they have recognized in particular the cost savings in enforcing compulsory rules. For instance, the water suppliers take on a great part of the monitoring costs, since they are directly interested in controlling the compliance with the voluntarily agreed obligations. Furthermore, in most of those CAs where water pollution caused by agriculture should be prevented, the water quality is stabilized at levels far below the maximum allowable concentrations (for example 50 mg/l for nitrate). This is true in many German cases. Consequently, the prevention of water pollution is more likely to be implemented in such agreements compared with a strict command and control policy.

CONCLUSIONS

In comparison with other agri-environmental instruments, such as compulsory rules and taxes, CAs seem to have essential advantages in terms of environmental effectivity and economic efficiency. However, there is no real conflict between CAs and mandatory measures. Voluntary arrangements prove more and more to be a prerequisite for implementing environmental legislation. Thanks to the main characteristics of CAs (self-determination, mutual trust, focus on site-specific conditions, specialized knowledge of the participants about the local conditions, agricultural advisory service, payment-by-result) the outcomes of such agreements go, in many cases, beyond the standards laid down in environmental laws.

While, initially, in Germany and in the Netherlands CAs between water suppliers and farmers are practised ('pure' cases), this instrument is not common in several EU member states, especially in the Mediterranean countries. In France, a special type of voluntary arrangement can be found which is initiated mainly by the agricultural sector and the authorities. Whilst the 'Ferti-Mieux' operations aim to reach agreement on a better use of fertilizers in water catchment areas, the 'Irri-Mieux' (which can be translated as 'irrigate better') operations focus on more sustainable water utilization. A third type, named 'Phytomieux', aim at improving the application of pesticides. In all these operations the water suppliers play a minor role. The main goal is to change the farming practices by communication and education, especially in the case of the 'Phytomieux'. These voluntary arrangements are not the result of direct negotiations between water suppliers and farmers and therefore do not represent the 'pure' case of CAs. In some other member states, such as in Austria, Denmark and in Great Britain, the first steps towards negotiations between water suppliers and farmers can be observed.

The main reasons for this unbalanced occurrence of such agreements in the EU include institutional factors, such as the management of water supply companies and the attitudes of their customers, as well as natural factors, such as groundwater resources available and the size of large river basins as the basis for drinking water supply. In Great Britain, for example, it is not allowed to pass the costs of CAs, especially compensation payments for farmers, to customers. Moreover, the planning of the water suppliers operates on too short a time-scale compared with the long-term perspectives of CAs. In addition, since in this country water abstraction from large river basins prevails, in many catchment areas the costs of establishing and managing CAs might be prohibitively high. In the Mediterranean countries, especially in Italy, most of the water suppliers have reacted to increasing water pollution and to more severe environmental standards by treatment measures or shutting down wells. Why they do so, is difficult to explain. The lack of motivation of the municipalities which manage the drinking water supply might be one of the decisive reasons. In France, the delegation of water supply services to private companies which are only responsible for the operation results in a minor role of water suppliers in CAs, so that the possibilities for entering into direct negotiations with farmers are very restricted.

Since the costs of establishing and managing CAs (transaction costs) are a key influencing factor, the governments should promote co-operative arrangements by compensating such costs, at least in part. This is to be recommended especially in those cases where ecosystems are protected as a side-effect of the agreements, because the total net benefits resulting from CAs would be increased. Moreover, under certain circumstances, the use of revenues from water abstraction charges and/or other supporting measures, such as agri-environmental programmes for promoting such agreements, can be helpful. However, in regions where CAs have already been established, the introduction of water abstraction charges might be counterproductive. Taxes on the use of pesticides or fertilizers can also hamper the establishment and running of CAs. In those countries where such taxes exist, an exemption of farmers participating in CAs with water suppliers and/or nature protection groups should therefore be considered.

It should be emphasized that CAs cannot replace mandatory measures, such as rules which are obligatory for farmers and which correspond to the minimum or indispensable requirements of good agricultural practice. Examples are the ban on using certain pesticides or on spreading semi-liquid manure on frozen soils during the winter period. The responsibility of the governments in prescribing environmental laws and in checking the compliance with regulations cannot be questioned. But the way in which such regulations are implemented should be delegated more and more to the farmers and water suppliers concerned (possibly including nature protection groups). The achievement of economic gains through better farm management resulting from agricultural advice is an essential outcome of the CAs.

One obstacle to creating CAs may be an uncompromising insistence on the enforcement of the Polluter Pays Principle, even though this principle obviously belongs to the fundamental doctrine of environmental policy in the EU member states and, especially, of the EU Water Framework Directive. However, in the special case of agriculture, where water pollution from diffuse sources and long-term hydrogeological processes are typical, the enforcement of mandatory rules is often difficult. As mentioned before, this does not mean that the farmers are not obliged to fulfil indispensable requirements of good agricultural practice. It should be pointed out that a broader application of the voluntary approach can contribute essentially to the implementation of EU environmental legislation (such as the Nitrate Directive and the Drinking Water Directive) and to the agri-environmental measures (such as the 2078/ 92, 1259/1999 and 1257/1999 regulations) as well. The establishment of CAs can be facilitated by a greater flexibility in enforcing mandatory measures and in granting direct payments for enhancing the environment and improving the landscape. For instance, the possibilities of paying compensations for changes in farming practice should be extended and voluntarily agreed obligations for farmers should have, to some extent, priority over compulsory rules.

Because CAs between water suppliers and farmers are locally targeted and self-regulated they can provide useful guidelines for a more purposeful EU agri-environmental and water policy. Consequently, the EU member governments and the EU Commission would be well-advised to think about how this voluntary approach can be promoted by incorporating it into their legislation or agri-environmental programmes.

ACKNOWLEDGEMENT

The author and his project partners Floor Brouwer at the Agricultural Economics Research Institute (LEI) in The Hague and Tom Zabel at the Water Research Centre (WRC) in Medmenham, would like to thank the European Commission (DG Research) for funding the project 'Co-operative agreements in agriculture as an instrument to improve the economic and ecological efficiency of the European Union water policy' (Contract No. ENV4–CT98– 0782).

REFERENCES

Bahner, T. (1996), *Landwirtschaft und Naturschutz – vom Konflikt zur Kooperation*, Frankfurt am Main: Peter Lang.

Brouwer, F. and P. Lowe (eds) (2000), *CAP Regimes and the European Countryside: Prospects for Integration between Agricultural, Regional and Environmental Policies*, Wallingford: CAB International.

Brouwer, F., I. Heinz and T. Zabel (1999), 'The role of CAs in agriculture to achieve EU water policy targets', in: Proceedings of the 64th EAAE Seminar, organized by the Humboldt University of Berlin (European Association of Agricultural Economics): *Co-operative Strategies to Cope with Agri-environmental Problems*, Berlin.

Buller, H., G.A. Wilson and A. Höll (eds) (2000), *Agri-environmental Policy in the European Union,* Perspectives on Europe, Contemporary Interdisciplinary Research, Aldershot: Ashgate.

Carlson, G.A., D. Zilbermann and J.A. Miranowski (1993), *Agricultural and Environmental Resource Economics*, Oxford: Oxford University Press.

Coase, R.H. (1960), 'The problem of social cost', *Journal of Law and Economics*, **17**, 1–44.

Glachant, M. (1999), 'The cost efficiency of voluntary agreements for regulating industrial pollution: A Coasean approach', in C. Carrado and F. Lévêque (eds), *Voluntary Approaches in Environmental Policy*, Dordrecht: Kluwer Academic Publishers, pp. 75–89.

Heinz, I. (1998), 'Costs and benefits of pesticide reduction: best solutions', in G.A.A. Wossink, G.C. van Kooten and G.H. Peters (eds), *Economics of Agro-Chemicals: An International Overview of Use Pattern, Technical and Institutional Determinants, Policies and Perspectives*, Aldershot: Ashgate, pp. 333–44.

Heinz, I., F. Brouwer and T. Zabel (2000), *Summary Report of the 1st workshop to the EU project 'CAs in agriculture as an instruments to improve the economic and ecological efficiency of the European Union water policy'*, Dortmund: University of Dortmund, Institute of Environmental Research (INFU).

Just, F. and I. Heinz (2000), 'Do 'soft' regulations matter?' in F. Brouwer and P. Lowe (eds), *CAP Regimes and the European Countryside: Prospects for Integration between Agricultural, Regional and Environmental Policies*, Wallingford: CAB International, pp. 241–55.

Meyer, C. (1999), 'Wasserentnahmeentgelte – ein taugliches Instrument zum Gewässerschutz?' in *Wasserversorgung in Deutschland im Rahmen europäischer Wasserpolitik*, 13. Trinkwasserkolloquium 18 February 1999, Munich: Kommissionsverlag R. Oldenbourg, pp. 107–132.

OECD (1998), *Sustainable Management of Water in Agriculture: Issues and Policies, The Athens Workshop*, Paris: Organization for Economic Co-operation and Development.

Oskam, A.J., R.A.N. Vijftigschild and C. Graveland (1998), *Additional EU Policy Instruments for Plant Protection Products*, Wageningen: Wageningen Pers.

Polman, N.B.P. and L.H.G. Slangen (1999), 'Wildlife and landscape preservation: Incomplete contracting', in *Proceedings of the IX Congress of European Association of Agricultural Economists*, 24–28 August 1999, Warsaw.

Wossink, G.A.A., G.C. van Kooten and G.H. Peters (eds) (1998), *Economics of Agro-Chemicals: An International Overview of Use Patterns, Technical and Institutional Determinants, Policies and Perspectives*, Aldershot: Ashgate Publishing.

Zeijts, H. van (ed.) (1999), *Economic Instruments for Nitrogen Control in European Agriculture*, Utrecht: Centre for Agriculture and Environment.

12. Integrated rural development

Markus F. Hofreither

INTRODUCTION

In the 1950s agriculture was still a key factor for the well-being of rural regions in Europe. Since then the economic weight of agriculture has declined in a way that today significant contributions to the economic viability of a region are an exception. This holds both for agricultural value added and farm employment. Farm output has lost its regional focus, being mainly produced for internationalized markets. Farm input structures have changed by replacing intra-farm production of intermediary goods by traded inputs. In many regions the full-time family farm dwindled to a phenomenon of secondary importance, but with part-time farming the maintenance of agricultural activities depends on non-farm job opportunities at local labour markets. Farmers remaining self-employed often have to enter new fields of non-agricultural activities and so gradually may turn into non-agricultural entrepreneurs. At the outset of this process traditional regional policies have supported these transformations in their attempts to enhance regional economic conditions via top-down measures, mainly in the form of providing infrastructure support and adjustment subsidies.

With commodity markets gradually moving to a more liberal setting, the regional function of agricultural production activities partly shifted towards the provision of local public goods, predominantly in the form of environmental services. At the same time, however, agricultural production may contribute to local environmental objectives through reducing negative externalities caused for example by effluents, monocultures, or erosion. Agricultural policy responded to rising environmental concerns by introducing agri-environmental programmes, which intend to curb negative effects and to foster positive ones.

Integrating the environment into farm policies can be seen as the first step of an 'integrated' policy. The indispensable and much more difficult second integration step is the move from a predominantly sectorial to a truly territorial concept. Farm interests would then be only one component in an all-embracing regional perspective. One reason for the still insufficient integration between community policies relevant for rural areas today may be the structure of private and public decision making, which is basically organized by sectors (Freshwater, 1997). Moreover, as nearly all sectors have their central focus of attention in urban areas, only agriculture and perhaps forestry may have a clear non-urban orientation. In combination with a comparably strong political position of farm and agribusiness interests in the formation of farm-relevant policies (Salhofer *et al.*, 2000) the result is often a marked difference between agricultural and non-agricultural policies and regulations relevant for rural areas and inhabitants. This for example holds for trade regulations on regional markets, for environmental policies, and even for social support of rural people.[1] Differing consequences for farm and non-farm individuals may also be the result of macroeconomic policies influencing inflation, interest rates, employment, or exchange rates.[2] At times, macro policies may have an even greater impact on rural areas than agricultural policies do.

In general, unbalanced development patterns of rural regions may be either the result of insufficiently co-ordinated public policies and measures (policy failure*)* or of deficits with respect to the exploitation of the endogenous potential of rural regions, as private or public markets as well as the information flows between actors may be deficient (market failure*).*

The following section provides a brief survey on various theoretical contributions relevant for the complex problem of policy integration. Then a description of the characteristics and the historical changes of rural areas in Europe is provided, both in general as well as with respect to their agricultural dimension. The main shortcomings of current agricultural policies with respect to integrating their effects into rural development processes are illustrated in the next section. An exposition of actual development paths of two mountainous rural regions in Austria provides illustrative insights into rural development processes. The conclusions summarize the main requirements for positive achievements with respect to Integrated Rural Development.

THEORETICAL ASPECTS OF INTEGRATED RURAL DEVELOPMENT

Growth and Trade Theories

An integrated policy setting intertwines the sectoral and spatial aspects of different policies in establishing logically coherent and socially accepted links between the production of food and fibre, regional development of production factors and infrastructure, the environment, and social structures. Designing effective policies for a prosperous development of rural regions requires a thorough understanding of the relevant forces at work. To shed light on the development of leading and lagging regions[3] all factors determining economic growth processes may be suitable, embracing trade relations, the endowment of a region with respect to factors of production, but also the internal flows of information as well as the mode of decision making. While appropriate theoretical groundwork is easily available for the individual parts, the integrated whole is much more difficult to analyse.

Traditional (neo-classical) trade theory assumes that free trade between countries and regions influences prices, production, and trade volumes in a way that ensures welfare maximization across all regions. However, as the initial endowment with factors as well as the technology used have an impact on the outcome, not all regions will profit equally. In taking on board elements of Industrial Organization the so-called 'New Trade Theory' emphasized the role of different returns to scale as well as technologies applied, but also took into account imperfect competition (Helpman and Krugman, 1992). Moreover, in considering externalities new trade theory provided a well-taken starting point for 'new' agricultural trade issues emphasizing 'non-trade concerns' as being highly relevant from a territorial viewpoint.

Traditional growth theory would predict long-term convergence of regional growth patterns, as technical innovations[4] are available free to all. Obviously, this is not what we observe in practice. Regions exhibit grossly divergent growth patterns, which can only be explained by differences in the endogenous growth potential. 'New growth theory', nested in the same economic framework as new trade theory, thus focuses in more detail on the accumulation of production factors. The recommendations for policymakers trying to foster economic growth of a region are not surprising: support for education, stimulating investment in physical capital, support for R&D, protection for intellectual property rights or avoidance of government-induced market distortions (Barro and Romer, 1990).

Although new growth theory in general provides useful starting points for the analysis of regional development, due to its narrow focus on 'formalization' quite a few economists consider these approaches as insufficient to address the key questions (Nelson, 1997). As the highly important institutional setting of a region or a nation is particularly difficult to formalize, Nelson suggests that 'formal' theorizing should co-operate more closely with 'appreciative' theorizing.[5]

One 'appreciative' way of looking at integrated processes at the regional level distinguishes between various types of rural capital (for example Castle, 1998): natural capital, man-made capital, human capital, and social capital. Here, social capital is more or less tantamount to economic institutions, embracing features like common trust, social rules, enforcement mechanisms, or reciprocity. In combining elements of industrial, trade, and regional economics, agglomeration models do play a noticeable role with respect to regional development questions, although their direct focus is on urban areas. Here the fate of a region is primarily the result of the interplay of economies of scale, land competition, and transportation costs. Urbanization as well as its opposite is always a compromise across these determinants. More traditional regional or rural economic analyses employ empirical models concentrating on the flow characteristics of commodities, income and employment (for example Batten and Boyce, 1986). This bias towards 'flows' at the expense of 'stocks' poses the risk of neglecting asset creation within a region and its accumulation over time, which is a crucial determinant of rural well-being (Kraybill, 1998). This warning nicely corroborates the above mentioned position of Nelson that co-operation between 'formal' and 'appreciative' theorizing is necessary to get sound results in the end.

Importance of Collective Action

Besides the logical coherence of top-down measures an important facet of the contemporary understanding of integrated rural development is subsidiarity, which not only embraces important rights of regional and local constituencies, but also the responsibility of a spatially defined entity to come to balanced decisions about the key objectives as well as the ways to realize them. Collective action in this sense implies that 'the efforts of two or more individuals are needed to accomplish an outcome' (Sandler, 1992). In practice this may occur in the form of fierce battles between local and regional interest groups, often additionally fuelled by conflicting political party interests.

Traditional economic approaches

A widely known argument says that if local resources are shared by a group of people this is likely to end in the resource itself being destroyed, as individual use would always face only a fraction of the common cost incurred. This problem often occurs as the result of an 'open access' situation caused by insufficient rules to guide the use of the common property. Intensive tourism in many regions of the globe provides warning illustrations.

Considerable influence on research about collective action also had a group of economists addressing lobbying activities of interest groups (Becker, 1983; 1985) as well as forms of collective action (Olson, 1965; 1990) including voluntary compliance. In this respect the important characteristics, among others, are group size and group asymmetry (Sandler, 1992, 9f.), but also the proper design of institutions as well as selective incentives for individuals. Voting models in the tradition of Downs (1957), assuming that politicians formulate only such policies that provide the maximum chance of (re-)election, also fit quite well to many problems of rural development.[6]

Methodically, problems with respect to local decision-making have for a long time nearly exclusively been embedded in the field of non-co-operative game theory, with the 'prisoners' dilemma' game as a well known starting-point. Due to the fact that the assumptions are quite restrictive, the outcome that the dominant strategy for each player is to defect remains of limited relevance for practical rural development processes. Empirical evidence in fact provides a great number of examples with quite successful forms of managing common resources, mostly based on voluntary acceptance of conventions, rules and norms. Hence, subsequent theoretical developments tried to incorporate co-operative behaviour by introducing repeated forms of non-co-operative games, and introducing communication, persuasion or coercion, possibilities for reciprocity, but also forms of social disclosure of individual choices (Rupasingha and Boadu, 1998). Longer time horizons increase the tricky impact of the social time preference or discount rate, which also plays an important role in determining policy decisions in real-life, such as measures to curb greenhouse gas emissions, resource depletion processes at the regional level, and so on.

Of practical relevance also is the so-called 'assurance problem', where players establish mutual contracts with respect to different forms of co-operation. The willingness to co-operate in order to solve specific common property externalities increases with the probability that the other player(s) will stick to the contract and so joint co-operation may become the preferred strategy. Here, as an important new element, the collective design of institutional rules allows socially desirable outcomes (Rupasinga and Boadu, 1998).

Evolutionary approaches
In practice, creative processes including reciprocity, learning and adaption, as well as habit formation among agents often lead to the creation of a new social order with respect to local commons. Here the key issue is the collective desire to use a common resource base 'sustainably', which stands for simultaneously optimizing the environmental, economic, and social dimensions of a specific resource use. Self-organization is a typical phenomenon of evolutionary approaches to solve problems of local commons. In a trial-and-error process strategies, which work well for individuals or groups, are systematically taken up by the collective and so a development path towards the 'collective optimum' materializes. The concept of self-organization was initially applied to social systems by Jantsch (1980), and later on refined by Ayres (1988), Leifer (1989) and others. Also in a social framework self-organization is the result of communication, selection, and adaptation. Such a system follows a cycle starting from an equilibrium that changes into a situation with increasing instability, which finally leads to a bifurcation point, where the system takes a decision between alternative development paths. In

structuring regional development processes adequately, in many cases these stages are clearly identifiable.

Solving a regional development problem nearly always requires some minimum amount of mutual trust and reciprocal altruism among group members. Important factors in this respect identified by evolutionary scientists are learning and cultural transmission, kin relations, and altruistic partnerships. The emerging social patterns help to establish mutual trust and thereby reduce the risk of counterproductive opportunism. Recent socio-economic research increasingly emphasizes networks: 'Internal networks' are relationships between private managers, local administrators, financial institutions and organized interest groups within a region. 'External networks' are directed towards functioning relationships with upper level authorities in administration, politics or private business organizations.

Presently, these evolutionary elements of research are integrated back into standard economic analyses via technical developments in evolutionary game theory and computer simulation modelling. However, despite remarkable advances in this domain of social science research the applicability of the results and methods as tools in practical problem solving remains to be a matter of the coming years. Perhaps research on integrated regional development is itself plagued by insufficient integration between disciplines. This, however, does not lessen the value of the results achieved so far out of this highly diversified and elaborated research domain.

RURAL AREAS IN EUROPE

Dimensions and Types

Defining the term 'rural area' is not an easy task today. In the past, the strong dependence on the economic status of the farming community made finding a typology of rural areas relatively simple: the share of agricultural production activities made up the single central feature. In the meantime, however, we observe a sharp increase in the structural differences between rural regions. At least four sets of characteristics have to be taken into account to categorize rural regions:

- the *physical endowment* of a region, including for example topography, natural resources and latitude, but also the existing infrastructure, including transportation and communication systems;
- the *economic situation* of a region, dealing with characteristics like per capita income, employment and job structure, but also for example the development potential of the regional industry structure;

- the *social structure* of a region in its broadest meaning, covering population density, age structure, educational status, but also features like
  cultural aspects;
- the individual *policy setting* of a region, embracing the capacities of
  regional or local actors, formal decision structures or informal leader-
  ship profiles.

Nearly all of the popular classifications refer only to a subset of the above
mentioned criteria, mainly with respect to area and population. The OECD
Rural Development Programme is based on a standardized territorial framework and distinguishes between three types of regions: *predominantly rural*
areas with more than 50 per cent of the population living in 'rural' communities, *significantly rural*, with a share of 15 to 50 per cent, and the rest being
predominantly urbanized areas. Alternatively, absolute thresholds could be
used to separate types of rural regions. EUROSTAT for example distinguishes between *densely populated* zones (more than 500 inhabitants/km^2
and a total population of at least 50 000), *intermediate* zones (between 100
and 500 inhabitants/km^2 and a total population of at least 50 000 or being
adjacent to a densely populated zone), and *sparsely populated* zones (not
falling in either of the first two categories).

The share of people living in 'Rural Europe' covering 84.4 per cent of the
EUR-15 area amounts to 39.5 per cent. Only 9.7 per cent of the population
live in predominantly rural regions covering 47 per cent of EUR-15. If the
EUROSTAT typology, relying on absolute numbers of inhabitants, is applied,
17.5 per cent of European citizens live in areas with less than 100 inhabitants
per km^2, which make up slightly more than 80 per cent of the area of EUR-15
(see Table 12.1). From a dynamic viewpoint population changes are different
between these types of areas, however, without a clear pattern across all
countries. So, at the same time, we observe predominantly rural regions with
increasing (46 per cent) as well as decreasing population (42 per cent).
Although compared to the averages across EUR-15, predominantly rural
regions exhibit a moderate relative decline of population, this does not hold
uniformly for the individual Member States (European Commission, 1997).

Regarding regional value added, measured as Gross Domestic Product
(GDP) in 1994, a more coherent picture emerges. Relative to the EU average,
predominantly rural regions produce only about 80 per cent of GDP, significantly rural regions about 88 per cent and predominantly urbanized regions
about 110 per cent. Although the national averages of the 15 Member States
exhibit significant deviations from the EU average, the relative relationship
of the three types of regions within each member state is remarkably uniform
to the EU average as such. This means that if for example a country like
Spain shows 62.5 per cent of the average GDP of the community, the pre-

Table 12.1   Rural population and rural areas in Europe (share in per cent of national population)

	Population in rural communities[a]	Population by type of regions		
		Predominantly rural	Significantly rural	Predominantly urbanized
Belgium	4.9	3.4	4.9	91.7
Denmark	32.4	39.6	31.3	29.1
Germany	12.0	5.4	25.2	69.3
Greece	30.8	28.1	28.3	43.6
Spain	24.4	12.7	41.5	45.8
France	23.7	10.5	56.5	32.9
Ireland	43.1	46.6	15.1	38.3
Italy	14.1	4.1	27.1	68.8
Luxembourg	19.3	–	100.0	–
The Netherlands	3.1	0.0	6.7	93.3
Austria	34.6	30.2	28.9	41.0
Portugal	21.2	18.1	22.8	59.1
Finland	50.6	58.9	41.1	0.0
Sweden	66.8	63.2	17.7	19.1
United Kingdom	8.7	1.0	18.7	80.3
EUR-15	17.5	9.7	29.8	60.5
EUR-15 area	80.9	47.0	37.4	15.6

Note: a.   Population of local communities with population density below 100 inhabitants/ km^2 (EUROSTAT definition).

Source: European Commission (1997, p. 8)

dominantly rural regions of Spain are about 20 per cent below this level and the predominantly urbanized areas are about 10 per cent above (European Commission, 1997, Table 3a, 12).

Agricultural employment in rural areas has steadily declined since the 1950s. In 1990/91 the EUR-15 average was about 5.8 per cent, and even in the predominantly rural areas this figure was only 12.4 per cent (European Commission, 1997, Table 7, p. 15). This corroborates the notion that agriculture no longer is a decisive factor for the economic viability of rural regions.[7] In order to be able to analyse the development of a particular region and even more for designing an integrated rural policy strategy, many other elements have to be included. Among them, the endogenous capacity to actually exploit the local or regional comparative advantages, which is related to the above mentioned social and political characteristics, may be of central importance. So, despite numerous efforts to systematize rural regions (for example Marsden, 1995) it still may happen that distinct characteristics of a region not covered by common classifications may be the true key to understanding individual development patterns.[8]

Integrating European Policies for Rural Areas

Already in the Treaty of Rome (Art. 39, para 2) the intention was formulated that '… account shall be taken of the particular nature of agricultural activity, which results from the social structure of agriculture and from structural and natural disparities between the various agricultural regions'. Ten years after that, the first concrete idea of a European structural policy was born with the so-called 'Mansholt Plan' and put in force at the legislative level by three 'socio-structural' directives in 1972 (159/72/EEC, 160/72/EEC, 161/72/EEC), which addressed the modernization of agricultural holdings, the cessation of agricultural activities and qualification issues.

In the subsequent years these measures have been supplemented by the first regional measures, notably the LFA Directive (268/75/EEC) in support of agriculture in mountainous and certain less-favoured areas. In formulating criteria that enabled the delineation of territories with respect to the eligibility for these measures this directive for the first time brought in an explicit territorial approach. This development was driven by the broad and increasing agricultural and rural exodus of people moving towards more agglomerated areas at this time. This was perceived as a severe threat for the economic and social viability of rural regions, while environmental concerns did not play an important role at this time. In the following years similar measures were created first for selected northern areas, followed by the 'Integrated Mediterranean Programmes', which continued along these lines for southern France and Italy as well as Greece.

The next important step in the development of European policies for rural regions was part of the initiatives to establish a single European market across all Member States. This required effective measures to alleviate the differences between leading and lagging regions in Europe. At the institutional level this was done by fundamentally reorganizing the Structural Funds in 1988 (European Commission, 1988) with introducing Objectives 1 to 5a and 5b.[9] The intention to integrate the resulting measures better is visible in the guiding principles of these structural polices, which emphasize:

- partnership between the different levels of regional interests between the local and the Community level;
- additionality of funding including financial participation at the lower levels;

- concentration of funding on selected regions and actions;
- programming of measures to ensure a clear and detailed picture on objectives to be reached and measures to be taken.

The need to improve the existing links between agricultural and rural policies was also reiterated. The practical outcome of this intention was the integrated approach across the different funds with respect to regions targeted by Objectives 1 and 5b of the Structural Funds. These two policy domains represented the narrow link between the agricultural policy setting decided with the MacSharry Reform in 1992 and rural development objectives. Although the MacSharry Reform brought about a basic switch from price support to direct payments as the main instrument for farm income support, no significant spatial redistribution effects did occur, as compensation payments quite exactly eliminated the income losses from the price reductions.

The CAP reform 1992 did not accomplish significant steps with respect to a broad integration of agricultural and rural policies, but it represented the first marked step with respect to integrating agriculture and environment with the so-called Accompanying Measures. Regulation (EEC) 2078/92 tried to accomplish a more coherent structure for agri-environmental measures as an attempt to support the expected general reduction in specific intensity of agricultural production as a consequence of the decided price reductions. Additionally, some Common Market Organizations (CMO) introduced ceilings on the number of animals eligible for premiums, which acted as an ecological restraint on stocking rates.

Initiated by the need for a new Financial Framework for the period 2000–2006 the last fundamental reform of community policies (Agenda 2000) was intended as a seamless continuation of the Reform 1992 and thus provided further attempts to integrate agricultural, environmental and rural policies. In general, there is increased emphasis on subsidiarity, entitling Member States to shape the details of CMOs as well as Accompanying Measures of 1992 in a way which best matches national or regional requirements. This also includes the possibility of sanctions to enforce the correct execution of measures and programmes.

With the final agreement on Agenda 2000 in April 1999 the framework for structural policies also changed in more than one respect: the number of Structural Fund Objectives was cut back to three, which terminated the previously separated treatment of agricultural issues:

- Objective 1 remains directed towards lagging regions, with regional GDP being less than 75 per cent of the Community average, but includes also peripheral regions as well as arctic zones;
- Objective 2 targets areas with restructuring problems, particularly re-

gions with economic decline, areas undergoing socio-economic change in industry and services, and urban areas under pressure;

- Objective 3 explicitly addresses the development of human skills and includes the adaptation of education policies, training and employment in areas not covered by Objectives 1 and 2.

In addition, the details of implementing measures to serve environmental and regional objectives have been further developed and refined. The concrete rules for measures targeted to realize these objectives are laid down in subsequent regulations, mainly Regulation (EEC) 1257/1999 (Support for rural development from EAGGF) and Regulation (EEC) 1259/99 (Common rules for direct support schemes under the CAP).[10] Continuing on the existing legal framework regarding structural measures (Regulation [EEC] 2052/88) and the accompanying measures of the MacSharry-Reform (Regulation [EEC] 2078/92, 2079/92, 2080/92) the explicit coverage of problems of less-favoured areas, including mountain areas and areas affected by specific handicaps, and areas with environmental restrictions broadened the scope of this policy development. Some important but so far isolated prescriptions aiming at the 'adaptation and development of rural areas' have been united into the so-called 'Article-33–Measures' (Regulation [EEC] 1257/1999). Also the renewed 'LEADER+' is focused more than so far on integrated strategies in order to speed up the development of rural areas.

In emphasizing the key principle of subsidiarity and the importance of 'bottom-up' activities these regulations represent an important step in the right direction: they allow Member States to pinpoint agri-environmental as well as rural development measures in accordance with the distinct national requirements. From a political economic viewpoint, however, it remains to be seen to what extent Member States will actually take up these possibilities in a way that truly serves the public interest.[11]

RURAL AREAS AND AGRICULTURE

Historical Development and Characteristics

While in the late 1950s, although varying across countries, agriculture contributed to about a third of value added and embraced up to significantly more than 50 per cent of the labour force, in the course of time two characteristics of farm development changed this picture significantly: first, the high pace of technical progress as well as organizational changes induced outstanding increases in labour productivity; secondly, due to the emphasis on food production the limitations on the demand side illustrated by Engel's law reduced the share of agriculture within the overall economy. The inevitable joint effect of both factors was an unprecedented decline in labour demand.

Nowadays European agriculture contributes only about 1.5 per cent to gross value added at market prices. Depending on the particular characteristics of EU-Member States this figure varies between more than 5 per cent of GDP for Greece and less than 0.5 per cent for Sweden.

A characteristic feature of this development is a slow but steady tendency to part time farming in Europe. Between 1987 and 1995 across EU-12 the number of full time farmers has declined at a faster pace (-33 per cent) than the number of part time farmers working less than 50 per cent of the annual working time of a full-time worker (-18 per cent). However, this trend is not at all uniform across Member States. So for example in Greece or Ireland the number of people working at 100 per cent of average working hours on their farm has even increased since 1997. Italy, on the other hand, shows hardly any structural changes within this period (http://europa.eu.int/comm/dg06/archiveagrista/table_en/index.htm). For 1995, statistics show a share of 58 per cent of people working less than 50 per cent of the average annual working hours on their farms, with Ireland or the Netherlands exhibiting very low shares (about 15 per cent), but for example Greece and Italy featuring more than 65 per cent.

So in general, the immediate importance of agriculture and agricultural policy for the economic well-being of rural areas has diminished considerably. This also reduced the previously dominating social role of agriculture within rural regions. However, despite this relative decline in terms of value added and employment, agriculture still features a unique characteristic: it is the dominating user of land in Europe. This implies that agriculture is the dominant force in shaping the rural landscape and has a considerable impact on environmental conditions in rural areas. This brings into play an indirect, but important effect on the economic viability of rural regions, as farm activities may provide important inputs for the tourism industry or contribute to the well-being of local residents through rural amenities or disaster prevention in mountainous regions (Hofreither, 1998).

The 'Sectoral' Bias of European Agricultural Policy

Imperfections of the Common Agricultural Policy

Since the basic outline of the Common Agricultural Policy (CAP) was laid down in the late 1950s questions about the consistency of its objectives, its instruments and the particular ways of implementing them in a complex mix of measures have been under discussion. Across this entire time-span the setting of agricultural policy objectives was dominated by the long-term goal to increase or at least maintain agricultural incomes, while regional and spatial aspects never played an influential role. During the last decade, a tendency to integrate agricultural and environmental interests through agri-environmental measures is to be observed, which, however, exhibits quite different interpretations across Member States and still is far from being optimal (Brouwer and Van Berkum, 1996; Hofreither, 2000).

Normally, a policy is deemed to be acceptable if it reflects the current priorities of society. Whether the poor integration of farm and environmental policies as well as regional policies was intended or simply the consequence of insufficient information and co-ordination of non-farm interests, remains an open question. In any way, a fundamentally changing world forces policy to steadily adjust to changes in societal priorities. This also holds for the CAP.

Many observers maintain that European agricultural policy is still predominantly sectoral, farmer and commodity oriented, although there are first steps in reforming market, structural and agri-environmental policies (Buckwell *et al.*, 1997). The rural development aspects of the structures programme and the agri-environmental measures still appear as artificial supplements to the core measures concerning CMOs. The remaining overdependence on the use of market policy and farm-related subsidies at the expense of structural, environmental and rural development incentives is one of the most disturbing factors of the CAP, even after its most recent reform as part of Agenda 2000. As a consequence, rent-seeking activities ('farming the subsidies') often provides higher payoffs than taking the risk to engage in new market segments.

Market organizations and agri-environment
In the long run, the tenet to raise agricultural incomes via price support measures has spurred capital intensive production methods. There is a widespread notion that during the last decades in many farming regions the net effect with respect to the environment has not turned to the better (for example Nowicki, 1997). Among the key problems are plant protection chemicals, nitrate leaching, loss of habitats, declining quality of landscape, and threats to biodiversity. However, due to variations in natural conditions, these problems appear with marked differences across farming regions. The historic policy reaction was not to lessen the negative incentives in the CMOs, but first to give a positive environmental meaning to set-asides and later to invent agri-environmental policy measures.

The primary purpose of set-aside is to control production and this normally has only marginal, accidental and transient environmental benefits (Buckwell *et al.*, 1997). The main reason is that there is no incentive for farmers to put the environmentally most fragile land into set-aside. Moreover, if set-aside is rotational, the environmental benefits to wildlife and habitats are often lost as soon as the land returns to production. Environmentalists are also concerned about certain forms of set-aside which can actually damage the environment.[12]

Agri-environmental policies try to address environmental problems related to farming directly. Due to the complex relationship between agriculture and the environment a lot of agri-environmental issues are dominated by site-specific characteristics and, moreover, may be subject to changes in the course of time. The lack of data or incomplete knowledge with respect to the underlying causal relationships may lead to diverging opinions with respect to the causes for the problems observed. Additionally, experts may arrive at different views with respect to the optimal response to a specific problem. So, reducing agri-environmental deficiencies often requires developing problem-specific and even location-specific policy measures fitting closely to the different objectives pursued.[13] This task is to be mastered only if subsidiarity and co-operation between farm and non-farm interests at the local level is part of the institutional setting.

However, as long as CMOs include market price support as a means of maintaining incomes, this not only may add to environmental problems, it also increases the compensation payments required to achieve voluntary participation of farmers in agri-environmental programmes. Yet, curbing high and biased national commodity prices may be a necessary, but not always a sufficient precondition for agri-environmental improvements.[14]

In summing up, agri-environmental policies may have a twofold impact on rural regions: first, if they are successful with respect to their key objective, namely improving the state of the environment, they add to the well-being of rural inhabitants and other users of the rural landscape. Secondly, if such programmes do transfer substantial amounts of money into rural regions via agri-environmental payments to farmers, the economic status of this region in principle is affected in a positive way.

Spatial implications of common farm policies

With respect to market policies unbalanced support between commodities may have substantial effects with respect to the spatial distribution of CAP support. Examples can be found in the different treatment of cereal and oilseed prices compared to milk and sugar prices since 1992, with these differences not in any way being related to incomes, natural conditions or other objective factors. Other examples occur with respect to headage payments, often providing different rates for animals under extensification programmes, in less favoured areas and under agri-environmental schemes.

However, even structural policies themselves are not always sufficiently integrated. Until Agenda 2000, for example, structural policy followed a horizontal approach with respect to Objective 5a measures, but a territorial one with respect to Objective 5b. The consequence often was an accidental overlap of territories situated within zones declared by Member States as eligible for certain measures, with the resulting complexities causing confusion both for the subjects of the measures and those trying to implement them. There are also examples that two distinct measures try to achieve the same objective (for example LEADER initiatives[15] and 5b measures working towards rural development), but also that they may be working in conflict, for example afforestation and agri-environment. In some cases EU programmes complement Member State activities, in others there is duplication (for example LEADER support for small and medium enterprises for which there are often national schemes). Again, making regions rather than sectors the basis of such policies may provide an important chance to bring in more rationality and simplicity in this policy area. Such a policy move would also provide opportunities to indirectly adjust the market balance of the main commodities.

INTEGRATED RURAL DEVELOPMENT AND MOUNTAIN AREAS

Introduction and Problem

In Europe, mountainous areas cover about 30 per cent of the territory and make up 20 per cent of the total utilized agricultural area (UAA). Although in general, the population densities remain below average, in mountain areas large cities with central administration and schools, a well-elaborated traffic system, and industrial production structures are also regular features.

Often the links and the potential conflicts between the economic, environmental, societal, and cultural dimensions of human life are more pronounced in mountainous regions. The diversity of living conditions within close quarters, varying between urban-like valleys and isolated locations within distances of a few kilometres, raises the awareness for economic and social problems. At the same time, the potential impact of natural disasters is a very direct one, with avalanches, mud slides and torrents posing a realistic threat to many settlements. Often there is also a direct link between natural threats and changes in agricultural production activities. Under such circumstances there is not only an increased need for integrated policies, but normally also a higher than usual willingness to support such measures. So it is not surprising that mountain areas have been among the first targets of attempts to integrate related, but so far isolated policy areas.

With 70 per cent of total area, providing living space for more than one third of the population, Austria is the country with the highest share of mountain areas in the EU (Dax, 1997). Concerning population densities the situation in the Austrian Alps, which comprise about 90 per cent of national mountain areas, is characterized by an extreme diversity of conditions. Population density varies widely around the average value of 50 to 60 inhabitants per km², including zones of more than 500 inhabitants per km² and nearly depopulated stretches. Interestingly, mountain regions exhibit a higher population growth than Austria on average.[16] This combination of natural handicaps, but also advantages, disadvantaged location and divergent economic development patterns makes these regions an interesting object of development studies.

In this section a practical illustration of integrated rural development processes is provided by briefly looking at two rural regions in the Austrian Alps. Osttirol is an example of a leading rural region, while Liezen is a lagging one, with non-agricultural employment growth for the period 1981–91 as the differentiating characteristic. The two regions have been analysed in detail as a contribution to a major study on agriculture and employment in rural regions of the EU, with results being based on the analysis of data[17] and literature, but also on interviews with entrepreneurs and representatives of institutions in these regions.

In order to provide an illustration for the theoretical and political elements touched in the preceding sections this part tries to demonstrate the actual development of these regions, to identify the most important driving forces and to point out the influence of policies relevant for rural areas. Due to space limitations the analysis of course has to remain quite selective.

Outline of Study Regions

Overall economic setting

The two study regions selected are quite similar with respect to size and economic structures and are even located at close quarters in the central area of the Austrian Alps. In the 'leading' region, Osttirol, being a district of the province of Tyrol, the annual rate of non-agricultural employment growth in the period analysed was 1.3 per cent and thereby more than 0.5 per cent above the Austrian average of 0.8 per cent. On the other hand, in the 'lagging' region Liezen, a district of the province Styria, employment is more or less stagnated. Some of the key features of the regions are presented in the following Table 12.2.

Osttirol is strongly concentrated around a regional centre, with 48 per cent of the population and 63 per cent of total employment being located there.[18] The outstanding natural resource is a very pleasant Alpine landscape, which provides the basis for both summer and winter tourism. The regional structure of education institutions is very balanced. Employment in both the

Table 12.2   Statistical information on Austrian case study regions

Characteristics	Period	Region		Austria	
		Osttirol	Liezen	Total/ Average	Predominant rural
Population and area					
Population (in 1000s)	1991	48.3	81.4	7795.8	3797.7
Area (in 1000 km)		2	3.2	82.5	67.4
Population density (inhab./km)	1991	24	25	94	56
Growth (% per annum)					
Population	81–91	0.20	0.10	0.30	0.30
Total employment	81–91	0.60	–0.40	0.40	0.20
Non-agricult.employment	81–91	1.30	–0.04	0.80	0.80
Employment					
Agriculture (share in %)	1981	16	13	9	–
	1991	10	10	6	12
Industries (share in %)	1981	34	40	38	–
	1991	35	34	35	38
Services (share in %)	1981	50	47	53	–
	1991	55	56	59	49
Unemployment	1981	3	2.10	2	2.10
	1995	8.50	9.40	5.70	5.40
Value added					
GVA/capita (ECU)	1991	11 885	12 145	16 530	12 161
GVA/capita growth (% p.a.)	81–91	8.50	5.70	7.80	7.50

Source: Terluin *et al.* (1999), Weiss (1999), own calculations.

industry and the service sector increased substantially, while farm jobs decreased. Despite the remarkable increase in labour demand, unemployment also grew during the 1980s and 1990s, maintaining unemployment rates still above the average level of rural regions. However, the dominant share of unemployment is related to tourism and construction and thus is merely seasonal.

Liezen is an alpine region with settlement in various valleys with no concentration around a particular centre. Important local resources are the beauty of the landscape, extensive forests and alpine pastures, mineral resources and a number of hydro-power plants. This region is at the same time engaged in tourism and in industrial activities, both with a long tradition and with clear geographical demarcations. Since 1981 employment development worsened substantially, with agriculture and industries facing a strong decline, and services increasing below average. The unemployment rate of Liezen is one of the highest in the country and is characterized by high shares of long-term unemployment and unemployed women, being strong indicators of structural unemployment.

The development of productivity and thus income levels also differs sharply between these two regions. Although the leading region Osttirol exhibits a slightly lower level of Gross Value Added (GVA) per person than the lagging region, the growth rates are revealing: GVA in Osttirol grew at 8.5 per cent p.a. during 1981–91 and thus at a higher pace than the national average, while Liezen with 5.7 per cent lagged about 2 per cent behind this average. Surprising for quite remote rural regions, in both cases the main driving force for employment changes came from an increase (and decrease) in metal manufacturing. Other important industries in this respect have been construction and transport.

Mountain farming

The actual share of farm employment in the mountainous regions of Austria is about 9 per cent, thus being 50 per cent higher than the national average, however, with strong regional differences.[19] With managed grassland being the dominating pattern, cattle and milk production are the leading farming activities. Due to the significantly lower factor productivity of mountain farming the average income of these farms is less than two thirds of the income of non-mountain farms (BMLF, 1999). In making up only 28 per cent of the total forest area in Austria and unit value added remaining far below national averages, the main function of mountain forestry more and more switches to its positive external effects with respect to avalanche and torrent regulation (Dax and Wiesinger, 1998). Alpine pasture grazing has a similar function in protecting against specific natural hazards, but at the same time may also damage these fragile environments. Nearly all mountain farms have joined the Austrian agri-environmental programme based on Regulation 2078/92 (ÖPUL). These farm characteristics are likewise relevant for both Osttirol and Liezen.

The employment share of agriculture in the two case study regions was 10 per cent each in 1991 and has further decreased in the meanwhile. As farm expansion is often limited by natural conditions and a high labour demand per hectare, the main adaptation strategies of farming are a move towards specialization through production of higher quality output, niche products, or the switch to organic farming. The share of part time farming in 1991 was 53 per cent in Osttirol and 44 per cent in Liezen, with on-farm pluriactivity mainly concentrated on agritourism and processing of farm products. Off-farm pluri-activity is dependent on job availability in the region as well as on commuting conditions and covers a wide range from seasonal engagements in tourism to highly specialized industrial jobs.

Actors, networks, policies

In both regions important private investment projects were related to firms from the outside, which indicates an exogenous development strategy. However, in many cases this was the consequence of local actors being very active in attracting those new firms. In addition to politicians and public servants important local actors are the interest groups forming the chambers of commerce, labour and agriculture. Besides official networks many things happen on the basis of informal personal relations. Particularly in Osttirol local actors played a decisive role in using personal contacts to get in touch with firms from the outside and attracting them by creating favourable preconditions for industrial development.

Both regions predominantly emphasized infrastructure improvements, mainly with respect to tourism and the road system. Financial support for these projects primarily came from funds at the national and provincial level. While the availability of national funds was similar in both regions, important differences existed with respect to regional and local funds. While in Liezen (Province Styria) decisions were almost exclusively made at the provincial or national level, in Osttirol (Province Tyrol) again local actors played a dominating role in all decisions about the actual use of the available provincial funds.

Of course, both regions are eligible for regional support measures after EU accession. Osttirol so far was an Objective 5b region with 100 per cent Less Favoured Areas (LFA). Also the western part of Liezen took profit from Objective 5b measures, while the eastern, industrial part was under Objective 2. Due to the unfavourable conditions for agricultural production the whole region is also classified as an LFA. A similar pattern will emerge under the new Community legislation concerning regional support described earlier.

Key Development Drivers

Non-farm sectors

In an attempt to summarize the key factors of the observed employment dynamics in the two case study regions non-agricultural forces obviously played a dominating role. In the leading region (Osttirol) the dominating driving force was an industrial settlement process starting in the early 1980s, which did not impair the environment or landscape features. The following factors have played an essential role in inducing this process:

- a well-educated labour force with above basic-level technical skills, high flexibility and problem-solving capacities as an outcome of a balanced structure of schooling institutions within the region, providing an important advantage in the competition with low-wage countries;
- lower unit cost of labour, being the result of solid qualifications in combination with slightly lower wage rates, but also a reasonable transportation infrastructure through capable connections across the Alps both in northern and southern direction;
- a truly 'bottom up' approach in the form of decentralized decision-making with respect to the funds available from the province in combination with a very co-operative attitude of local actors towards companies being willing and suitable to move into the region.

On the other hand, the key factors of the negative employment dynamics in the lagging region (Liezen), which for decades has been a region with both considerable industry production and traditional tourism activities, may be summarized as follows:

- the existing industry, mainly large enterprises in basic industries with strong exogenous dependence, did not react in time to bring above average labour unit cost as well as an outdated product mix in line with changing world market conditions;
- political pressure and strong labour union resistance, particularly in the state-owned firms, provided an important reason for this delayed adjustment process in the form of a detrimental political concentration on supporting obsolete industry structures instead of investing money and ideas in new branches;
- the depressed endogenous growth potential of this region as a consequence of the high wages in the existing industries, which caused a low propensity to self-employment and at the same time introduced a strong cost disadvantage for local firms;
- the poor performance of local networks, which may be traced back first to a pronounced 'top down' situation in the Province Styria, where decisions are mainly taken from bodies not situated in the region, but secondly also to a lack of local awareness, which together resulted in not enough endogenous activities to bring new firms to the region.

Taking into account that both regions are of similar size, are located in comparable, difficult mountain settings, have a similarly well-developed traffic system, and access to the same funds at the national and the Community level, the conclusion from these two case studies is straightforward: the difference in the economic development of these regions, making them a leading and a lagging one, is mainly caused by the difference in the exploitation of endogenous potentials in the form of activism and creativity of local actors. The favourable preconditions to take decisions within the leading region spurred the emergence of formal and informal networks which subsequently improved the odds to effectively deploy the opportunities available. So over a time horizon of only ten years the resulting difference is already remarkable.

Mountain farming

The long-term development of agriculture fitted exactly into the general picture described earlier, characterized by below-average income levels and thus out-migration. In order to mitigate the resulting burdens for regional labour markets as well as the environment, in 1970 a specific support programme for mountain farmers ('Bergbauernsonderprogramm') was designed and subsequently developed (Dax, 1997). The key instrument of this programme was the provision of direct payments. In joining the EU in 1995 Austria's mountain policy came under pressure, as the community setting, based on compensatory allowances, was less targeted than the previous system. Austria successfully negotiated for a transitional solution in the form of a supplementary national support grant, which allows those farmers being hurt by the new rules to be compensated for a period of ten years.

Although there is only limited empirical work on this segment of rural policies in Austria the key drivers for retaining agricultural activities under these unfavourable mountain conditions can be identified as (OECD, 1998).

- the enterprise-specific graduation of farm aid, which allowed mountain farming to continue under calculable economic conditions, but also secured a socially acceptable income distribution as well as an efficient use of public funds;
- the new emphasis on a careful treatment of natural resources in face of the fragile ecological setting of these mountainous areas, which helped to secure the important function of mountain farming with respect to the provision of positive externalities.

These activities mainly followed a top-down philosophy, although with respect to the environmental contributions of mountain farming local interests have also taken part in designing programmes. In general, the relatively high share of farming activities in the study regions is the result of the interplay of farm-related support and the impact of regional policy attempts to provide job opportunities and thus income in the region, which allows farming either on a full-time or part-time basis.

In the meantime, however, in the mountain farming community a shift towards bottom-up initiatives is apparent. To give an example, a group of farmers in one study region has abandoned cattle farming in favour of keeping sheep, which not only reduced the production cost of related milk products, but also allowed them to engage in a non-food market by producing high quality insulating boards from sheep wool. This move significantly boosted the income of the engaged farmers via higher market revenue. Another very successful example is a special form of agri-tourism in a valley of Osttirol, where guests are able to live in remote alpine huts under very traditional conditions,[20] which can be ordered via global reservation systems. These examples have in common that farmers increasingly engage in non-regulated private markets by producing high quality niche products or services, which are marketed far beyond the borders of the region. These successful strategies strictly pursue the endogenous approach of integrated rural development.

However, it would be misleading to expect similar success stories by simply copying the strategy of a leading to a lagging region, as the individual particularities may be quite diverse. However, in analysing an increasing number of such case studies it should be possible to find out the general valid success factors, which then have to be gradually implemented in political measures targeted to support integrated rural development processes.

SUMMARY AND CONCLUSIONS

From a historic perspective the decline of agricultural activities can be seen as the origin of rural development concepts. Such concepts to stimulate local development are conventionally subdivided into an exogenous approach (industrial recruitment strategies) and an endogenous approach (local growth strategies). While the first approach is characterized by attempts to attract outside producers in offering cheap production factors, mainly land and labour; cost advantages with respect to local taxes and fees; and perhaps subsidies for the move into the region, the second one views improvements in local assets, be they physical or human, as prerequisites to stimulate the economic growth of a region. While these strategies appear to be quite distinct in various dimensions, in practice either a combination of both approaches takes place within one development project or we observe projects following the exogenous or the endogenous philosophy in parallel. In any case, both strategies normally require a straightforward integration of different policy areas in order to function.

In general, the success of an integrated development strategy depends on three elements: the resource endowment of a region, the ability and activity of actors and the actual measures realized. This finding is not only the clear message of the previous case studies, it is also the result of the huge number of other attempts to single out common factors being relevant for the employment growth of rural regions in Europe.[21] So the following characteristics may be seen as key factors for improving the probability of a successful integrated development of rural regions:

1. *Infrastructure investment* is important for the economic well-being of a region as a necessary, but not a sufficient condition for a comprehensive local development strategy.
2. A *multisectoral approach* with a healthy mix of different, but compatible sectors may be preferable to a specialization strategy if a continuous long-term growth path is aimed at. Specialization always increases the economic vulnerability with respect to sectoral business cycles, and sometimes brings in a seasonal pattern in economic activities. Farming is an integral part of the regional economy, with commodities produced as well as (positive) externalities generated at the output side, but also with respect to its factor market linkages.
3. Related to the sectoral mix of a region the *qualifications of the work force* with the available employment opportunities is also of relevance. The number and the qualification level of the regional work force is an important issue in setting up new business activities. Regions with a strong growth in manufacturing industries are nearly always characterized by a sufficient availability of workers with medium level technical skills. An inadequate mix of regional skills may be fixed by improving commuting activities. In the long run the qualification structure is shaped by appropriate regional education opportunities.
4. Perhaps the most important element determining the development path of a region in practice remains the *capability and creativity of actors*. Such persons may be part of official decision bodies or may simply act in private interest. Their ability to analyse the regional situation with respect to the available assets and to develop appropriate strategies and projects in practice to a large extent determines the growth path of a region. 'Appreciative theorizing' in this field emphasizes the importance of a long-term perspective with respect to innovation goals, the courage to apply experimental behaviour apart from tested routines, but also the need to outsource specific tasks.
5. Closely connected with the abilities of actors and of similar importance is the existence of *internal and external networks*. The functioning of such networks and the build-up of more formal 'clusters' was found to be a decisive element in many development processes. An efficient coordination among different actors is necessary for bringing together providers

of knowledge and information on the one hand, and innovators using this information on the other.

The increased emphasis on bottom-up factors however does not imply that top-down policies are not relevant any more. Both the rules and the budgets of national and community-level policies dedicated to support rural regions of course remain an important top-down element. Yet, for the actual success of regional development processes an active and skilful bottom-up incentive is of indispensable importance in order to complement the top-down measures available. 'Integrated Rural Development' therefore must not be confined to improving the coherence and compatibility of community and national initiatives. It has to put at least the same weight on the endogenous ability and willingness of a region to act efficiently in favour of its own interests.

In its attempts to curb both policy failures as well as market failures the actual development of European policy incentives regarding IRD seems to proceed slowly, but steadily in the right direction. The high complexity of this subject becomes evident through the fact that the related scientific work is also quite strictly separated along the individual segments of integrated development processes. In taking into account that political attempts to integrate policies not only have to overcome this functional complexity, but disagreeing party interests as well, the expectations with respect to the speed of the further development of an integrated rural development in Europe should not be too ambitious.

NOTES

1. One example in this respect is fully decoupled direct payments, which *per se* exhibit characteristics of genuine transfers (for example retirement plans, minimum income allowances, and so on), however, often without reference to the accepted rules of social policies.
2. While US and UK economists already looked very early at the 'macro linkages' of the farm sector (for example Kirk, 1933; Schultz, 1945) and the discussion entered a very active period of research after the seminal contribution of Schuh (1974) with respect to exchange rate impacts on the US farm sector, this field of research was never high on the agenda in continental Europe (Hofreither *et al.*, 1991).
3. The definition of 'leading' vs. 'lagging' is inherently vague, as these terms refer to the relative position of regions on a time axis. This raises the question of the relevant benchmark, as regions may differ with respect to natural conditions, physical infrastructure and labour force quantity and quality. An example of a detailed analysis based on European employment dynamics as the benchmark criterion is Terluin and Post (1999). A basic theoretical explanation of 'leader regions' vs. 'follower regions' is provided by Batten and Boyce (1986).
4. A basic theoretical introduction of innovation in a regional development context is provided by Malecki and Varaiya (1986).
5. Nelson characterizes 'formal theorizing' as proceeding at some intellectual distance from what is known empirically, being mainly caused by emphasizing general equilibria. 'Ap-

preciative theorizing', on the other hand, includes the relevant substance of empirical research in this field, if necessary at the expense of mathematical rigour (Nelson, 1997, 33f.).

6. For a more comprehensive look at the applicability of political economy approaches to agriculture please refer for example to Swinnen and Van der Zee (1993).

7. This statement may not be true for all regions of rural Europe. For the possibility of exceptions refer for example to Doyle *et al.* (1997).

8. A resolution of this problem is often attempted by establishing a more qualitative typology, for example distinguishing regions with respect to their main problems (pressure of modern life, rural decline, marginal areas, and so on) or according to their degree of integration with the national economy (integrated, intermediate, remote, and so on)

9. The objectives primarily relevant for rural areas were Objective 1, which applied to lagging regions with a GDP of less than 75 per cent of the EU average, and Objective 5b focusing on rural areas with a low level of socio-economic development, a high dependency on agricultural employment, low agricultural incomes and population problems. In connection with EFTA-enlargement Objective 6 was introduced later and applied to regions north of the 62nd parallel with less than 8 inhabitants per km[2].

10. Regulation (EEC) 1260/99 is also to be mentioned in this respect, as it lays down general provisions of the Structural Funds, but also refers to the details of implementation of related measures.

11. As an example quite a few authors express doubts whether agricultural decision makers at the national level will have an interest in setting strict environmental regulations as a prerequisite for farmers to obtain direct payments ('cross-compliance'), as any such attempt in turn would be criticized as a threat to farm competitiveness within the EU-15 (Dabbert *et al.*, 1998). Similar arguments may apply to the programmes designed to provide payments to ecologically valuable land in less-favoured areas.

12. This for example may happen as a consequence of establishing green cover too late or incompletely, but also if green cover is periodically removed. Problems of non-food set-aside are analysed in Brouwer and Van Berkum (1996).

13. Examples regarding the interdependence between CMOs and the agri-environmental measures as well as their objectives can be found in Buckwell *et al.* (1997, 45).

14. Despite stiff price reductions for field crops in the MacSharry Reform of 1992, the expected positive environmental consequences remained negligible. A possible reason for this effect may be the fact that farmers mistakenly aggregate the lower product price with the area premium, which entails a more or less unchanged marginal revenue and thus intensity of production of these crops.

15. The Community Initiative LEADER did operate within Objective 1, 5b and 6 regions and aimed at stimulating rural development initiatives at the local level. With Agenda 2000 this Initiative has been 'upgraded' to LEADER+ and now features an explicit focus on integrated rural development processes. For further information please refer to http://www.rural-europe.aeidl.be.

16. This fact may be traced back to the positive economic development in the western, mountainous parts of Austria and a less pronounced drop in birth rates in relation to non-mountainous areas.

17. The reason for choosing this somewhat outdated period for the official data base was that quite a few of the required statistical data at the district level are updated only at ten-year intervals.

18. The following paragraphs draw primarily on the related parts in the Project summary (Terluin and Post, 1999) as well as Weiss (1999).

19. In the eastern regions of Austria agriculture still counts for nearly 20 per cent of total employment, while in the western parts this share, ranging between 2.9 per cent and 4.7 per cent, already falls below the national average (BMLF, 1999).

20. In detail this means water from wells, no electricity, no phone, and of course no cars, which may be a nightmarish vision for some convinced urbanites. However, despite not very moderate pricing the waiting period for reservations is about two years.

21. One already mentioned example is the European research project carried out in the 4th

Framework Programme which looked at the key factors explaining the development of 18 selected rural regions in Europe (Terluin and Post, 1999), but similar positions for example are held by Rutten and Van Oosten (1999) in looking at innovation oriented strategies for rural regions, in the case studies presented in Dax and Wiesinger (1998) or from a more 'appreciative' theoretical viewpoint by Marsden (1995).

REFERENCES

Ayres, R.U. (1988), *Self-organization in biology and economics*, Research Report 88-1, Laxenburg: International Institute for Applied System Analysis (IIASA).

Barro, R.J. and P.M. Romer (1990), *Economic Growth*, NBER Reporter, Cambridge MA: National Bureau of Economic Research, pp. 1–5.

Batten, D.F. and D.E. Boyce (1986), 'Spatial interaction, transportation and interregional commodity flow models', in P. Nijkamp (ed.), *Handbook of Regional and Urban Economics*, vol. I, Amsterdam: North-Holland, pp. 357–406.

Becker, G.S. (1983), 'A theory of competition among pressure groups for political influence', *The Quarterly Journal of Economics*, **XCVIII**, 371–400.

Becker, G.S. (1985), 'Public policies, pressure groups and dead weight costs', *Journal of Public Economics*, **28**, 329–47.

Brouwer, F.M. and S. van Berkum (1996), *CAP and Environment in the European Union: Analysis of the effects of the CAP on the environment and assessment of existing environmental conditions in policy*, Wageningen: Wageningen Pers.

Buckwell, A., J. Blom, P. Commins, B. Hervieu, M.F. Hofreither, H. v. Meyer, E. Rabinowicz, F. Sotte and J.M. Sumpsi Vina (1997), 'Towards a Common Agricultural and Rural Policy for Europe', *European Economy*, Reports and Studies, No. 5, Brussels: European Commission.

Bundesministerium für Land- und Forstwirtschaft (BMLF) (1999), *Grüner Bericht 1998*, Vienna: Herold Druck.

Castle, E.N. (1998), 'A conceptual framework for the study of rural places', *American Journal of Agricultural Economics*, **80**, 621–31.

Dabbert, St., B. Kilian and J. Umstätter (1998), 'The Environmental Effects of Agenda 2000 in the Agricultural Sector', English transcript of: Umweltwirkungen der Agenda 2000 im Agrarbereich, *Agra-Europe*, **19**, 1–14.

Dax, Th. (1997), 'Mountain Policies in Austria – experiences and outlook on an integrated approach', paper presented at 'Quale futuro per l'agricoltura montana in Europe: politiche di sviluppo, di stegno o di tutela', 7 Oct. 1997, Milan.

Dax, Th. and G. Wiesinger (1998), *Mountain Farming and the Environment: Towards Integration, Perspectives for mountain policies in Central and Eastern Alps*, Research Report No. 44, Vienna: Bundesanstalt für Bergbauernfragen.

Downs, A. (1957), *An Economic Theory of Democracy*, New York: Harper and Row.

Doyle, Ch. J., M. Mitchell and K. Topp (1997), 'Effectiveness of farm policies on social and economic development in rural areas', *European Review of Agricultural Economics*, **24**, 530–46.

European Commission (1988), *The Future of Rural Society*, COM (88) 501 final, Brussels: European Commission.

European Commission (1997), Rural Developments, *CAP 2000 Working Document*, Brussels: Directorate General for Agriculture.

Freshwater, D. (1997), 'Farm production policy versus rural life policy', *American Journal of Agricultural Economics*, **79**, 1515–24.

Helpman, E. and P. Krugman (1992), *Trade Policy and Market Structure*, Cambridge, London: The MIT Press.

Hofreither, M.F. (1998), 'Amenities in rural areas: responding to a new social demand', in G. Paillotin (ed.), *European Agricultural Research in the 21st Century*, INRA Editions, Berlin: Springer, pp. 209–21.

Hofreither, M.F. (2000), 'Socio-economic aspects of agri-environmental programs – an introspective survey', in M. Härdtlein, M. Kaltschmitt, I. Lewandowski and H. N. Wurl (eds), *Nachhaltigkeit in der Landwirtschaft*, Berlin: Erwin Schmidt, pp. 165–90.

Hofreither, M.F., G. Pruckner and Ch.R. Weiss (1991), *Ökonomische Interaktionen zwischen Gesamtwirtschaft und Agrarsektor*, Kiel: Wissenschaftsverlag Vauk Kiel KG.

Jantsch, E. (1980), *The Self-Organizing Universe: Scientific and Human Implications of the Emerging Paradigm of Evolution*, New York: Pergamon Press.

Kirk, J.H. (1933), *Agriculture and the Trade Cycle*, London: King.

Kraybill, D.S. (1998), 'The view from economics: discussion of Castle's conceptual framework', *American Journal of Agricultural Economics*, **80**, 635–6.

Leifer, R. (1989), 'Understanding organizational transformation using a dissipative structure model', *Human Relations*, **42**, 899–915.

Malecki, E.J. and P. Varaiya (1986): 'Innovation and changes in regional structure', in P. Nijkamp (ed.), *Handbook of Regional and Urban Economics*, vol. I, Amsterdam: North-Holland, pp. 629–45.

Marsden, T. (1995), 'Beyond agriculture? Regulating the new rural spaces', *Journal of Rural Studies*, **11**(3), 285–96.

Nelson, R. (1997), 'How new is new growth theory?', *Challenge*, **40**(5), 29–58.

Nowicki, P.L. (1997), 'Environmental Benefits of Agriculture: European OECD Countries', in: *Environmental Benefits from Agriculture: Issues and Policies – The Helsinki Seminar*, Paris: OECD, pp. 55–80.

OECD (1998), *Rural Amenity in Austria, A Case Study of Cultural Landscape*, Unclassified paper no. C/RUR(98)4, Paris: OECD.

Olson, M. (1965), *The Logic of Collective Action: Public Goods and the Theory of Groups*, Cambridge MA: Harvard University Press.

Olson, M. (1990), 'The exploitation and subsidization of agriculture: There is an explanation', *Choices*, 4th Quarter, 8–11.

Rupasingha, A. and F.O. Boadu (1998), 'Evolutionary theories and the community management of local commons: A survey', *Review of Agricultural Economics*, **20**(2), 530–46.

Rutten, H. and H. van Oosten (eds) (1999), *Innovating with ambition – opportunities for agribusiness, rural areas and the fishing industry*, The Hague: National Council for Agricultural Research.

Salhofer, K., M.F. Hofreither and F. Sinabell (2000), 'Promotion of the agricultural sector and political power in Austria', *Public Choice*, **102**, 229–46.

Sandler, T. (1992), *Collective Action, Theory and Applications*, Ann Arbor: University of Michigan Press.

Schuh, E.G. (1974), 'The exchange rate and U.S. agriculture', *American Journal of Agricultural Economics*, **56**, 1–13.

Schultz, T.W. (1945), *Agriculture in an Unstable Economy*, New York: McGraw-Hill.

Swinnen, J. and F.A. Van der Zee (1993), 'The political economy of agricultural policies: A survey', *European Review of Agricultural Economics*, **20**, 261–90.

Terluin, I. and J. Post (1999), *Employment in leading and lagging rural regions of the*

EU, Summary report of the RUREMPLO project (FAIR CT96 1766), The Hague: Agricultural Economics Research Institute (LEI).

Terluin, I., J. Post and A. Sjöström (eds) (1999), *Comparative analysis of employment dynamics in leading and lagging rural regions of the EU, 1980–1997*, Rapport 4.99.09, The Hague: Agricultural Economics Research Institute (LEI).

Weiss, F. (1999), *Employment in rural regions of Austria – The case study regions Osttirol and Liezen*, Working paper, No. 78b-W-99, Vienna: Agricultural University Vienna, Department of Economics, Politics and Law.

PART IV

Outlook

13. Agriculture and nature: retrospect and prospect

Floor Brouwer and Jan van der Straaten

INTRODUCTION

The preceding chapters have given a 'state of the art' analysis of agricultural and nature policies in the European Union (EU). The main theme in this text has been the development and selection of suitable instruments to strengthen the interaction between agriculture and nature. From the various contributions we can draw a number of conclusions about the interactions and their role for policy design and evaluation. These are:

- Intensification and extensification of farming practices are main threats to the management of land. They have brought major changes in European land use and a wide range of factors and conditions have contributed to these. Declining trends in agriculture extensified production, which might be affected by a combination of environmental, agricultural, socio-economic and political conditions. A combination of factors could cause the cessation of farming, usually leading to a change of land use or even land abandonment. Favourable socio-economic conditions caused agriculture to intensify, and again altered the relationship between agriculture, biodiversity and nature management.

- The economic viability of agriculture and the targeted use of agri-environmental programmes are essential for areas with high nature conservation values. Such conditions could prevent inadequate management practices and even abandonment of agricultural land. They could also promote more sustainable farming practices that manage habitats better than they did some decades ago. A further integration of policy instruments within a broad EU framework, covering agricultural and nature interests could be beneficial to the farming community and local economies.

- A range of actors and institutional settings could strengthen the interaction between agriculture and nature in the EU. Farming practices change in response to improved relationships with actors involved in the sustainable use of the rural countryside. The policy challenge will be to devise a set of policy instruments that give market incentives strengthening the market values of public goods and externalities provided by agriculture and forestry.

• A range of instruments could enhance the interaction between agricultural and nature policies in the EU. Traditionally, public policies are the main instruments applied to change farming practices. A more recent instrument is the adoption of the Beneficiary Pays Principle, with a limited group of beneficiaries who are willing to pay for the benefits created by agriculture.

THE PROPERTY RIGHT OF NATURE

The property right of nature is an important issue for the design of policy instruments. Nature and biodiversity essentially are public goods and therefore are subject to public intervention. Payments provided to farmers who join the agri-environmental measures of the CAP depend on the effort made, the loss of net income and the costs incurred as a result of compliance with the additional requirements. Under Regulation 2078/92, and the more recent Regulation 1257/1999, the premium may be increased by a margin not exceeding 20 per cent to encourage participation in the scheme. However, farming practices have resumed a high level of biodiversity over the past century, which was essentially a by-product of agriculture practices. The provision of such external commodities was not rewarded by society and farmers did not get any payment for the provision of such common goods. This, however, changed with the increasing demand for public services, and society being prepared to compensate farmers for these services delivered. Intensification has increased considerably during the past decades, and harmful effects of agricultural practices on nature gained importance. This, then, raises the question whether farmers have the right to reduce biodiversity and what degree of biodiversity needs to be maintained at the expenses of the farming community. And a related question is to what extent the Polluter Pays Principle is relevant in this respect.

Public policies have been formulated at national and EU level to protect nature, landscape and biodiversity. The relationship between agriculture and nature is of particular significance because of the limited remaining area of natural habitat. However, this protection has until now mainly been achieved by special laws, regulations and conventions in the policy field of nature protection. As long as the objectives of nature protection are not adequately reflected in agricultural policy, the quality and quantity of nature and biodiversity might remain harmfully affected by agricultural practices. An adequate protection of nature, landscape and biodiversity would require the establishment of agri-environmental schemes. Such schemes should include clear environmental objectives, clarify property rights in environmental resources and also establish scientific linkage of objectives with instruments. In addition, the schemes require the implementation of monitoring and evaluation. Ervin (1999) provides a set of criteria for the agri-environmental schemes that contribute to meeting environmental objectives and that are also a suitable basis for multilateral trade negotiations. Various options for the management of nature will be discussed in the next section.

OPTIONS FOR NATURE MANAGEMENT

Some options are discussed in this section, which are considered vital in the interaction between agriculture and nature management and deserve attention in Europe.

The Regional Context

Price support measures currently offer support regardless of the location of the farmer. Nature management aspects are not considered, unless they are a condition for direct payments (also called cross-compliance). In the event of cross-compliance, the amount of income support is only reduced if a farmer fails to meet the relevant environmental and conservation conditions. The provision of price support implies that in all regions the same impetus to intensify production can be recognized. However, one can question whether this makes any sense.

The viability of farming is limited in many remote regions of Europe. It includes the Cevennes, the Appenines, the Spanish Sierras and the Northern regions in the UK. In these regions, agriculture hardly has any chance to survive and villages are increasingly being abandoned. An increasing number of schools, churches and shops are closed. The possibilities for new jobs are very limited, which leads again to emigration of people. A further intensification may be an option for an individual farmer. However, intensification of production again may reduce employment in agriculture.

The objectives of the Regional Funds and the Structural Funds are to neutralize these negative effects in regions with limited employment possibilities. However, the impetus to intensify resulting from the price support measures remains. The future perspective of the remote rural areas cannot benefit from such a dual policy. The abandonment of land and villages will continue, unless regionally targeted programmes are established (for example through agri-environmental programmes).

The nature and biodiversity value of the remote areas mentioned before is rather high. In hilly and mountain regions the barriers against intensification were, generally speaking, more significant than in the flat fertile soils. This resulted in still favourable conditions for wild plants and animals. So far, national parks are, by definition, only established in nature areas in which agriculture or other economic activities are forbidden or strictly controlled. This concept of national parks is strongly related with the idea that it is possible to define nature. According to this perspective, nature is different from agricultural land. This concept is ready for revision.

The value of nature and biodiversity can benefit from the establishment of national parks in agricultural areas with a low population density and a low level of agricultural activities. The costs of these national parks can be relatively low as the land in these remote areas is hardly used for economic activities. The economic value of the land is also low due to the low population density. Perhaps it is better to define these parks as regional parks, as the generally accepted definition of a national park can be a barrier to establishing a national park. In France, the authorities confronted with serious problems of rural development established the Parcs Naturels Régionaux. The total number of these parks in France is 38 with a surface of 45,000 km^2 (Reille, 2000). These parks contribute to rural development and the protection of nature. Generally speaking, the effects of the establishment of these regional parks in France are quite positive.

Such regional parks might also be a good option for other European countries. However, this is only possible if sufficient financial resources would be made available for the establishment of such parks. A suitable option would be to generate special funds at Community level, which are only used for the establishment of these parks in all European countries. One should bear in mind that setting up these parks only makes sense if they are not too small. An average French regional park, for example, has a surface of more than 1000 km^2.

The Employment Concept

Maintaining employment is a vital issue of regional development in the remote areas. Emigration will continue without a sufficient level of employment. Tourism is an option, which is often identified to resolve a range of threats to remote areas. However, tourism as such can be a danger in these vulnerable areas. Therefore, only a low impact type of tourism can be a serious option in these regional parks. Nijkamp and Verdonkschot (1995) present a general overview of how to develop such a type of tourism. Special attention has to be given to the possibilities of the combination of farming preserving biotic resources, and low-impact tourism. This type of farming does not have harmful effects upon nature and biodiversity. Furthermore, biotic products can be used as a label in the development of low impact tourism as is demonstrated by 't Zelfde *et al.* (1998).

The establishment of regional parks does not necessarily limit the development of employment in rural areas. On the contrary, if the type of agriculture is organic, the value of nature and biodiversity will be considerably higher than in the case of an intensification or extensification of agriculture in those areas. However, there are always pitfalls and dangers in tourism development, even in the case of low-impact tourism. Downhill skiing, for example, is often propagated as a new instrument for rural development in mountain areas. However, the effects of ski tows, parking places and infrastructure on nature and landscapes can be dramatic. Furthermore, downhill skiing is often accompanied by the cutting of forests and an increase in erosion. In mountain and hilly areas cross-country skiing can be a better option, as its effect on nature and the environment is considerably lower than downhill skiing.

Nature and Revealed Preference

In environmental economics it is understood that the demand on nature and biodiversity is not always reflected on a recognizable market. Spash and Carter (Chapter 5) discuss the possibilities of different instruments evaluating nature. Of course, many problems can be recognized by using these instruments. However, one cannot overlook the high value that people give to nature, regardless whether this value is the 'correct' economic value (van der Straaten, 2000). The contribution of Maurizio Merlo (Chapter 10) demonstrates that nature, landscape and biodiversity are inputs in the economic process.

Additionally, there is the emerging discussion regarding the long-term viability of current agriculture in the European Union. For example, the BSE crisis in the EU opened the political discussion concerning to what extent agricultural policies should be better targeted to the demand of consumers. It is increasingly argued that the CAP is currently too supply orientated. Of course, we cannot discuss here the relevance of the BSE crisis; however, it cannot be overlooked that both nature and the current debate on consumer concerns are related to current agricultural policies in the European Union.

Nature and Agriculture in Central and Eastern Europe

Enlargement is one of the main challenges the EU will face in the years to come. The enlargement process includes the adoption by the candidate countries of the EU *acquis communautaire* in sectors such as agriculture and the environment. As far as biodiversity, in particular nature conservation, is concerned, the adoption of the environmental *acquis communautaire* involves the implementation of the Habitats and Birds Directives. Brouwer *et al.* (2001) offer an overview on the key interactions between agriculture and nature conservation in the candidate countries. In particular, policy options and strategies are identified, which integrate environmental concerns with agriculture, nature conservation and rural development. In Central and Eastern Europe the value of nature and biodiversity is often high. As an illustration, we compare the breeding populations for some species (Table 13.1).

Table 13.1   *Populations of some breeding birds in 15 member states, compared with the 13 candidate countries*

Species	Minimum population in candidate countries	Minimum population in EU-15
Corn crake	92 225	4 000
Lesser Grey Shrike	46 255	3 098
Lesser Spotted Eagle	5 950	190
Red Footed Falcon	2 300	2
White Stork	79 809	15 439

Source: Tucker and Evans (1997).

Though collectivization of farms has eroded the quality of many landscapes in various regions, there are still many rich landscapes, hardly disturbed by 'modern' agriculture. Intensification and extensification of agriculture may induce pressures similar to those that were observed in the EU (Mander and Jongman, 1999). Low-input agriculture is the dominant farming practice in most of the candidate countries, and a range of policy options is currently available.

The Special Assistance Programme for Agriculture and Rural Development (SAPARD) contains measures that benefit biodiversity. The programme was introduced to support the Central and Eastern European Countries (CEECs) in adapting their agricultural sector and adopting the rural development *acquis* as it relates to agriculture and rural development. Most CEECs have submitted one or more pilot agri-environmental schemes to the European Commission. Nine countries will receive funding under SAPARD to implement these schemes (Table 13.2).

In addition to the agri-environment schemes, other policy approaches and strategies might be adopted as well. Brouwer *et al.* (2001) list the following options:

Table 13.2 Summary of proposed annual expenditure on agri-environment programmes under SAPARD

Country	Agri-environment SAPARD measure?	EU contribution (in thousand euros)	SAPARD budget (%)	Area (in hectares)	Number of pilot areas	Expected date of implementation
Bulgaria	Yes	9,000	2.4	32,000	1	2001
Czech Republic	Yes	4,584	2.9	5–20,000	5	2001
Estonia	Yes	1,210	1.4	?	3+	2003
Hungary	Yes	11,330	4.2	400,000	15	2001
Latvia	Yes[1]	6,970	4.5	43,000[3]	?	2001
Lithuania	Yes	2,124	1.0	4,700	2+	2002
Poland	Yes[2]	22,920	1.9	33,000	6	2001
Romania	Yes	26,571	2.5	36,000	7	2003
Slovakia	Yes	4,500	3.5	10,000	5	2002
Slovenia	No	–	–	–	–	–
CEECs		89,209	2.4	>578,700	–	–

Notes:
1. Includes 3 measures of the plan;
2. Includes afforestation of agricultural land;
3. Estimated.

Source: Brouwer et al. (2001)

- Agri-environment schemes, which are particularly relevant in regions that require specific measures to manage biodiversity, manage nature and protect landscape.
- Other rural development measures under the CAP, which have the potential to gain benefits from the interaction between economic, social and environmental conditions.
- Environmental appraisal of agricultural and rural development plans. This process allows the environmental implications of policies, plans or projects in decision making to be taken into account.
- Promoting sustainable agriculture
- Capacity and institution building by offering training, extension and R&D programmes to support farmers to prepare for implementing agri-environmental programmes.

These tools are mutually supportive and a combination of approaches could strengthen their achievement. The nature conservation aspects of different options for integrating nature in future debates on agricultural policy merit due attention.

REFERENCES

Brouwer, F., D. Baldock and C. la Chapelle (coordination) (2001), *Agriculture and nature conservation in the candidate countries: Perspectives in interaction*, Report for the Netherlands' Ministry of Agriculture, Nature Management and Fisheries, The Hague.

Ervin, D. (1999), 'Toward GATT-proofing environmental programmes for agriculture', *Journal of World Trade*, **33**(2), 63–82.

Mander, U. and R.H.G. Jongman (1999), 'Ecological and socio-economic consequences of land use changes', in: A. Farina (ed.), *Perspectives in Ecology*, Leiden: Backhuys Publishers, pp. 269–80.

Nijkamp, P. and S. Verdonkschot (1995), 'Sustainable tourism development; a case study of Lesbos', in H. Coccossi and P. Nijkamp (eds), *Sustainable Tourism Development*, Avebury: Aldershot, pp. 127–40.

Reille, A. (2000), *Guide des Parcs Naturels Régionaux*, Lausanne: Delachaux et Niestlé.

Straaten, J. van der (2000), 'The Economic Value of Nature', in Helen Briassoulis and Jan van der Straaten (eds), *Tourism and the Environment, revised second edition*, Dordrecht: Kluwer Academic Publishers, pp. 123–32.

Tucker, G.M. and M.I. Evans (eds) (1997), *Habitats for Birds in Europe. A conservation strategy for the wider Environment*, Birdlife, UK, Birdlife Conservation Series No. 6.

't Zelfde, J., G. Richards and J. van der Straaten (1998), 'Developing Sustainability in the Alps', in Bill Bramwell, Ian Henry, Guy Jackson, Ana Goytia Prat, Greg Richards and Jan van der Straaten (eds), *Sustainable Tourism Management: Principles and Practices*, Tilburg: Tilburg University Press, pp. 73–86.

Index

abandonment 2, 4, 187, 283
abatement (pollution) 29–30, 33–4
  command-and-control schemes
    (quantity regulation) 31, 32
  and taxation 30–33
aesthetics, valuation of 92–3, 99, 103,
  109, 110
Agenda 2000 78–82, 210, 261–2
  and cross-compliance 133, 134,
    135–6, 137
  Greece 187–8
agri-environmental policy 34–6, 64,
  284–5
  Central/Eastern Europe 82, 287–90
  costs 74–5, 77–8
  current intervention framework 81–2
  development of 4–6, 8, 67–8
  economic incentives, importance of 7
  environmental impacts (externalities)
    model 71–3
  future prospects 9, 82–6
  Greece 12, 13, 191–7, 198–200
  implementation strategies, member
    states 75–6
  'paid stewardship' 72–3, 74
  policy instruments, types 234–5,
    283–4
  policy options within EU 129–31
  problems 76–8
  productivist policy model 67–71
  reform 78–81, 82–3
  'sectoral' nature of 263–6
  voluntary measures 233–4, 235–6
  see also UK, agri-environmental
    policy
agricultural incomes, and Environmentally Sensitive Areas (ESAs) 155,
  159
agricultural methods, and nature values
  of land 1–3, 4
agricultural policy

and consumer interests 287
  market distortions caused by 36–7
  purpose 19, 20–21, 36
  'sectoral' nature of 263–6
  see also agri-environmental policy;
    Common Agricultural Policy
    (CAP)
'agricultural terms of trade' 167
agriculture, significance to economy/
  society 1, 252, 262–3
agro-tourism, Greece 188–91, 198
air quality 94
  valuation of 110
Amsterdam, Treaty of (1997) 6
'appreciative theorising,' and regional
  development 254–5
aquifers *see* groundwater, depletion of
Austria, mountainous regions
  agriculture 269–70, 272–3
  employment 267–8, 269, 270–71
  non-agricultural sectors 270–72
  population 267, 268

Beneficiary Pays Principle 211, 214,
  284
biodiversity
  benefits due to agri-environmental
    schemes (UK) 151–3
  Central/Eastern Europe 287–8
  effect of enhancement scheme
    participation rates 150–51
  loss of 2, 3, 4
  and national parks 286
  valuation of 95, 110
biotopes, Greece 195–6

cadmium, in agricultural soils 63
CAP *see* Common Agricultural Policy
  (CAP)
capital substitution 20, 21
carbon dioxide, as 'greenhouse' gas 49